D0875881

MY BROTHER ADLAI

MY BROTHER
ADLAI

BY

Elizabeth Stevenson Ives

AND

Hildegarde Dolson

*"Let gratitude for the past inspire us
with trust for the future."*
—Fénelon

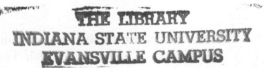
WILLIAM MORROW & COMPANY

NEW YORK, 1956

Published simultaneously in the Dominion of Canada
by George J. McLeod Limited, Toronto

Printed in the United States

Library of Congress Catalog Card No. 56-7134

To My Husband

MY BROTHER ADLAI

Chapter 1

ADLAI MADE HIS FIRST political appearance as a child in Bloomington, Illinois, sitting up stiffly on the speakers' platform at a big Democratic rally. One of the speakers was our Grandfather Adlai Stevenson I, who had been Vice-President under Mr. Cleveland, and we were dressed to do him proud, my brother in starched Eton collar, and I with a monstrously large hair bow.

We sat frozen to our chairs, not daring to squirm, while Grandfather introduced his friend William Jennings Bryan, whom he considered the finest orator in the country, and praised long and eloquently. Then Mr. Bryan gave a thunderous declamation, tossing his great head, and pushing his hand out palm forward. In the midst of all this, and the wild applause, I glanced at Adlai, to see how he was taking our exciting platform prominence. My young brother had gone peacefully to sleep. I felt utterly disgraced.

Father loved politics, and seemed continuously involved, but there was very little that Father *wasn't* involved in. He bubbled over with ideas, and his humor spilled out; he told stories for the sheer joy of it, especially jokes on himself.

1

One favorite was about his honeymoon abroad with Mother, in 1893. Father got off the train during a stop at a small Swiss town and was strolling around the station when suddenly bells rang, whistles blew, and away went the train carrying his bride. When the frantic bridegroom finally reached their destination—Vevey—late that night, the hotel manager led him up to Mother's room. Father exclaimed, "Helen! I'm here at last." Mother stared at him blankly, then turned to the manager and asked "Who, *who* is this impostor?"

Another story we loved was about how Father tried to impress Mother on that same trip. Being very young and very much in love, he was eager to show her he could cut quite a dashing international figure armed with letters of introduction from Grandfather Stevenson and other prominent Americans to important people in Europe. Of course the newlyweds were handsomely entertained, but Father decided that as a grand climax, to show how worldly he was, he would take his lovely, dark haired, distinguished-looking bride to the gambling casino at Monte Carlo. "The doorman bowed low to Helen," Father would say, when he told this story. "Probably thought she was royalty incognito. But he said I was too young to gamble. He wouldn't even let me inside."

Coming as he did from a strict Presbyterian household, brought up by a mother who had refused even Ulysses S. Grant's request for a whiskey with a gentle, "We don't serve spirits in our home, but do have a lemonade," perhaps Father didn't try very hard to get inside a gambling casino. Otherwise, he'd have managed. He had a warm, winning, almost irresistible smile, and the kind of gaiety and charm that could light up a roomful of strangers. Nobody stayed

a stranger for long, around Father. He introduced Adlai
and me, as children, to a variety ranging from flying trapeze
artists to Woodrow Wilson. (I wrote in my diary: "President
Wilson is a dear!!! His wife is fair, fat, and fortish.") We
always took it for granted that Father knew everybody, and
I guess he did. Certainly he always had an eager audience,
at home or wherever he went.

Home, from the time Adlai was six and I was eight, was
a ten-room gray stucco house on Washington Street, with
the high, narrow Gothic gable that came to its incongruous
peak in the Midwest architecture of the early 1900's. Bloomington, sixty miles north of Springfield, had a population of
25,000, hitching posts on every curb, and the wide-lawned,
leisurely look of a non-industrial town encircled by rich farm
country—the golden tasseled corn belt.

Adlai and I knew the price of corn per bushel almost before we could spell, because Father was the manager of
forty-five farms—thousands of acres—belonging mostly to
Grandmother Stevenson's sister, our great-aunt Julia Scott,
and he traveled endless miles by buggy or "jerkwater" trains
(before we had a car) visiting tenant farmers in Illinois,
Iowa and Indiana. Father's ideas flew so far ahead of his
time that he had vast areas planted with soy beans when
people still hooted at the notion of encouraging such
"weeds." He loved farming on this large, no-hand-to-the-
plow scale, but he was much too restless to be a home gardener. He left that to Mother.

She had chosen our house not because it was handsome
or in a fashionable section, like our two grandfathers' big
brick houses a few blocks away, but because it was in the
newer end of town, where empty lots separated the houses,
and yards were measured in acres instead of skimpy feet,

with room for children and trees to grow in freedom. Washington Street was a beautiful wide archway of elms, with our public school just down the block.

Our own yard was about an acre deep, sloping down in back to a pasture and a little stream crossed by two rickety planks, where Adlai caught crayfish and sailed his homemade boats. Just beyond the back fence, cows grazed tranquilly. At least, some of them did, but our neighbors', the Grahams', cow kept getting loose and eating flowers out of Mother's garden. This cow got her comeuppance the day my friend Dora Mooney came to see me in a new spring coat with a brilliant red lining, which she rashly left on the ground near my small brother. I don't know whether Dora or the Grahams' cow was more astonished to see Adlai, suddenly turned bullfighter, with Dora's new coat providing the cape-work, as he waved the red lining frenziedly and danced around the loudly mooing beast. The young bullfighter's explanation to his anxious parent was, "But Mother, you know the Grahams' cow doesn't have horns."

My lively, imaginative little brother had a healthy dislike of being restrained in starched Eton collars and too-starched manners, and he was always on the go. He had brown hair that never stayed flattened, a round face that always looked sunburned, and his favorite costume was corduroy pants topped by a visor cap worn backwards. I thought he was a "sight" most of the time.

"You and Adlai were such different children," an old and dear friend of our family's, Mrs. John Fletcher Wight, said to me recently. "I could tell you a story your mother told me about that, but I don't know if *you'd* like it, Buffie."

A child we went to school with had gotten into some kind of boyish scrape, and mother decided impetuously he wasn't a suitable influence. She told Adlai and me we must promise never to have anything to do with him, from then on. I said, "Certainly, Mother, I understand. I'll never speak to him again," and probably pictured myself piously cutting the wrongdoer dead in geography class. "But Adlai couldn't be stampeded," Mrs. Wight said. "He was an obedient little boy, but his eyes filled with tears and he told your mother, 'Don't ask me to do that. He's my friend.' "

I think the very fact that Mother told this story on herself shows she thought Adlai was right. She was never small-minded, but at times her devotion to her children took the form of overprotectiveness. She had rather a phobia about "germs," and would try to keep us home from school at the slightest real or fancied sniffle, or a rumored case of mumps. I always seized on any such excuse and yielded happily to coddling, but not Adlai. "I don't have a sore throat. I feel *fine*," he'd say hoarsely, and occasionally he got away with no more than an extra muffler and rubbers! Instinctively, he reached out for the freedom of making his own friends, and independence from the oversolicitude of a mother we both adored.

She had beautiful, deep-set gray eyes, and shining, almost black hair which she wore rippled back from her high forehead, and fastened in a low knot. My great ambition was to look just like her. I remember once walking with Adlai behind my parents, on an uneven brick sidewalk, and looking at Mother's tall, slim back. She was wearing a bottle-green velvet suit with a snug little basque jacket, a brown velvet platter-brimmed hat with two dashingly long plumes, and she was holding up her heavy skirt gracefully with one ecru-kid-gloved hand, to keep it from trailing in the dust. I felt overcome with pride, to think this elegant lady was our mother.

Although she was astonishingly ahead of her time in some ways—she fed us orange juice long before vitamins were table talk—she encased us in the strict upbringing of that day, just as she encased our feet in high shoes. When Adlai pleaded for a pair of sneakers, I backed him up, because we always sided with each other's campaigns to convert parents, but Mother thought sneakers were too "soft." We always left our overshoes in a box at the side door (we weren't allowed to use the front door) and hung our coats neatly on our own two wall hooks in the back hall. My sunbonnet hung there for years, then a Maud Mullerish straw hat, because sun on the bare head was still considered dangerous enough to addle one's brain, and certainly to ruin the complexion.

Fortunately, Mother loved trees and flowers so much herself that she encouraged us to run free, outdoors. She often said, "Remember, nature is the great restorer and the perfect guide." For gardening, she wore a large faded duster and gloves riddled with holes; each spring she'd take us out to Funks Grove to dig spiderwort and columbine for her wild-flower garden.

She had started us as small children on Nature Observation walks, and taught us to keep a sharp eye peeled for everything from a leaf's veins to Petoskey stones, those lovely compound cup corals with fernlike tracery designs. Adlai and I had to draw pictures of our finds, and tie the pages together with red cord, to make portfolios. Mother often read us the scene in Kipling's *Kim,* when Kim and a little Hindu boy play a memory game, describing minutely each kind of stone they'd seen on a tray: "There is one piece of old greenish pipe amber . . . a carved ivory from China representing a rat sucking an egg; and there is last—ah ha!— a ball of crystal as big as a bean, set in a gold leaf." After the Hindu child wins every game, Kim asks plaintively, "But how is it done?" and Lurgan Sahib answers, "By doing it many times over till it is done perfectly—for it is worth doing." Mother always stressed the moral of this—"Observe! Persist! Learn!"—when she read aloud to us in the small library that was Adlai's and my real living room.

Like the dining room and drawing room, the library opened off a square front hall that was lavishly decorated with mementoes of father's trip as a young reporter to the Orient: Egyptian embroideries, a carved elephant tusk, Japanese and Korean ceremonial swords hung in crossed array flanking the doorway. In contrast, the library was casual and comfortable, with a cheerful red carpet, and a shabby brown leather sofa where I'd sit beside Mother while she read. Adlai often sprawled on the floor in front of the acrid-smelling coal fire. Father had the big fireside chair, when he was home, but my strongest recollection of him is rushing in generating a great air of excitement, whenever he returned from a farm inspection trip or political doings, or a journey to that mysterious place—New York. He always had some new project he could hardly wait to tell Mother about: he'd enrolled forty tenant farmers for a short-term agricultural course at the University of Illinois. Or he'd bought a wonderful new health invention—a "rough mitt" to rub up friction and circulation. Once he told Mother he'd been boosting Teddy Roosevelt's Bull Moose party wherever he went, because he thought if Teddy drew enough votes away from the Republicans, then the Democrats would easily win. (As they did.) Often Mother's Quaker-bred, intellectual's mind reacted against Father's more exuberant projects, but never against his gaiety, and she'd laugh in spite of herself.

Almost the only time Father played a quiet-listener role at home was during our reading-aloud evenings in the library. He himself seldom read "literature," (he was a passionate newspaper and magazine reader) but he enjoyed the family closeness, in those sessions, as much as the stories Mother read. She gave us a magnificent variety: *Les Miserables,* Hawthorne's *Wonder Book,* Greek mythology, Dicken's *Tale of Two Cities,* the *Jungle Books,* Scott's Waverley novels and *The Last of the Mohicans.* Later, when Adlai and I were old enough to take turns reading, Mother would put in an occasional quiet criticism: "Pitch your voice lower. It must have *timbre*"; or she'd help us with pronunciation. She had a warm, lovely voice, and she read superbly. She never said "Don't read Elinor Glyn or Hall Caine. They're trash." But she made the big doses of the classics so exciting that they never had for us the bitter medicinal taste of compulsory education.

Although she and Father were opposites in so many ways, when it came to repartée and telling stories, they were like a brilliantly matched tennis team. The dinner table was their court; a small boy in knee pants and long black cotton stockings, and his sister in white lawn guimpe or middy blouse, could only sit and watch from the sidelines. I can't remember that we ever opened our mouths, except to eat. This was harder on me than on my brother. He already had a gift for listening (except to orators like Mr. Bryan!) but I was flyaway and emotional, and enough of an extrovert, like Father, to long for an audience. While our parents volleyed remarks back and forth, laughing gaily and returning each serve faster and faster, I used to think despairingly, "How do you get *into* this?"

Adlai and I certainly didn't do much talking in the drawing room, either. This was a long narrow room with floor-to-ceiling windows along the street side framed by heavy red curtains. The other walls were covered with gray grass cloth. At one end was a Baldwin piano with a Chinese mandarin coat draped down the side; the statue of a Chinese goddess crouched on a high carved seventeenth-century Italian cabinet, near a simple old walnut table brought west by Mother's Quaker ancestors. The white-tiled hearth with gas grate had a fire screen flaunting a brilliant cut-velvet peacock; on the mantel was a white marble leopard with a naked lady recumbent and a Sèvres clock that never ran, but to children, the most glamorous part of the décor was the tiger-skin rug that sprawled before the hearth with outstretched claws. We used to point it out grandly to our friends as "the tiger that Father brought home from China."

That reminds me of something even more spectacular Father brought home. On a trip down the Nile, he had gone to a museum in Luxor and was looking at a glass case full of Egyptian mummy heads 3,000 years old. A whiny vendor kept yanking at his elbow, nagging at him to buy some scarabs. Father refused, and said jokingly, "All I want is a mummy's head. I'd give a dollar for one of these." The vendor disappeared, but he turned up later at the hotel carrying a package carefully wrapped in cloth. Father was appalled to discover it was one of the mummy heads. The man got his dollar, and Father had nervous tremors until he'd got his startling memento safely out of Egypt. Once back in Bloomington, he wanted to give the mummy's head a featured spot in our drawing room, but Mother said she wouldn't have the thing in the house. She made him give it to the Historical Society.

Mother's own special treasures were the beautiful Dresden kerosene lamps she had bought in Germany as a young girl, when she'd gone abroad to study "voice culture." On company occasions, the lamp wicks were lit just before guests arrived, so that the sky blues of the Dresden made shimmering reflections in the tortoise-shell buhl table, and Mother arranged silver vases of red roses that matched the draperies.

If she and Father were having a dinner party, Adlai and I had dinner in the kitchen with Agnes Hagerty. Ag looked exactly the way a child imagines a cook: red-faced, jolly, and built on a bountiful shape. She always let us examine the pictures on the best china, called the Game Set because each plate had a different bird. The guinea hen and pheasant were our favorites. Then we sampled each company delicacy before it was carried off. The dining room was like a hundred thousand others of that period: muddy-brown walls, massive oak furniture, and a low-hanging center gas jet with a Tiffany shade that cast a greenish light. But party airs transformed it: silver-filagree shades with bead fringe and rosy silk linings glowed over tall candles, and over a white linen and lace dinner cloth with a mammoth monogram at one end. Katy Gambon, our special-occasion maid, was another festive touch, black-haired, fresh-cheeked, as pretty as a Rose of Killarney in her pink cotton uniforms, or in a frilled white apron billowing over black, and a fluted cap with velvet ribbons. She had originally worked for Aunt Julia Scott, and when Aunt Julia's daughter Letty was married, she took Katy along on the honeymoon to Yellowstone Park, because she said she was afraid to go off alone with a strange man to the wild west. Soon after that, Katy had a honeymoon of her own, but her husband had died and left her with young children, and to support them she worked for Stevensons, Scotts and our numerous other relatives during emergencies or, preferably, parties.

Sometime during the evening, Adlai, in the stiff collar he detested, and I, with freshly brushed Alice-in-Wonderland hairdo and a spanking sash, would file into the drawing room to greet the guests, and bow or curtsey. Then we stood quietly and took turns winding the high, shiny mahogany Victrola. (*The Walkyrie,* sung by Gadski, and Madame Schumann-Heink's *Selections from Samson and Delilah,* stay in my mind as theme songs of those command appearances.) Later mother would tell us, "You appeared very well." The expression "appeared well" became a horror to me, and made me feel I was putting on some kind of act to win the grownups' approval.

One of the teen-age entries in my diary is: "Adlai and I had dinner alone tonight and laughed ourselves nearly sick." From the time we were very small, we had fun together. One of our favorite stunts, when our parents were out in the evening, was to crawl out my bedroom window and squat on the roof, laughing uproariously, and hoping the people on the passing street car saw us.

Adlai's room was almost too cluttered to get into. Like any small boy, he was already a passionate collector; he saved the midget-size pictures of baseball players, boxers, actresses and what not that came in cigarette packages. In fact, one of his more repulsive habits was to examine each crumpled cigarette package in the gutter for "cards." He collected coins, luggage tags, baggage checks, tadpoles in Mason jars, wood for his boat carving. The only hobby I objected to violently was his collecting stray cats.

One of his four-footed protégés, a scrawny kitten, had a fit in the kitchen one night, and hissed and gyrated so wildly I jumped up on top of a table screaming, and had quite a fit myself. Being a brother, Adlai wasn't impressed with my hysterics, and told me not to be a "goop." (A book called *The Goops* had supplied us with our choicest epithets.) Another time he smuggled a black cat upstairs and put it on my bed, as a friendly surprise, but my hackles rose higher than the cat's, and we both boded evil for Adlai.

It was a relief when he switched to machinery, and began to give us bafflingly technical descriptions of pet cocks and valves. He and his friends in the neighborhood—Harry Mc-Murray, Tip Fredericks, Harold Eckart and Hesketh Coolidge—were acquiring grease spots and a new vocabulary in the machine shop Walter Williams had rigged up in his father's barn down the street. Walter was in his teens, and the grownups spoke tolerantly of his tinkering. Some years later, they were surprised to hear that Walter's tinkering had resulted in some highly profitable inventions in oil heating. But back in those coal-shovel days, Adlai and the others hustled through their home chores of pumping water from the cistern and carrying out ashes, and gathered at Walt's garage to talk about the most fascinating thing on earth: motorcars.

We were to get one of the first cars in Bloomington, but I'm glad we had a taste of that end-of-Victorian era our grandparents had thrived in, when horses and people had plenty of time. As for our beloved Grandfather Davis, and Grandfather and Grandmother Stevenson—they were so important a part of our happiness and security I can't imagine growing up without them.

I remember once being sick, with a high fever, and waking up to find my gentle-voiced Grandmother Stevenson sitting beside my bed, smiling. I felt so comforted and reassured I thought drowsily, I must be in Heaven.

She was small and dainty, with skin like porcelain, and at home she wore lavender or silvery gray silks, and full-skirted black velvet collared in Brussels lace. She always had a radiant serenity about her, although she wasn't one to sit with folded hands. During her years with Grandfather in Washington, she had been one of the founders of the Congress of Mothers, which became the Parent-Teachers Association, and she had worked to organize the Daughters of the American Revolution, hoping it would help heal the breach between the women of the North and South. She was also four times president general of the D.A.R., but she once said firmly, "I hope the day will never come when club women are not also home women." For her grandchildren, she had a never-ending supply of affection and peppermints and hot chocolate with whipped cream.

It was always a great event when her dashing little one-horse brougham, driven by the colored coachman, George Meaderds, came up our driveway. The brougham had her initials on the door, and it was lined in gray satin, with compartments for her smelling-salts bottles and calling cards. I remember once when she walked into our hall, she tsk-tsked Mother's adopting the new fad for uncarpeted stairs, and predicted we'd all break our necks. Her own winding stairway, in the big Victorian house on Franklin Square, was of course heavily carpeted and ended under a dome of stained glass.

Every Sunday we were taken to Grandfather Stevenson's for heavy noon dinners that began with a long Presbyterian grace—"May our spirit be humbled and our transgressions forgiven in the sight of the Lord"—and ended with Grand-father's best (therefore longest) stories.

Grandmother would sit at one end of the dinner table, smiling and nodding while Grandfather, impressively hand-some in a Prince Albert coat, entertained the guests. He was a great raconteur, and no one ever tired of his tales—nor did he! His stories were apt, full of good humor and en-riched with the Bible. Although one of Grandmother's say-ings was "An honest tale speeds best, being plainly told," she was much too good a wife to spoil his stories. In fact, she always laughed at the right spots, with as much delight as if she'd never heard the story before. She handled Grand-father with a velvety iron guile, and like the rest of us, he adored her. They were always very formal, and addressed each other as Mr. and Mrs. Stevenson.

Grandfather was six feet tall and straight, bald, with bril-liant, merry blue eyes, and very bushy brows that he'd draw together with a fine grimace, during his dramatic pauses. Father's sister, our Aunt Letitia, used to take advantage of the pauses to slip a second helping of dessert—always brick ice cream with chocolate sauce—to Adlai.

Aunt Letitia seemed to me like a fairy princess sort of aunt, with her red-gold hair, very white skin, and her lovely gaiety. Once Grandmother said to her beautiful daughter, "I notice you don't accept compliments gracefully, and that's an art every woman must learn. Even if the compliment is insincere, if somebody has gone to the trouble to make it, then you must take the trouble to receive it charmingly."

Certainly Aunt Letitia never rebuffed Adlai's and my open adoration. She and Grandmother always sensed when we'd reached the limit of dutiful listening, and to reward us for not squirming, or to forestall it, they'd maneuver an end to the after-dinner stories, so that Grandfather would take us into his study for the high spot of our Sundays—examining what we called his Treasure Cabinet. This was a glass-front cabinet that reached almost to the ceiling, crammed with mementoes of his long public life. I'm afraid Adlai and I ignored one of Grandfather's own favorites, a framed letter from Grover Cleveland saying: "I am extremely well pleased that I am to be in harness with you, and I believe we shall prove a fast team." This couldn't compare—for us—with the charms of a dagger once owned by a cannibal chieftain, with a blade over two feet long and a handle carved like a man's head and inlaid with *human teeth.*

Another one that fascinated us was the real hornet's nest, and the story Grandfather told us about it. An ancestor of ours, Ephraim Brevard, helped draw up the Mecklenburg declaration of independence, to launch the Colonies' first protest against British tyranny, in North Carolina, and General Cornwallis reported to King George there was a regular hornet's nest of rebels in that county, so the rebels promptly adopted that for their emblem.

Adlai and I used to eye the hornet's nest longingly, but we were never allowed to touch, just look and listen. Aunt Letitia says she overheard us once discussing, with that rather horrifying matter-of-factness of children, which treasures we'd take "when Grandfather dies." We both coveted the tiny gold bell that was an exact copy of the original Liberty Bell, crack and all. Adlai had a hankering for the good-luck coins, and a gavel made of wood from Lincoln's birthplace, and naturally, the cannibal dagger.

Like Lincoln, our Grandfather Stevenson was born in Kentucky, one of six sons of a farmer of Scotch-Irish descent who moved his family to Illinois in 1852 and died soon afterward. Grandfather worked his way through school, helped support his young brothers and sister, and went to Centre College in Kentucky with his double first cousin James S. Ewing. He then practiced law in Metamora, and went to Washington as Democratic congressman elected on the heels of the Civil War in strong Union territory. He served as assistant postmaster general during Cleveland's first term, and got the nickname of The Headsman when he lopped 40,000 Republican postmasters off the payroll with such grace and decision they almost liked it! Mr. Cleveland was so impressed with the way The Headsman wielded the political axe that it's no wonder he wanted Grandfather in harness with him, as Vice-President, when he was re-elected in 1892. Grandfather never made an enemy of a political opponent.

Grandmother's inaugural ball gown, which was carefully preserved in a trunk in their attic, was one of the costumes my friend Elizabeth Linn and I longed to play dress-up in, but never did. It was white watered silk with mammoth puff sleeves of purple velvet, a lace Bertha, and a skirt surely twelve yards around. Once Grandmother remarked that to keep pace with the First Lady, Mrs. Cleveland, in stylishness, took a lot of "pleasant thought and effort."

An old newspaper clipping describes another costume she wore which must have outshone even the First Lady's: "Mrs. Stevenson received in a gown of white satin trimmed with ermine, over a petticoat of light blue silk veiled in crystal lace. The corsage was trimmed with crystal passementeries and ermine." What the clipping didn't say was that under this creation, Grandmother wore iron braces on her legs (she had had severe rheumatism) to enable her to stand for hours in a receiving line.

Another old clipping, from the *Bloomington Observer*,

gives a reader's poetic outburst after an election night of Grandfather Stevenson's:

> The streets that night were full of cheering men.
> Beneath the swaying, spluttering torches' glare
> The marchers paused, e'er moving on again
> Before a lighted house on Franklin Square.
> When an erect, broad-shouldered man came out,
> A boy delirious in the evening's fun
> Inquired, "Who's that?" amidst tumultuous shout,
> His father said, "That's Adlai Stevenson."

This reminds me of a rather startling encounter that Adlai, as Grandfather's namesake, had in 1948 when he was running for governor. A very old farmer came up to him after a speech, shook hands, and inquired solicitously after his health. Adlai said he was fine, and the old man seemed relieved to hear this. "I been wonderin'," he muttered. "Ain't seen you since I voted for you last time you run, in 1908."

Nineteen hundred and eight was Grandfather's last campaign, and I wish my brother and I could remember it as clearly as the old farmer did. But Adlai was eight then, and even my two-years vantage hasn't aided my memory much. Grandfather, at the age of seventy-three, ran for governor of Illinois and lost to Charles Deneen by only 23,000 votes, while his party lost the state, to William Howard Taft, by 179,000. We were at Grandfather's house that losing election night (Father was campaign manager) and I remember being impressed because there were *two* telephones for receiving returns, and one was the new-fangled sort that sat on the marble-topped table, and had no crank.

In defeat, Grandfather was exactly the same charming, affable, family-loving man he'd always been. My earliest

memory of him is sitting on the top stair with Adlai and me
behind him pushing, playing a game with the rather irrever-
ent title of "Kicking gaw-gaw downstairs." Another of our
early treats, on overnight visits, was a bath in the huge tin
tub built into a wooden block, that made us feel we'd gone
to sea. The first time we stayed overnight, when Adlai was
about five, we were put to bed in the dressing room adjoining our grandparents' bedroom, separated only by portieres.
In the middle of the night, I woke up terrified by a loud,
strange roaring sound. (I had never heard anyone snore
before, and Grandfather's snores were as dramatic as his
oratory.) I shook Adlai awake, wailing, "Listen! What is it?"

My brother listened sleepily and said in an interested tone,
"Lions, I think."

There were often other kinds of lions present at the Stevensons', including William Jennings Bryan. (He and Grandfather had been running mates in 1900, on the People's
party ticket.) One of our favorite family jokes was about a
reception at Grandfather's, when Mother wore a string of
brilliant blue glass beads and one of the distinguished guests,
Henry Wellcome of London, exclaimed, "Madam, what magnificent sapphires!"

Mother repeated this delightedly to Adlai and me, and for
years afterward, when she was dressing for a gala evening,
we'd ask, "Madam, will you wear your sapphires?"

As small children, we often sat on either side of her dressing table while she did her hair and told us a story. Being
a girl, I had the privilege of combing and rerolling the false
hair pieces—puffs—that she pinned at the back of her head.
She had a beautiful throat and shoulders, and she carried
her head very high, so that in evening clothes there was a
regal upness about her. I remember a pink lace dress with

long tight sleeves and a great flounce behind, and a black dress studded all over with jet, with jet loops cascading down her arms.

If Father had had his way, she probably *would* have been wearing sapphires. He was so extravagantly generous that Mother's Quaker sense of thrift was often outraged. I remember her looking at an elaborate new silver toilet set, saying, "But, Lewis, it's folly. My old set is perfectly good." Another time, he brought her a coiled gold snake bracelet with glittering diamond eyes. I thought it was the most glamorous thing I'd ever seen, and I couldn't understand why Mother was so lukewarm toward this gift.

The Stevensons were never wealthy, but Father had the generous giving nature of his Southern ancestors. Some of his gestures were incredibly impractical, but done with such love. When his sister Mary died in her teens, Father, who was then on his first job, used all his savings to buy a diamond ring for her to be buried in. He told Grandmother, "Because Mary always wanted a diamond."

Mother believed in spending money on education, travel, health, or furnishing a home, but Father had no such limitations, and this naturally led to some spirited arguments. Not that Father needed an excuse to make a scene. When he was in a good mood, nobody could be more charming, but he had a temper that would come up as unexpectedly as a summer storm. One of the later entries in my diary was: "Father is still easily flustrated." Thanks to my always-shaky spelling, I'd coined the perfect word to describe his tempers.

Mother never raised her voice, in these scenes, but she had a quick tongue, and she certainly wasn't the woman to back down if she thought she was right. Once when she and Father were having a spirited set-to, Father said, "Well, you took me for better or for worse." Mother snapped, "Well, you're worse than I took you for!" The contestants then burst out laughing.

When I started this book, one of my parents' closest friends in Bloomington, beautiful Miss Julia Hodge, remarked, "You were a very loving family, but very explosive. Adlai was always the peacemaker."

It wasn't so much what Adlai did that brought peace, but the very fact that he was around. I think the best explanation of that is a letter Father wrote him on New Year's Day, when he was ten.

My splendid boy: My heart is full of good wishes to every one of you, and I want my smiling, blessed boy to be the carrier of them. I know of no one on earth whose heart is more kindly or who is better suited to carry a message of good will. Keep it up, old boy, & you will continue to be a pleasure & a source of joy all your life. I can wish you no more desirable trait than the one you already have—that of being able to give joy by your mere presence. Pop is proud of you and believes he will be more so all the days of his life.

This is Sunday and I hope a letter will be started on its journey to me. . . . Write me fully and tell me something of your daily life. Buffie says you are bringing in the coal. Am glad to know this. Help Mama every way you can. . . . Grandfather was much pleased by your paper box. It is on the mantle. He is sitting just back of me and says send the good old boy a "buss" (kiss) for me.

This is my first letter this year, & is, very properly, to the first boy of this or any other year. . . . Devotedly, Pop.

My brother's sweet disposition didn't prevent his being a normal small boy and getting into some lively neighborhood scraps. Mother had asked him not to fight, but he managed to get his nose broken twice, in honest battle. The second time it happened, he put off telling Mother, and as a result his nose is still slightly crooked because it wasn't set until a week later, when the truth leaked out—that one of his friendly opponents had thrown a brick, in the heat of the fray. It was Adlai's first brickbat.

During the 1952 campaign, when reporters swarmed down on Bloomington to collect facts (or fancy) about the Democratic nominee for President, a brisk Chicago newspaperman of the opposition press asked a charming old lady who had been a neighbor of ours, and a staunch Republican, "What was Stevenson like as a boy?" Perhaps he wanted to hear that Adlai had tortured frogs and trampled her garden. If so, he heard no such thing. Bursting with kind intentions, the lady said vivaciously, "Why, that boy was an angel— just an angel."

But I'll bear witness that the "angel" often had a bloody nose, a black eye and torn pants!

Chapter 2

ADLAI AND I are the fifth generation of our family to live in Illinois, and there is no other place so close to our hearts. An Easterner friend said recently, "Whenever your brother says 'Illinois' he gives it such a special, loving sound that I find myself feeling wistful because I didn't grow up there."

The house on Washington Street is the home I came back to, with my husband Ernest Ives and our son Timothy, when Ernest retired after thirty years abroad in the Foreign Service. The ginkos, maples and chestnut trees Mother planted are now a high, leafy awning over the porch and lawn. As a girl back from boarding school, I exulted in my diary, "Home again! Home—the sweetest, freshest, greenest place in all the world!" Now that I've lived over a good bit of the world, I still feel that way. It has always seemed to me that the prairie sky is vaster and nearer to earth, and I get a sense of peaceful purpose and fulfillment from the rich, black, rolling prairie country.

Even in our early years out west, Mother told Adlai and me so many stories of "When I was a little girl" that Illinois stayed fresh and green in our minds.

She and Father had been childhood sweethearts in Bloomington, where mother's father, Pennsylvania-born Quaker William O. Davis, was publisher of the staunchly Republican *Pantagraph*. When Mother married Lewis Green Stevenson, the son of the Democratic Vice-President, in 1893, newspaper accounts called it "a triumph of love over politics."

When I was born, in 1897, Father was working for the Hearst Estate, as a superintendent at the Santa Rita copper mines in New Mexico. Senator George Hearst of Nevada had been a great friend of Grandfather's during their years in Washington, and while his wife, Mrs. Phoebe Hearst, and Grandmother Stevenson were working busily to assemble the first Congress of Mothers, their sons, Father and William Randolph, were boyhood friends. Father went to Philips Exeter, but didn't go on to college; a gun had backfired freakishly when he was hunting, leaving a wound that developed into tuberculosis of the shoulder. He said that he learned in those weary years of illness to be patient and trust God to take care of him. Even after he was cured, the lame shoulder and a rather stiff arm were handicaps he refused to surrender to. The year after his marriage he went off to the Far East as a newspaper correspondent. When he came back, he needed a stay in a better climate than Illinois, and also a job, I suppose. Mrs. Hearst, by then a widow, hired Father and put him to work as manager of several mines in the Southwest.

Mother stayed in Bloomington for the birth of her first child—me—in a blue silk canopied bed in her parents' house. When she went to New Mexico, Cora Galbraith went along as my nurse, and stayed with us till my brother was six. Cora—Codie—was as slim and straight and blonde as a corn

stalk, in blue-and-white striped uniforms that reached to her
high-buttoned shoes. The warmhearted Illinois country girl
and my elegant homesick young mother must have been a
great comfort to each other in the wild, desolate country
around Fort Bayard, where coyotes howled through the
night. (The little community was almost wholly Mexican.)
A New Year's letter from Grandfather Davis written to me
when I was six months old undoubtedly cheered mother:

> To our sweet little Elizabeth: We hope that you may grow
> large enough to wear Cora's shoes, your father's hat, and to
> eat your mother's slice of cake. We urge you to kick strenu-
> ously for your vested rights, as a citizen of the sage brush
> territory. We urge you to raise your voice by night or day
> until the dwelling of the Aztecs resounds with its vibrations,
> and your privileges are fully recognized. Cut your eye teeth as
> quick as you can, get a rocky mountain lion for playmate, and
> have a pair of Jackass rabbits trained to draw your little car-
> riage. Be a live active part of the resistless [restless?] enthu-
> siasm of your western civilization so that when you return to
> this land of steady habits the Stevensons and Davis' will greet
> you with awe and admiration. So bidding you goodbye with
> Mark Twain's maxim, "Be good and you'll be lonely," we
> subscribe ourselves . . . Daddy Davis.

We moved to Los Angeles when Father became assistant
manager of his friend Mr. Hearst's first newspaper venture,
the *Examiner,* and Adlai was born there in a rented house
on Monmouth Avenue, on February 5, 1900. I was two and
a half; Codie told me later that she took me out for a walk
that morning, to pick oranges. When we got back to the
house, I had a new brother weighing eleven and a half
pounds, named Adlai Ewing Stevenson II. (Grandfather got
his first name from Adlai Osborne of North Carolina. It
must have come from the First Book of Chronicles, twenty-

ninth verse of the twenty-seventh chapter, in which Shapat is identified as "the son of Adlai.")

When the news reached Bloomington, both the Democrat and Republican sides of the family rejoiced, and Grandfather Davis wrote mother teasingly, "We are all highly gratified to hear of the successful launching of this little Presidential craft."

To mark the great event of his son's birth, Father gave mother a gold bracelet with the date engraved inside, and the baby soon teethed on it so lustily that the bracelet bears formidable toothmarks to this day.

I was always the mothering type, and I must have wanted to treat my new brother like a doll, but he was so big no one could lift him, and besides, he had other ideas, even that young; from the time he could walk, he was very independent. I have a hazy recollection of another small girl and myself sitting on his stomach trying to make him be our "baby" when we played house. One of his first words, trying to say my name, was "Lizbuff," and I've been "Buffie" ever since. A letter from Grandmother Stevenson to father remarks: "I am so glad Elizabeth loves the boy. A child is apt to carry through life the feelings it had when its first rival arrives into the world."

It would have been hard *not* to love so smiling, eager a little boy; in just one of the early snapshots, he looks ready to howl, and with good reason: a bee stung him just as mother clicked the Kodak.

With all his contentment, he was deeply sensitive. When he was about three, he yanked at a cloth on a table set for a dinner party, and brought china and silver crashing down. Mother slapped his hands, and he was told to go upstairs, the usual punishment for misdeeds. Hours later, our worried parents, after searching all over the house, discovered my small brother peacefully asleep in the kennel with the dog. (His fondness for strays showed up first in California; a homeless dog with an advanced case of mange was an acquisition he clung to like grim death.)

Father also worked on the San Francisco *Examiner,* and we lived in Berkeley, in a house rented from Mrs. Phoebe Hearst. The stable at the back was converted into a little school where neighborhood children were taught French. My first lessons were in that language, and I've loved it ever since. Mother wrote Daddy Davis, in 1905: "If Elizabeth continues at the same rate in poetry, French and flirting, she will afford me all the aesthetic diversion I need."

My young brother's own aesthetic diversions were feeding swans in the park, being read to, and building things. He would work quietly for hours building an "engine" of boxes and chairs. He says now that one of his earliest recollections is of Mrs. Hearst making "colored fire" for his delight, in the great fireplace of her hacienda across the bay.

While we were living in Berkeley, mother had such a serious bout of pneumonia she was never really healthy again. When the San Francisco earthquake struck, in 1906, we were back in Los Angeles, and Father was in charge of the first relief train sent into the devastated area, by the Los Angeles *Examiner.* Many of the babies born in tent hospitals during those nightmare days were named after Mr. Hearst or Father and Mother.

Perhaps the earthquake made Mother long more than ever for the safe, solid ground of her home state. She was also worried about being so far away from Grandfather Davis, after Grandmother died in 1900. On one of our yearly trips back to Bloomington, she took Adlai and me to visit her mother's mother, our Great-grandmother Fell, who was still living in the adjoining town of Normal. Great-grandmother was already in her nineties, and wore her hair skinned back so tightly I thought it must hurt her. I remember the scratchy horsehair upholstery, a big glass case full of wonderful, bright-hued stuffed birds, and a trellised back porch with the ripe fragrance of fruit that had just thudded to earth.

A plaque on the gateway of the Normal University campus where we both went to high school, says:

TO THE FOUNDER OF NORMAL
J. W. FELL
LOVER AND PLANTER OF TREES
PHILANTHROPIST OF MIGHTY VISION
THIS GATE IS DEDICATED BY
THE WOMEN'S IMPROVEMENT LEAGUE
AND HIS MANY FRIENDS

This farseeing, extraordinary little Quaker and friend of Lincoln is Adlai's favorite ancestor. Great-grandfather came to Bloomington because John Todd Stuart, Lincoln's future law partner, told him it was a promising community. At the age of twenty, he had left Chester County (in Pennsylvania near Philadelphia), and started out on foot, stopping in Wheeling, Virginia to work on an Abolitionist newspaper for a year, and in Steubenville, Ohio, to study law. When John Stuart directed him to Bloomington, in 1832, the town had ninety-seven citizens, and hardly enough legal business to keep a young lawyer's horse in oats. This didn't daunt Jesse Fell. He was a pioneer in developing central Illinois, and he often covered eighty miles a day on horseback, looking for good, fertile land. He not only founded many new towns but acquired sizable property in most of them, and

secured the right-of-way for Bloomington's first railroad. As
he rode around the country, two shabby volumes of Shakespeare jounced in his saddlebags, and when he stopped to
eat by the roadside, his meal would be enriched with sonnets
or scenes from *Richard III.*

In 1836, he started a Bloomington newspaper that lasted
for twenty issues. He tried again, and managed to keep it
alive for a year. On the third try, in 1851, he brought new
printing equipment from Philadelphia up the Illinois River
and launched the *Intelligencer.* Soon he had an assistant—a
scholar of the classics—who rechristened the paper the *Pantagraph,* derived from the Greek words "Pan" and "Graf,"
meaning "write all things."

Great-grandfather's own motto might have been "Do all
things—well." While he was still practicing law, he prepared
his briefs at home, then rode all night to reach Vandalia, the
first capital of Illinois, where he'd present his case or appear
before the Legislature. And it was in a Vandalia boarding-
house that he first met the gangling young legislator, Abra-
ham Lincoln. He became Lincoln's devoted friend, and as
a dissident Whig, was one of the founders of the Republican
party in Illinois.

It was Great-grandfather who suggested the Lincoln-Doug-
las debates, and their success convinced him all the more
that Mr. Lincoln should be President. Knowing that his
native Pennsylvania was a stronghold of the new Republican party, he persuaded his friend Joseph J. Lewis to begin
an active campaign there to spread the facts about Lincoln,
and he himself traveled through the eastern states talking
to politicians and other influential people. To help this
campaign along, Jesse Fell got Lincoln to write a three-page
autobiography. (Carl Sandburg mentions Great-grandfather's

persistence in this task.) This document circulated all through the East, and played an important part in Lincoln's election. The original is now in the Library of Congress, but both Adlai and I have copies of the facsimile edition Great-grandfather published.

In the letter Lincoln sent with the original autobiography, he wrote Jesse Fell, "Herewith is a little sketch, as you requested. There is not much of it, for this reason, I suppose, that there is not much of me. If anything be made out of it, I wish it to be modest, and not to go beyond the material."

Great-grandfather was also modest; he wasn't interested in politics for himself, although he served Lincoln as paymaster and major during the Civil War, and was urged to run for Congress. His real passion was the land, and horticulture. He wanted the great, rolling prairie planted with fine trees. He planted 10,000 trees in Normal alone, before the town was even laid out, and many more for a campus when he inspired the founding of the state normal school there, the first one west of the Alleghenies.

He also built the cupola-topped house of his dreams on the exact spot in Normal where, as a penniless lawyer, he had reined his horse and exclaimed, "This is where I'll have my home someday!" He bought Great-grandmother the first piano and the first ice-cream freezer in that section of Illinois. Nobody tried to borrow the piano, but the freezer was such an exotic new gadget that it was constantly carted off by the neighbors, until Great-grandfather finally, in exasperation, bought a spare, known as the Neighborhood Freezer. This ensured his having homemade cherry ice cream for a constant stream of guests, including Horace Mann, Susan B. Anthony, Robert Ingersoll and Mr. Lincoln. We loved to hear Mother tell about the deer he brought to roam in the big wooded park around the estate, and how his young grandchildren could "help" with the bird houses he built, and with his planting.

By the time we moved back to the Midwest, that land had all been sold, and the house sadly changed, but one of the many memorials to Great-grandfather, Fell Avenue, ran the three miles from Bloomington to Normal. As we drove along it in the buggy that Mother often rented from the livery stable, Adlai and I sat beside her while she held the reins skillfully in one hand, and just as skillfully held us enthralled with her stories.

She'd tell us about Great-grandfather's horses Dolly and Pet—and this reminds me of a letter I came across recently, which Father wrote Mother from California the year before they were married, when he was about to come home for a visit: "Have both Pet and Dolly re-shod, lay in an extra supply of carriage grease and bid the family a fond farewell— you are mine for six weeks. . . . This poor moustache that I thought you would be so proud of is, I see, doomed. . . ."

On our own buggy rides, Mother would tell Adlai and me how she and the other children played circus with the horses. "We hung from Dolly's tail and rode around a little sawdust ring in the barn, doing stunts," Mother would say gaily. Even my engine-minded brother was overwhelmed with envy at this picture of Mother hanging from a horse's tail.

Both of us begged for stories about the Grandmother Davis we'd never known. She loved animals so devotedly that she often sat up all night in the barn, while a sick horse lay with its head in her lap. But it was the story about her dog we found most dramatic. On a camping trip in Nebraska he caught fire when a kerosene lamp tipped over, and ran off in flames across the prairie, but Grandmother Davis raced after him, on and on, till she caught the poor frantic animal and wrapped him in wet cloths and unguents, and nursed him for weeks. As a result, the dog worshiped her, and when she came back from her only trip abroad, he leaped up to greet her and dropped dead at her feet—"from joy," Mother said.

Grandfather Davis wasn't sentimental about animals, but he had a wonderful way with children. He was very tall, with thick wavy gray hair, and he walked so fast we had to trot to keep up. Like all born editors and reporters, he had an enormous curiosity about everything and everybody. When he'd say to Adlai and me, "Tell me what you did today," this was no social pleasantry. He expected a good, full account. "But what *kind* of wagon?" he'd ask. "Sky blue? Nine feet high? Drawn by elephants?"

His eyes twinkled encouragement, and he listened so perceptively, not just with his ears but with his whole brilliant mind, that we sharpened our wits to please him.

His office at the *Pantagraph* was a cubbyhole with a rolltop desk piled with books and proofs, and with its own door onto the street, so that he could slip out and jump into his buggy hitched there, whenever he took a notion to gather his own news. On our visits, the printers always let Adlai and me set our names in type, and the clerks in the business office—called the counting room—gave us long yellow ruled pads, the kind my brother still uses for the first drafts of speeches.

Adlai's literary style has changed considerably since his first essay, published in the *Pantagraph:*

MY PET BUNNY

When I was eight years old, my father brought me from his farm a wee bunny that seemed to me not more than three weeks old.

At first bunny was very much frightened. I got a large box for his home and fixed it up very comfortably, where bunny lived cosily for some time, never running away.

His box was kept in the upper half during the night, and one morning when I went out to see how bunny was, I found he was gone. Then everyone in the house started to look for bunny, but nowhere was he to be found until the cook, coming into the dining room saw bunny sitting on a register as comfy as could be. This was only a taste of adventure for bunny, and every day he was in some new mischief. One bright day bunny was sunning himself on a window sill, when a thievish cat suddenly snatched him and ran away. I hunted everywhere, but I could not find him, and I never saw my pet bunny again.

Adlai E. Stevenson

Age 9 years old.

1316 East Washington Street

I suspect Grandfather or Uncle Bert fixed up the spelling before "My Pet Bunny" went to press.

Mother's brother Uncle Bert—H. O. Davis—became editor of the *Pantagraph*. He was a small, lovable man who used swear words as casually as if he were sprinkling pepper on mashed potatoes. The whole staff adored him; he had practically been raised in that newspaper office, and he loved every inch of it. In those days, the *Pantagraph* was a morning paper, and he often spent most of the night in the press rooms, "putting the baby to bed." The only time he lost his genial manner was during elections; he was violently Republican, and he never supported Father or any other Democrat. The rival paper, the *Bulletin,* owned by the Braleys and O'Donnells, was soundly on "our side." I think this lack of support from her own family's paper caused Mother many a twinge, because she was loyally Democratic from the day she married

Father (or even earlier). It was undoubtedly a relief whenever a lull in politics brought "friendly relations," literally.

Cousin James Ewing, another relative who often called on us, was a courtly old gentleman who wore a long black frock coat with a crisply pleated shirt front. (He had been Minister to Belgium, and a friend of King Leopold's.) Adlai and I would sit and watch him suck in his mustaches and make faces, while he talked. Whenever he told a story that had something to do with "fast horses" and "fast women," he twirled the walrus ends of his mustaches, imitating a Kentucky colonel. I wish I could remember the whole story, but I pictured "fast women" as fleet-footed females, so it's possible I missed the point. One phrase he used I've never forgotten, which I finally discovered referred to a drink of whiskey, was "a touch of the ardent."

Cousin Jim was quite a gourmet, and he seemed to enjoy our "specialties of the house." Mother was a natural-born cook, and she and Ag were like two artists conferring, as they tasted and improvised. In disputes, the higher authority Mother consulted was *Mrs. Rohrer's Cookbook,* jacketed in black oilcloth. One of the dishes I've never had anywhere since was tomatoes simmered in cream. The dessert that was (and still is) Adlai's favorite was a kind of cherry pie called cherry "slump." (Ag also did a magnificent blueberry slump.) The crust on top was rather like a biscuit dough, with the juicy fruit bubbling through. Mother and her sister, Aunt Jessie Merwin, often used "receipts" they'd copied from Grandmother Davis, and maybe our "slump" came from there, too.

The Merwins lived in a house at the back of Grandfather Davis' property, and their oldest son, our cousin Davis, was just Adlai's age. The two boys would crouch for hours on their haunches, in the doorway of Grandfather's stable, throwing jackknives in endless games of mumblety-peg. Once Daddy Davis gave Adlai a handsome red-handled new knife which my brother, boy-fashion, promptly lost. Daddy Davis found it on the lawn, and thought he'd teach Adlai a little lesson, so he pocketed it and asked at lunch, "How's the new knife? All right for whittling?"

My brother was so stricken with remorse he burst into tears before Grandfather could reach in his pocket and produce the lost treasure.

We usually had early morning Christmas with the Merwins at Grandfather Davis', before we went on for the second half of the double-header day: more presents and another tree, at Grandfather Stevenson's. One of my most thrilling presents was a doll's brass bed with pillows, sheets and blankets, from Aunt Letitia. Another was the silver comb, brush and mirror Grandmother gave me, piece by piece, engraved with a rose and my name, Elizabeth. Adlai's favorite was his toy train, which he kept set up in the attic, where he could crash his cars in harrowing imitation of the wrecks that were all too frequent in that day.

One year our pre-Christmas curiosity reached such a pitch we sneaked into the guestroom when our parents were out, crawled up on the closet shelf, and examined every one of the presents Mother and Father had carefully hidden away. Then our guilty consciences made us exclaim all the louder on Christmas morning, over "surprises" that included a tool chest for Adlai, and for me a doll's purple velvet coat and matching hat with plumes that Mother had made.

Whenever our Hardin cousins came for the holidays, they

livened things up considerably. Our handsome Aunt Julia, father's sister, was married to a Presbyterian minister, Reverend Martin Hardin II, and they had a daughter Letitia and three rambunctious sons. There was a great uproar the time young Letitia was missing all day, and by late afternoon the frantic grownups called the police, to help search. Eventually they found our cousin sitting peacefully upstairs in Grandfather's attic, surrounded by three thousand books, reading her way through them as a mouse nibbles through cheese.

Her brothers were active in a less literary way, and Adlai went right along. Once at dinner the boys snapped butter balls up at the ceiling, and a few stuck there and quivered suspensefully over the chatting grownups' oblivious heads. They also staged shooting frays with Concord grapes—one strategic squeeze and the grape's innards would squirt out and plop juicily on the target.

For more conventional amusement, at family parties, we played charades. Once Adlai lay down on the floor, curled up in a ball, and stymied all guessers. It turned out he was "a sunbeam on a rug." Then I came leaping in waving my arms wildly; this was intended to depict "the soaring of a soul."

Father often performed, pulling coins out of his ear, and doing hilarious imitations of a monkey. Or all the children would crowd around while he told us the latest adventures of two fabulous creatures he'd invented, named Whangdoodle and Whiffenpoof. Once Whangdoodle ran away to the Orient and had to be rescued from Chinese dragons. Each time, the escapades were brand new and more exciting than ever. I used to think Father must lie awake all night thinking up stories.

We always said good-by to him just after the Christmas
holidays, and went off south with Mother and Daddy Davis.
Even a train trip, with Grandfather Davis, was a unique kind
of adventure.

Chapter 3

SUSIE ANDERSON, a maid who went south with us one winter, complained because Grandfather Davis ordered her to put away the magazine she was reading and improve her mind by looking out the train window.

That was typical of our highly cerebral, delicate grandfather, but Susie was a capable, Viking-like blonde, with a Scandinavian will of her own. At home, the streetcar conductors were so smitten with her that they'd clang the bell and stop the streetcar exactly in front of our house, to let us off. But when she traveled with Grandfather Davis, it was he who called the halts, and if he told her not to read, even high-spirited Susie obeyed. He said the only point in going anywhere was to see new sights and learn from them.

Adlai, who would rather travel, read and listen than anything else, often reminds me of Grandfather. My brother never had to be coerced, especially when it came to learning about trains. He dogged the footsteps of every conductor and porter, pestering them with questions, and he hopped off at each stop, to consult with his friends the brakemen, and bear up-to-the-minute reports back to Grandfather. In a letter written en route, decorated with drawings of engines and

decorously signed, "Your trutly, Adlai Stevenson," he sent
home some of the news:

> "We are about 200 miles from Chicago. We will reach New-
> orleans in the morning at ten fifteen. There is very much to
> see. The land is very good for farming. . . . The train is a very
> nice one and my sister and myselfe are having a fine time."

While we watched out the window, Adlai and I played a
game of observation with freight cars. Keeping score was
noisy, because the idea was to call out the name of the railroad line a passing car belonged to—"Wabash! Lackawanna!
Baltimore and Ohio! Santa Fe!" we'd shout, and whoever
yelled first (or loudest) could add that freight car to his score.

To keep out the soot at night, Mother draped sheets up
over the windows, but her children always managed to fix
peepholes. By day, whatever we saw—a tobacco-shed, a mule,
a glimpse of a plantation house beyond a cotton field—Daddy
Davis filled in the picture, while Mother wiped soot from the
window sills. He explained what sharecroppers were, told us
how farmers dried tobacco, and gave us bits of Confederate
history livened by firsthand accounts of the Civil War, when
he served on the Union side as Great-grandfather Fell's pay-
master-clerk. He also told us about driving out as a young
man to Leadville, Colorado, in the 1860 gold rush, to sell
supplies to prospectors. Adlai never had much use for that
story, because he thought anybody who went to a gold rush,
especially one's own grandfather, should come back with real
gold nuggets.

When Daddy Davis talked about thrift, he would point to
his gold watch and say, "I had to pawn this to pay my printer,
the first year I owned the *Pantagraph*. Always save half of
what you make, and keep accounts of every penny."

Mother and Aunt Jessie sometimes complained that Grandfather kept entirely too strict account of his own "fortune," which he made by hard work and a real genius for publishing. He believed in a family paper that reported the news straight and clean—truth without fear, favor or filth—that "could be read even by children." His faith in people's intelligence had been borne out, and both he and his paper prospered, but Daddy Davis wasn't one to depend on idealistic theories alone. Even in his last years, he still drove around the countryside in his buggy, tacking up "Read the *Pantagraph*" posters on fences.

He also went right on practicing the thrift he preached to Adlai and me. One of his economies and health precautions was to carry all our food along on train trips. He said it was safer and cheaper than anything you could get in the old-fashioned dining car which Adlai and I loved. He had become a devotee of Battle Creek health foods, so one hamper contained great masses of Zweiback, odd protose concoctions and strained apple sauce in jars. After the porter set up a table, our abstemious grandfather always got out a small monogrammed silver flask, measured out one exact tablespoon of whiskey, and gulped it down with a distaste more feigned than real, I suspect.

He forgot about diets whenever we settled in that haven of gourmets, New Orleans, and would take Adlai and me on the streetcar to the fish market. I can't remember much about the houses we lived in, in New Orleans and Pass Christian. The only thing that stands out in my mind is beds draped with mosquito netting that hung from the ceiling. Our to-market expeditions were the big excitement, because they often ended in lagniappe adventures: one day Daddy Davis took us to see the battleship *Mississippi* anchored in the river.

The commander, having offered jovially to show us around, must have got more than he bargained for, because Adlai regarded ships, especially warships, with even more passionate enthusiasm than trains. He had to examine everything from the boiler room to the cannons, and went ashore wearing a sailor hatband contributed by a good-natured officer.

Grandfather kept a line-a-day notebook, which he always carried in his vest pocket, and recently I found a page of entries made in New Orleans. Along with quotations from Scott, Shakespeare and the Bible, he noted: "Took a ride around the Belt on the cars. Had the children recite this evening. Adlai has a sore foot, says he can't stand on it but when supper was called it became useful. Went to auto races, one mi. in 51 1/5 seconds, thrilling."

In a letter to Father, which Grandfather Davis dictated to me, a report on Adlai's lessons trails in second place after a report on the fish market: "Fine fresh oysters 10¢ a dozen, red snapper and pompano at a dime a pound, so you see good things are cheap. . . . Brother's taking French just as earnestly as he takes everything else except a scolding. The pronunciation puzzles him and [he's] like another French scholar of whom I heard it said that you would know by his French that he was English and by his English that he was Irish."

I was usually tutored, when we were away, but my brother went off to public schools. For so naturally friendly a child, this meant putting up a tough front among strangers, till he proved to the other boys he was no sissy. The first time he went to a new school was in Winter Park, Florida, and Grandfather Davis wrote father this account of seven-year-old Adlai's debut in the classroom:

He was dressed in the fringed suit Miss Woodbury gave him, so the scholars named him Indian. On his return home at noon, he felt quite a little chesty and told of his experience chiefly in the rough-house at the recess at 10 o'clock. He said, "There is one boy I must get rid of so I swatted him some good ones on the slats and soaked him a warm one in the face, and was oftener on top than under." Meanwhile some of the boys hollered, "Give it to him, Indian." It was altogether different from anything in his previous career.

Once he had cleared this hurdle, Adlai was blissfully happy that winter in Florida. The golf course was right in front of our rented cottage, and his new friends, the Negro caddies, loaned us an old, rusty set of clubs. Adlai, who longed for a brother, brought one of the littlest caddies into our kitchen and said to Ag, the cook, "Please give my brother some dinner." Ag did, and we were never without "brothers" from then on.

Being only a sister, I was flattered when he sought me out. In a letter to Father, I mentioned importantly, "Adlai is playing golf now and wantes me. So I will write more later. . . . We are still reading *Animals I Have Known*. . . . I love you alwas, your daughter."

It must have been Mother who was reading *Animals* to us, because Daddy Davis specialized in poetry. Our Quaker grandfather had a passion for "Bobby Burns," and he read brilliantly, with a relish and fine Scottish accent Adlai still recalls with delight.

Most of our Bobby Burns evenings were in Grandfather's cottage at Charlevoix, where we always spent our summers. It was a northern Michigan resort owned by fifty or sixty families who had built summer places on the lake. After supper, which was often planked white fish broiled and served on the blackened board, Grandfather would give us a reading in his small pinewalled bedroom. He always read sitting up in bed, wearing a high-necked, long-sleeved white nightshirt. There may be professional actors who would balk at this costume for poetry readings, but to us, and to the wearer, it seemed very right indeed.

Thus arrayed, with a pile of books by his bed and his audience of three, including Mother, waiting eagerly, Daddy Davis picked up the big red leather volume of Robert Burns he'd bought for two dollars in Philadelphia, when he started west in 1857. First he'd give us the "timorous beastie," "To a Mouse," and rollick through "The Cotter's Saturday Night." Then he read "To a Louse," with its lesson on false vanity as plain as the insect on the overdressed church-goer's bonnet. This was a moral after Daddy Davis' own heart:

> O wad some power the giftie gie us
> To see oursels as ithers see us!
> It wad frae mony a blunder free us,
> An' foolish notion:
> What airs in dress an' gait wad lea'e us,
> An' ev'n devotion!

For a climax, he'd do "Tam o' Shanter" in a way that chilled us to the marrow:

> There sat Auld Nick, in shape o'beast;
> A towzie tyke, black, grim and large,
> To gie them music was his charge; . . .
> And by some devilish cantraip sleight
> Each in its cauld hand held a light,
> By which heroic Tam was able
> To note upon the haly table . . .
> Five tomahawks, wi' blude red-rusted:
> Five scymitars, wi' murder crusted; . . .

Wi' mair, o' horrible and awefu',
Which ev'n to name wad be unlawfu'.

When he'd got us to such a pitch we saw witches and warlocks and murder-crusted weapons in every shadow, Grandfather would reach for William Cullen Bryant's: *The Family Library of Poetry and Song, Being a Choice Selection from the Best Poets.* He often read Goldsmith's elegy on the death of a mad dog, and Anthony's oration over Caesar's body, but my brother preferred Tennyson's "The Charge of the Light Brigade," and "How They Brought the Good News from Ghent to Aix." There were two he always shouted with laughter over: Bret Harte's "Plain Language from Truthful James," and Carroll's "The Hunting of the Snark." I myself was more the Byron, Browning and Wordsworth type, at that age, and my heart bled for beautiful Evelyn Hope, and for Lucy who "dwelt among the untrodden ways." Our beloved poetry reader had selections for every mood, and we were still begging, "Just one more," when Mother sent us off to bed. We didn't even know we were being inoculated with culture, and tastes for which I've been thankful ever since.

Grandfather's cottage was on a terraced bluff overlooking the lake, and our next-door neighbor was a dear old lady, Mrs. Ransom, one of a group commonly known as "Kalamazoo resorters—snip-snap snorters." She and my little brother were great friends. Once he appeared at her doorway clutching a dusty, wilted bouquet which he offered for sale, a gesture inspired by the Indians who went from door to door selling flowers and baskets. "Where did you get it?" Mrs. Ransom asked, looking dubiously at the bedraggled mess.

"Out of your garbage can," Adlai said gravely, as he took her nickel.

Indians had made the birch-bark flower boxes that bordered our cottage porch brightly, and the miniature house trimmed in porcupine quills that sat on the mantel of the huge stone fireplace. The head of the tribe, Chief McSaube, was also our postman. When he handed Mother the mail, with silent dignity, she said she felt as if she were getting important dispatches or a peace treaty. A high sand dune named after this postman-chief—Mt. McSaube—was three miles up the lake, and the scene of Adlai's first camping out. His camp mate was Joe Bohrer of Bloomington, who always spent summers with his grandfather, ex-Governor Fifer of Illinois. Joe and Adlai were inseparable (and have been close friends ever since). After elaborate preparations for their overnight safari, they trudged off under a great load of provisions, pans and blankets. The night must have seemed awfully long, because they were back home at 5 A.M. They thought it was already noon!

For our earliest nature observation, Mother rowed us over to Old River Island, where the kingfishers dove from the piles in the channel, and we walked in the thick woods of birches and pines. Our friends the Earl Babsts and the George Douglases, who stayed at the Chicago Club above the river, often joined us on these island expeditions. The boys preferred a dark and deep ravine so overgrown it seemed to us like a vast jungle, with martens and even an occasional fox. They also liked to prowl over the charred timbers of a burnt-out sugar-beet factory on Raspberry Bay. When Mother protested this was dangerous, Adlai reminded her, with calm logic, that he'd fractured his nose (the third time) by tripping over a garden wire. *Ergo,* walking in a garden was much more dangerous than leaping around on burned rafters.

Pine Lake was fourteen miles long and usually calm enough

for children in rowboats; it connected by channel with deep Round Lake, and through that to Lake Michigan. Whenever the drawbridge's warning bell rang, on Lake Michigan Channel, we rushed to see the long, flat lumber boats and the low-riding ore boats pass.

We knew many of the freight and passenger boats by their whistles, but it was the whistle of the train, the Pere Marquette, that always sent my brother into fast (and forbidden) activity. The tracks were down below the steep bank in front of the cottage. Scorning the wooden steps, he'd slide and roll down, arrive at a spot mercifully hidden from Mother's view, and proceed to lay pennies and pins on the tracks just before the train hurtled by. Then he'd rush back to get the flattened-out trophies. I never gave him away; we had a tacit two-way agreement that parents should be protected from foolish worries. But when he and Joe started the much more dangerous pastime of diving off the drawbridge as the train was coming, or jumping from the trestles as it thundered overhead, then I descended to the threat: "I'll tell Mother."

Their acrobatic act was done in full view of grownups. They rigged a wire pulley from a tree on the upper terrace to our cottage below, and would swing into midair, whooping and screeching, then drop by pulley-slide a mere thirty feet. I myself preferred playing paper dolls with my friend Dorothy Whitney, but I joined happily in another of Adlai's sports: we took turns sitting in a huge wooden chopping bowl, and sliding in this rather unusual craft down the steep sandy banks.

Every morning, we all gathered at the pier, and one of the star performers in the water was my friend Alice Stanley, now Mrs. Dean Acheson. Her swimming prowess seems all the more impressive now, when I think of our bathing costumes: ballooning black bloomers, a full skirt, a sleeved blouse with sailor collar, black cotton stockings, and a cap frilled like a Mack Sennett bathing beauty's. I noted modestly in my diary: "Brother & I have become fine swimmers, & he has learned all kinds of dives. I will never be able to dive because the minuet my eyes, ears, nose, & mouth fill with water, I scream for help."

I marvel that I didn't also scream for help on the tennis court a few years later, when I wore high-laced white buckskin shoes, a white serge pleated skirt, a Cossack blouse that sagged to my hips, and a straw hat that came down over my head like a diving bell. Even without these encumbrances, Adlai could have beat me at every game. He loved tennis, and in our later visits at Charlevoix, he spent whole days on the courts with his friends Joe Bohrer and "Lugi" Morrow. When I once won a set, I hastened to record the event for posterity: "I beat Adlai at tennis!!!!" Six exclamation points was my limit, usually reserved for romance.

Most of the resorters' social life centered around the big wooden Belvedere Hotel, and the bane of Adlai's small-boy summers was our Friday afternoon dancing class in the Casino there. Squeezed into a white suit and patent leather pumps, he was arrayed to face the music in more ways than one. Our dancing teacher, Miss Calla Travis, had yanked-up hair, protruding pointed teeth, a ramrod back, and a whistle she blew like a top sergeant. It blew rather often at Adlai. He persisted in gazing all around the room while he waltzed, and in stepping on his partner's feet and bumping into couples. He wasn't regarded as much of a partner by my sex. (Not then! Several years later, I recorded in my diary: "Ad dances like a prince. . . . We danced the Maxixe . . . We practiced the Bunny Hug. . . . I have been all afternoon at the Wood-

ruffs hearing how greatly the girls love my brother!") But in
his early dancing days, I was full of older-sister shame for
him. I was one of the three best dancers in the class—with
Lois De Sette and Clara Busch—and when Miss Calla Travis
had us help her with the younger pupils, Adlai didn't care at
all for my bossy "One, two, three, GLIDE," or the strong-
armed way I tried to lead him in a two-step.

The prize partner every girl prayed for was handsome
Gussie Busch. To lead a Grand March with him was an honor
we fought and shoved for. On cotillion nights, at the end of
each season, our parents gathered to watch us perform. One
year Clara and Lois and I, as a trio of ballerinas in black
gauze dotted with silver stars, did a number to the strains of
"The Glow Worm." We practiced so long and feverishly that
even now, if anybody struck up "The Glow Worm," I could
do every step of that dance. There is still a rumor that my
brother, at the age of ten, was featured with three other hap-
less boys in a Spanish dance with castanets, but he vigorously
denies this and insists it was a pirate dance.

Sunday nights at the Casino were much more to his liking,
when we gathered for a two-hour sing-fest, with Mr. Windsor
Aldrich waving his arms out front to lead us through the
hymns, while Miss Heaton accompanied on the piano. If
Adlai got so carried away he sang too loud, I shushed him
fiercely. I had been asked not to sing in school, because I was
always off key and it threw other pupils off too, so I tried to
make my young brother as self-conscious about his own tune-
lessness as I was, but he persisted in loving to sing. (He can't
carry a tune yet, but he'll still let loose joyfully in group-
harmonizing around a piano at parties, or in church.)

When Mr. Aldrich asked for requests, Adlai's hand always
shot up, and always the same request: "Throw Out the Life-

line." It reminded him of our heroes over at Michigan Beach, the coast guards at the lighthouse. Daddy Davis often took us over to watch the coast guard practice rescues, when they'd slide down a greased pole like firemen, and leap into their rowboats. Once, after a terrible storm, we even saw a real rescue. The *Illinois,* one of the overnight steamers from Chicago, was grounded off Michigan Beach, and the Coast Guard swung the passengers to safety in a basket-like conveyance that bobbed along a cable, a "breeches buoy."

Even on calm days, my brother usually managed to whip up excitement by clambering out on the breakwater, and to the dizzy top heights of the lookout tower. As I write this, I'm reminded of a story Senator Richard Neuberger tells, about going climbing with Adlai in Oregon. When their party reached a snow slope all the others hesitated about crossing, but Adlai strode forward like a mountain goat, calling back cheerfully, "What are you afraid of? Do you want to live forever?"

In their off-duty moments, the lighthouse coastguardmen wove handsome white string hammocks, which they sold to summer people. When we swung in the one on the porch at our cottage, it was high-flying indeed, until Daddy Davis ordered us down to a lower altitude "so as not to scuff the ceiling."

When he took us out in his beautiful mahogany rowboat, he always wore a visored yachting cap, with his usual stiff wing collar, and he barked orders like an admiral, trying to teach Adlai and me to row in perfect rhythm. "One, two— *steady Buffie.* . . . You're pulling too hard on your right oar, Adlai." After we got through Round Lake and tied up at the dock in town, Daddy Davis always had his shoes shined and bought the *Chicago Tribune* while Adlai and I watched the fishing boats come in and saw the enormous nets put on the racks to dry. Everytime we rowed back into the boathouse at the cottage, the crew of two had to look sharp, to keep from scraping Daddy Davis' cherished craft.

Once a season, he and Mother took us on the Dummy, the shuttle train, to nearby Petoskey, and we'd roam all day through the Oriental and Indian shops along the main street. That's where we developed a craze for leather-burning, from watching the Indians demonstrate this art, and both Adlai and I had leather-burning sets that gave off a terrible stench as we turned out decorated monstrosities. Another kind of stench rose on the Fourth of July, when Adlai and Joe Bohrer soaked cattails in kerosene, and lit them as torches which they stuck in the sand.

The peak event of the summer was our beach picnic, with bonfires of aromatic pine, and fresh corn boiling in big iron pots. Twenty or thirty of us rode over to Michigan Beach in a hired bus that was rather like a covered wagon, with wooden benches along the sides. It went so slowly that children hopped on and off the rear steps all the way to the beach.

Father usually arranged his visits to get in one of our annual picnics, and it was always a gayer occasion if he was on hand to do imitations of Leon Errol and his collapsible legs, and to show us how to skip stones. He often told us about rock formations, when we passed the boulders along the beach.

After Father had gone back to Illinois, we stayed on with Daddy Davis into the red-gold Michigan autumns, while Mother and Susie canned fruit and made jelly and jam, to refill the preserve cupboard in our cellar in Bloomington.

Each night Adlai and I crisscrossed the kindling as Grandfather had taught us, under the beech and birch logs, and by the time the fire was crackling, he was in his nightshirt and ready for Bobby Burns. When he died, in 1911, the loveliest part of our childhood had come to an end. That witty, sensitive, frail old man had a great influence on us, but his modesty and humility are much more apparent in Adlai than in me.

Chapter 4

RELIGION was never a duty, or church a mere ritual, in our family. Faith in God was as natural as loving Nature. Father, who was a Presbyterian, often went with us to Mother's church, the Unitarian, where Adlai and I went to Sunday school. One of our earliest memories is this little brick church at the corner of Jefferson and East Street in Bloomington, and it has always had for us a special gentle, sturdy grace and freeness of spirit.

The minister often read from Emerson, Thoreau or other philosophers, and talked about spiritual freedom through the ages. We learned there, as children, that nobody should be denied their choice of religion, and that to practice christianity in everyday living is to serve God most truly. We learned years later that our Presbyterian father always sent a Christmas "purse," donations he'd collected from businessmen, and that he and Mother provided toys for the minister's children. Mother, who sewed beautifully, made featherstitched sacques and embroidered bureau scarves for the church fairs, and was a member of the church Board of Trustees.

One of Father's close friends, and a fellow-worker on charity drives, was a Catholic priest, Father Weldon (later Monsignor). They met almost every week, for "discussion evenings," a game of checkers and probably some good stories, too.

Our cousins the Ewings were ardent Christian Scientists, and Mother read Mrs. Mary Baker Eddy's *Science and Health,* but she also read William James (and quoted him later in letters to Adlai). On a beautiful Sunday morning, she might excuse us from going to church—"You should be outdoors in this weather."

Our great-grandfather on Father's side, the Reverend Lewis Warner Green, D.D., of Kentucky, might have been shocked at the idea of letting children miss church, but in his day he was known as a great liberal, and a noted preacher and teacher of theology. In 1834, he took his bride abroad and studied theology in universities in Germany, Scotland and England. He believed that "religion and education are the two poles on which everything revolves," and he was president of Hampton-Sidney College, and then of Presbyterian Centre College in his native Danville.

When he inherited thirty slaves, he tried to send them to Liberia, through the Colonization Society, and when that plan failed, he freed them in Kentucky. During the Civil War, he was cruelly torn, because he was a strong Union man with kin and friends on the Confederate side. The battle of Perryville was fought just outside Danville, and Grandmother Stevenson, who had been in New York at Miss Hayes school, traveled through the battle lines to get home. She often gave Adlai and me exciting accounts of those times. One day she was lying on her bed and had just gotten up when a sniper's bullet whizzed through the window and into the pillow where her head had been.

A less harrowing but (to me) very sad tale was about her father and dancing. She and her sisters were allowed to have lessons in the ladylike art of quadrilles and such "in the parlor with a group of young ladies." Then Great-grandfather told them, "Now, my daughters, you've learned to dance. You must decide what to do, and you are free agents in God's sight, but you well know my views on dancing."

Grandmother would say gently, "So we put away our dancing slippers."

Perhaps the Reverend Lewis Warner Green would have frowned just as sternly on our love for such "godlessness" as theater and nonchurchly music. Mother had a lovely, true contralto voice, and she couldn't believe that children of hers had to sing like bullfrogs. Sitting at the piano, she'd strike a note and say hopefully, "Not da—it's *dee*. Now let's try once more." But it was no use. Even if we couldn't carry a tune, we were a rapt audience, with Father, when Mother sang the gentle, nostalgic lieder she'd learned in Germany, or the rollicking Cockney songs "Private Tommy Atkins" and "My Old Dutch," and two from Barrack Room Ballads— "Fuzzy-Wuzzy" and "Danny Deever." Then she'd do "Go Tell Aunt Rhody the Old Gray Goose Is Dead": "The one she was saving, the one she was saving, to make a feather bed."

Other favorites were "The Man Who Broke the Bank at Monte Carlo," "Kathleen Mavourneen, Don't Ye Cry, Ma Honey"; and Norah Bayes' newest hit, "Shine On, Harvest Moon." "Billy Boy" ("Can she bake a cherry pie, Billy boy?") had a special family meaning, because of Adlai's addiction to that dessert. And flat notes or no, we couldn't resist joining in when Mother sang:

"You can't holler down our rain barrel,
You can't climb our apple tree.
I don't want to play in your yard,
If you won't be good to me."

Father didn't share Mother's fondness for opera and concerts, but he was the most joyous theater-goer I've ever
known, and he loved vaudeville. He often took Adlai and
me to the Majestic, to see the Honey Boy Minstrels, Weber
& Fields, and the Flying Wards' World-Famous Trapeze Act.
When he took us backstage to meet the Wards, it was quite
an Old Home Week, because they had practiced their first
stunts in a local barn, and were one of Bloomington's claims
to fame. Rachel Crothers, the playwright, and Margaret
Illington, the actress who later married Major Bowes of the
Amateur Hour, were also famous native daughters. Father
used to tell the story of an Englishman who got tired of
hearing Bloomingtonians brag, at a dinner party, about how
many noted people had come from there. The stranger
sneered, "Next you'll be claiming Kipling." Father answered
serenely, "No, I don't believe Mr. Kipling lived in Bloomington, but his wife did." She did, too!

But to get back to vaudeville at the Majestic Theatre—
Adlai and Father liked magicians, next to high-wire artists
and comedians. I was charmed with lady singers, because
they always twirled a parasol and were surrounded by gen-
lemen who kept taking off their straw hats gallantly, while
they bowed from the waist. Mother wasn't too keen on
vaudeville, but she approved of our going to sit in Miss
Julia Hodge's box at the Chatterton Opera House, for mati-
nees. After we saw Maude Adams in *Peter Pan*, I wrote in
my diary: "Carried away!" My brother, as an old Charlevoix
pulley-slide expert, wasn't too carried away to speculate on

how they'd rigged up the wires to help Peter Pan fly. Billie Burke, in *The Mind-The-Paint-Girl,* drew this rave review from me: "She's a very pretty, dainty creature and really reaches quite a highth in the last act."

By that time, we were reaching quite a "highth" of our own, giving plays in our attic. I was usually the producer, and my cousin Hester Merwin and I pressed our younger brothers into forcible service, as stagehands. They hung the curtain (old draperies) from the rafters, and when I slapped on the upright beams that marked the two ends of our "stage," this was the signal for "End of scene—lower the curtain." If nothing happened, I'd keep on whacking the beams, in noisy agitation, and Adlai would whisper hoarsely, "What's *wrong?*" The paying audience was very tolerant of these distractions, and seemed to feel they'd got their money's worth, at ten cents a head.

As for us, we were delighted to get their money. Neither Adlai nor I had an allowance. (I believe strongly that children *should* have a regular weekly sum.) For years, a chief source of income was digging dandelion weeds out of the lawn for Mother, at twenty-five cents a bushel basket, or stoking the furnace "at a fair price." Adlai always held on to money better than I did. Later, in our teens, he used to take me aside and warn me whenever a domestic storm was brewing over my clothes extravagance. Even in our grade-school days, I was apt to spend a nickel freely. Father wrote Adlai, in 1910:

> My blessed boy: Papa owes you a great big apology for not having written you on your birthday. Enclosed is a dollar bill. It is for you to spend as you want and is not to be saved. [Our parents never had to tell *me* that!] You have been very good about saving money so you can do with this as you

want. . . . Be good to Grandfather always. Run his errands and always be on the lookout to help him everyway you can.

Adlai liked running errands for Grandfather, because he often got stories as a reward, as well as a dime. He also cleaned our walks and porches. Another chore he performed, less willingly, was working the hand pump which forced the rain water from a cistern in the backyard up to a copper tank in the attic. (Our washbasin and tub had two sets of faucets, one for rain water which we always used for washing our hair and for baths. City water was considered too harsh.) When Adlai took a turn at the pump, he had to heave and pull so strenuously that he "groaned like a galley slave."

But to lie under a car for hours, with oil dripping onto his face, was a glorious new freedom. In 1910, Father had bought a Locomobile, which we all referred to respectfully as The Machine. If The Machine got caught in a rain and came home wet, Mother always insisted it must be rubbed down at once, like a horse. Adlai took such zealous care of our autos that he was still sending back warnings and helpful hints on the care and feeding of The Machine after he went away to school. In 1916, he wrote from Choate: "Tell Buff to be very, *very* careful of the car and that I expect to see it in as good condition as when I left."

As a Freshman in Princeton, he was still a guardian: "I don't understand why the battery for the car should be no good. Tell Father to inquire if there is any guarantee on it, and if so, to see what can be done about it." (He says now that his sons write him exactly the same kind of letters.)

Our part-time chauffeurs were a series of Normal University students. These boys and my brother spent so much time lying on their backs tinkering that they were a perfect example of a hit-song of that era: "He'd have to get under, get out and get under, To fix his little machine."

On one of our first family outings in the car, when we went off enveloped in motoring veils, dusters and goggles, The Machine stalled on the railroad tracks on Oakland Avenue. Mother and I kept leaping in and out, fluttering and squealing, while Father and Adlai cranked and pushed frantically, to get the car off the tracks before a train came. On a drive out to our friends the Funks' farm, Mother complained that chickens flew into the radiator, and gave off a terrible odor of burning feathers. The chickens today must be faster.

As a very special treat, when I graduated from eighth grade, Father took me for a ride all by myself, in The Machine. He also took Adlai off overnight, on farm tours, when they carried a big tin box of provisions, a tent, water canteens, spirit stove, folding beds, and cooked and slept outdoors. Adlai would come home full of crop talk, and also confidential reports that it took most of the afternoon to make camp for the night in some farmer's yard. Once, like an early Spanish explorer, he brought us a report of a model farm where they made eighty-seven bushels of corn to an *acre*. (It was the start of the firsthand knowledge he applied to farmers' problems, when the government called him in during the depression to serve in the Agricultural Adjustment Administration.)

I remember his describing how he and Father once took their morning baths in a stream, with a cow standing on the bank, rolling its eyes in astonishment. Father had become a great exponent of cold baths—and not just in streams. He wrote Adlai from Indiana: "Are you taking your daily cold baths? I hope so. In a lecture the other day I heard a doctor say a man would gain thirty per cent resistance power (to prevent catching disease) if he had taken daily cold baths from childhood."

Now that I'm older I realize how courageously Father tried to build up his health and strengthen his injured shoulder. When we got up in the morning, he'd already be standing in the upstairs hall, swinging Indian clubs or dumbbells, and panting. "If you children would just do this religiously every day, you'd be strong as an ox. You'd save yourselves grief if you'd just listen to me."

Adlai and I occasionally swung the dumbbells to humor Father, but we never went in for regular indoor exercises.

Another fad we refused to share our parents' enthusiasm for was health foods. Like our Southern Grandmother Stevenson, who clung to her hot breads and watermelon pickle, we thought the new protose concoctions were "hay." To my parents' real credit, they never tried to force us to eat the hay, but they lectured us at the table: "You're bolting that down. You must fletcherize your food fifty times for each mouthful." And of course we weren't supposed to have our mouths full. Sam, a colored houseman and gardener Mother had brought from New Orleans after Susie got married, always heaped my brother's plate. (He and Adlai were friends from the start, and spent endless hours hovering over The Machine.) Once when Sam was serving table, his shoes squeaked so badly Father said, "What's the matter with your shoes?" Sam answered genially, "Mr. Stevenson, they're cryin' for a new pair." He got the new shoes.

When Mother protested his giving Adlai third helpings, at dinner, the squat, beamish Sam would say benignly, "He's just a growin' boy, Mrs. Stevenson. Let him eat his fill."

Adlai's fill was practically bottomless, especially for fresh homemade bread. For breakfast, we were stoked with oatmeal that cooked all night in a double boiler, on the back of the coal stove. We didn't mind the congealed oatmeal, but we loathed the gluey apple tapioca pudding that was an unchanging part of Sunday night suppers on the kitchen table. That was almost the only time my brother claimed a sudden loss of appetite.

I was allowed to make the cocoa on Sunday nights. One of the few other chores I enjoyed was to fix what were called "fomentations" when Mother had a bronchitis attack. I'd take a large, thick piece of cloth, twist it like a rope, dip it in boiling-hot water, and lay it on the congested spot—usually Mother's chest. But when Adlai or I had colds, Mother didn't try fomentations; she stuck to the good old remedies of camphorated oil, Antiphlogistine, and masses of cotton and warm flannel.

Once a week, Emma Smith, a remarkable colored woman, came to wash our hair and give Mother massages. Mother said Emma was one of the wisest natural philosophers she'd ever known, and they respected and loved each other. I think the only times Mother spoke in public were at Emma's church. Every time Emma asked her to "come give a talk," Mother accepted.

Although she wasn't a public speaker or much of a club woman, Mother was very civic-minded and campaigned, in the letter column of the *Pantagraph,* for more parks and children's playgrounds, and against Sunday performances in theaters. She took more direct action when she heard that the principal of our school had beaten a boy with a strap. As soon as Adlai and Dave brought this news home, Mother and Aunt Jessie Merwin pinned on their hats, leaped into

Aunt Jessie's electric, and descended on the principal like well-bred furies. I doubt if she beat any more boys with straps, after their visit.

The Merwins had moved to a house two doors away from us, where Loring, the youngest Merwin, still lives. He is now publisher of *The Daily Pantagraph,* which is still too Republican for my taste, and has suggested I call this book *The Egghead and I!* Politics notwithstanding, Loring and his pretty wife are two of our favorite people.

After the Merwins settled on Washington Street, Aunt Jessie came over every morning, to have a chat with Mother. For some reason, she always sat on the bottom stair, and Mother would lean over the upstairs hall banister, and they'd talk that way for sometimes two hours. Aunt Jessie often wanted Mother's advice on decorating her new home, because she thought Mother had a real flair. Mother never used wallpaper in our four bedrooms; her own airy large room had lavender walls and lilac-spray chintz with bold, black stripes. My room was in pale yellow, and Adlai's was dark green, with a pine chest of drawers and bed stained to match. The chest Aunt Jessie really yearned for was the one in our drawing room, a big carved oak chest brought over from England by our forebears, carved with the date 1626. When Mother returned from her first European trip, as a girl, she had acquired a new respect for antiques, and when she discovered this family heirloom chest being used as a feed bin in Grandfather Davis' stable, she promptly rescued it. Aunt Jessie often cast a wistful eye at this family antique on her morning calls.

Our neighbors two doors down to the right were the

Coolidges. Mrs. Coolidge's brother was Sidney Smith, who drew the Andy Gump cartoons we followed in the funny papers every Sunday morning. Whenever he came to visit, all the children on the street would rush down and beg for a ride in his car. The attractive, talented Coolidge family also supplied Adlai's and my first romances. Hesketh Coolidge once spent all day building me a tree house, but just as he was finishing it, Bob Whitmer called me to *his* yard, and although I was smitten with Hesketh, I dashed right off to see what Bob had to offer. Hesketh went home and reported gloomily to his mother, "I spent all day building Buffie a house in a tree, and then she left me. Women are certainly ungrateful."

Betty Coolidge, his sister, had curly red-gold hair, and she was so gay and pretty she always had a host of admirers. It took me some time to realize that Adlai was one of them. I would blurt out a full account of my crushes to friends, family and diary, but Adlai was even more close-mouthed than Penrod. I remember noticing that he was suddenly much more willing to perform in our attic plays. When Betty Coolidge was the princess, he seemed delighted to play the part of the frog who turned into a prince. In a letter to Father at the age of twelve, he managed to get in a mention of his beloved, but he was elaborately casual about it:

> Dear Father: I was over at Dave's house this afternoon. Betty Coolidge & Tip Frederick & Mary Frederick & Hester & Dave & I were there. We made pop corn balls and had lots of fun in the attick.
> We had considrel snow to day it is freezing so I think we will have some coasting. When you called up, Mother and Aunt Jessie were at Normal in Aunt Jessie's electric.
> I made a big Wind Mill with my American Model builder.

It works fine. I am going to attach my motor & see how fast
the fan will go round. I hope you are well.

Yours truly, Adlai E. Stevenson

We were definitely not sophisticated children. When Hesketh Coolidge pecked me on the cheek, as we roller skated
crossed-hands fashion, I was terrified that I'd have a baby!
One of our family stories illustrating Adlai's invincible
truthfulness dates from an earlier time. (He says now he
can't remember the incident at all, but I do!) Our cousin
Dave Merwin had a rather precocious talent for thinking up
mischief, and when my young brother came home late one
afternoon and said he'd been out in a field with Dave,
Mother asked, "What were you boys doing, dear?"

Adlai looked rather nonplused, but he spoke up bravely,
"We were watching the snakes do s-s-sex."

On our first trip to Europe, when Adlai was eleven, we
were innocents abroad, and startled to see ladies smoking.
Gold-tipped Turkish cigarettes, too.

We had been rereading Dickens' *A Child's History of
England,* in preparation for our travels. Adlai wanted to see
knights' armor, and the hiding place of Victor Hugo's Jean
Valjean—the sewers of Paris. We sailed with our parents on
the *Lusitania,* four years before its final tragic voyage.

Chapter 5

WE HAD already had a brief visit in New York. My ever-present diary reports: "We stayed at the Holland House. We saw the Statue of Liberty. I don't think it is very pretty but it means a good deal to us."

Now that I was about to see the world with my family, I was having a fourteen-year-old's agonies of self-consciousness over what the world would think of us: "Father began to play charades with Adlai on the street. It was awful."

The day we sailed, even I thought the grownups behaved very well. Father's closest friend, Edward Clark, who was manager of the Hearst estate, gave us a gala send-off, and his son brought me my first bouquet—violets. My shipboard account begins: "Hurrah for Europe!!! It is the steamer *Lusitania* we are sailing on. It is a very beautiful boat. Several of the saloons are mahogany, and the others are white and gold."

Our own quarters were less resplendent. Mother had insisted thriftily on inside cabins, down in the depths of the ship. She had inherited Grandfather Davis' estate, with Aunt Jessie and Uncle Bert, and now she was realizing her dream of showing the Europe she loved to her children. During the crossing, Adlai spent most of his time "fraternizing" with the crew and climbing over the lifeboats that were to be launched in such terrible haste and anguish a few years later. From my diary in midocean: "We have had very excalent sailing so far. I hope it continues, as Mother and Mrs. Funk get quite sick." My parents were having a gay time with their friends, the Dwight Funks of Bloomington, and far from being seasick, Mrs. Funk's beauty was causing a gratifying stir among passengers who included, I noted respectfully, "a Princess, a Baron, and other notable people."

The Funks also supplied a festive holiday celebration, just after we settled in London's Hotel Cecil. My diary continues: "Christmas Eve we had dinner with the Funks at the Ritz, and had champaign for the first time." At home, wine was served only at dinner parties, and my brother and I were surprised and flattered to be allowed a sip that night, although we agreed afterward that it tasted like getting water up your nose.

If "champaign at the Ritz" sounds as though Adlai and I had been plunged suddenly into riotous living, this was far from the case. We were being shepherded around London by a Bloomington schoolteacher, Miss Lucy Youngman, whom Mother had brought along to give us suitable lessons in each historic spot. My diary reports rather glumly: "We were not only taken to see St. Paul's Cathedral but told what it cost (850,000 £) & paid for by putting a tax on all coal coming into the harbor. . . . Sir Chris. Wren was the architect, and the cathedral does him justice."

In the Tower of London, I noted with blood-thirsty satisfaction: "We saw Execution Block where Ann Boleyn, Lady Jane Grey and other famous characters were executed." Adlai ran Miss Lucy ragged, because he had to see all the dungeons, and each joint of each piece of knights' armor, and ask a thousand questions. I also have a mental picture of my brother, wearing a little gray flannel jacket and knee pants, standing sturdily in a vast cold corridor at Windsor Castle, announcing politely, "But we haven't seen all the armor *here* yet."

His big enthusiasm, in Paris, was foreign stamps. While we were seeing the usual tourist sights, Adlai kept darting to kiosks and buying a new packet of stamps, with what was, for him, spendthrift abandon. He loved Paris, even then, although like any small boy, his reasons were hardly aesthetic. And he was revolted at the idea of *paying* to take a bath.

Mother took us to the opera, and I suppose Miss Lucy Youngman gave us statistics in the Louvre, but for me, the biggest excitement came in the dining room of our little hotel, when Mother pointed out a beautiful young woman at a nearby table. "Notice what lovely deportment. Listen to her voice—what perfect enunciation." It was Elsie Ferguson. As I gaped worshipfully, I had no notion that a dozen years later I'd be playing in the same theater with her.

I saw Sarah Bernhardt in *L'Aiglon,* and exclaimed in my diary: "I have decided to be an actress—I'll die if I am not. I 'Sarah Bernhart' all around the room all day. I dream about Sarah every night. It is really getting serious."

Father had to go back to America, and Mother must have been homesick, because she wrote him this verse, in a letter:

> I am thinking of the good old days
> When you and I were one
> And no thoughts of higher culture
> Troubled us from sun to sun
>
> And I'm wondering if my children
> In the years to come to them

Will thank me for this winter
So far from home and kin.

As they struggle with the Francaise
And wade through Table d'hote
I think they have a yearning
To be back in that old boat!

Her children were certainly a bit weary of trudging through galleries. In Florence, my brother was so excited by a basket of puppies on sale at the entrance of the Pitti Palace museum, and wanted one so badly that Miss Lucy could hardly get us inside to see Old Masters. To a homesick child, a dog looked better than all the Giorgiones and Titians. But a day or so later, in Rome, we went happily to see Keats' and Shelley's graves, and my diary records: "We took pictures and read their poetry aloud."

The influence of Miss Lucy's guidebook shows up strongly in my diary, in Milan: "We went to see Leonardi da Vinci's 'Last Supper.' The plaster is rotting and it is in bad condition as it was painted by oil instead of fresco. It is very beautiful and we all admired it greatly."

In Rome, Miss Lucy managed to corral her two lively charges in the Colosseum, supposedly to give us a Latin lesson, but Adlai and I were much more intent on finding where the lions had sprung from to devour their victims, and how the gladiators had made out. Poor, patient, sweet Miss Lucy, she must have left the Colosseum feeling like the newest recruit in a long line of Christian martyrs. She went back to Bloomington soon afterward.

Much as Mother loved Italian culture, she deplored a few aspects of traveling there. I wrote Father: "On the train we were attacked by flees!!! Fortunately Mother was spaired." My brother took the fleas as part of the charms of travel, and said we looked like Father doing his imitation of a monkey. Between scratching ourselves, he and I played two-handed casino.

He was blissful during a stay in the Swiss Alps, and immediately wrote to his friend Sam, our Negro houseman in Bloomington:

Dear Sam: We are at Val d'illiez Switzerland. Val d'illiez is a verry little village at the foot of the Dent du Midi.

The Dent du Midi is one of the highest Swisse mountains it is all coverded with snow. The chalet that we live in is all of wood, everything is of wood. We hear French spoken all the time. We are the only people in the Village that speak English. Everybody that comes [here] comes for Mountain climbing. They carry a large sack for food and things. Also an alpine stick which is a pole with a pick and hatchet on one end, and a point at the other. . . . Add

At the bottom of the letter, he drew a picture of an alpine stick, to make sure that Sam, in the flat Midwest, would grasp the beauties of this useful implement for scaling mountains.

My own report to Father was: "Brother & I take little climbes every day, but he is anxious to take some real climbes."

During the carnival season, our fashionable, charming cousin Letty Bromwell, who was living in Lausanne, swept us off in her Packard down to Nice. Part of the journey was hair-raising, over rough, twisting mountain roads, in a violent snowstorm that swirled through the Packard's flapping side curtains and froze us nearly numb. Adlai sat up front with the chauffeur, Louis, and the Pomeranian Ko-Ko, who had his own trunk. Every time we went around a curve, Cousin Letty shrieked emotionally and grabbed Mother's arm. Her pretty brunette daughter Millie, Adlai and I were more worried about Ko-Ko than the slippery curves; Ko-Ko refused to function, on the whole frenzied trip. Whenever we put him out on the road, he hopped right back in the car, no matter how we entreated.

By the time we reached Nice, the third day out, it was almost 10 P.M., and we were ravenous. Unfortunately, we landed in so fancy a restaurant, on the Boulevard des Anglais, that Mother took one look at the prices on the menu, and told Adlai and me to order soup. She also made Cousin Letty wait down the block with the Packard and chauffeur, while she went into a hotel to bargain for rooms. In a letter to Father, a nonbargainer, I mentioned happily that Mother had "made quite a 'hit' with the manager, and we have been given splended rates."

Nice was in a tumult of Mardi Gras spirits. When a masked young man darted out of a crowd on the street, seized my hand and kissed it fervently, I was intoxicated by this Old World atmosphere of romance. In Lugano, my diary still reflected this lyrical state: "When we look out from our tiny Paradise, we see that the mountains are bathed in rose and purple tints. I have declared that it is the very place where my lover and I will come. We will eat chocolates, smoke Turkish cigarettes, read, and have a glorious time all day."

Adlai must have gotten quite an overdose of this prattle, because he soon conspired to play an elaborate practical joke on his mooning, calf-eyed sister.

We had settled down for a few months stay in Lausanne, where Adlai was in a boys' day school at Ouchy. One of our new friends in the Hotel Savoy was an English girl named Dolly Clarkson, who spoke flawless French. She, Millie Bromwell, Adlai and I had riding lessons every day at a local academy, where we cantered around a ring while onlookers including parents watched from a balcony. One day I received a letter in French from "an anonymous admirer," saying that the writer had watched me every day as I rode, and had become deeply enamored. He adored me, he lived for the sight of me, he longed for a glance from my beautiful eyes, and so on and on, to ecstatic lengths. Overwhelmed, I showed this billet-doux to my brother and Dolly, who advised me gravely to keep mum about it and not tell Mother. From then on, I took my riding lessons in a blushing haze of self-consciousness, thinking, *He* must be watching me! It wasn't until months later that Adlai confessed he and Dolly had cooked up the whole scheme, and Dolly had produced the *lettre amoureuse,* because, as my brother said, "She knew how to gush in French."

Our own French was improving in Lausanne, Adlai's at school, and mine with two local tutors, one for conversation and one, as I noted, "for serious study." But much more important, we were losing our insular notion that people in foreign countries were peculiar if they seemed different from Americans. It was good for two Midwestern children to learn that no one is a foreigner to friendship. Every night we had early dinner in the hotel dining room with a half-dozen children—French, English, South American, German, Italian —and we all chattered happily.

The only thing Adlai couldn't get used to was the doll portions served at meals; he was always ravenous. When Mother took us to the famous (and expensive) tea place, Niffeneger's, on the Rue du Bourg, she had to caution her son not to eat more than two costly cakes at a sitting.

But even Mother couldn't resist splurging on Paris clothes.

At home, she had a dressmaker every spring and fall who sewed for weeks in the attic, making most of our clothes, including voluminous flannel nightgowns and petticoats, and summer pongees and voiles with exquisite tucking. My Peter Thompson suits were my only ready-made outfits. For ultra occasions, Mother ordered a dress for herself from Madam Glover's in Louisville. But even Madam Glover couldn't compare to Paris. I wrote Father, "Mother looked so young and handsome when she and Cousin Letty started off. I suppose you know it's a shopping expedition."

He knew it all right when he met us at the pier in midsummer, and paid $257 customs duty on mother's new Paris clothes. This sum impressed me so much I entered it carefully in my diary. I only wish I'd entered a description of the new clothes instead! All I can remember is an ermine scarf and muff, and a purple feather toque with two gay little wings.

I think Father enjoyed having Mother the extravagant one in the family, for a change; he was always proud of her chic. He himself was very fastidious about his clothes; he had his suits made to order, I think partly because his "game" shoulder was slightly higher than the other, and needed special tailoring to disguise it. His favorite jewelry was a pair of lapis lazuli cuff links set in gold, a present from William Randolph Hearst.

That July when we returned from Europe, Father insisted it was too hot to go right back to the Midwest, and he hurried us off to a hotel in Spring Lake, New Jersey. Looking back, I realize he was much more concerned with politics than sea breezes; he wanted to call on Governor Woodrow Wilson, who was already Democratic nominee for

President. When he set off for the Governor's summer mansion at nearby Sea Girt, he took Adlai along (my turn came a few years later) and my brother met the man who was to become one of his greatest heroes. On that first meeting, Adlai sat quietly on the wide verandah, while Father and Governor Wilson, a few feet away, conferred most of that afternoon.

When we got back to Bloomington, Grandfather Stevenson showed Father a letter from Governor Wilson:

> Sea Girt, N.J.
> August 22, 1912
> I am very much honored by your letter of August 13th, and have read it with the greatest interest. I also had the great pleasure of having a conversation with your son which was instructive and illuminating to me. It is delightful to look forward to your active support, and I want you to know how deeply I appreciate it.

Mother was as excited as Father about the new Presidential candidate. She told us Mr. Wilson had "a deep concern for humanity," as well as "a great mind." She was even more concerned about his chances than she was about the chances of finishing our new sleeping porch before winter set in. "Sleeping out" was a brand new fad, all over the country, and we were to spend some fiendishly healthy nights, with chattering teeth, on that porch. Even with hot-water bottles and warming stones in our bed, pajamas with feet on them, and improvised nightcaps, we never got warm. To complicate matters, Mother decided for some reason—perhaps belated thrift—that we didn't really need a door cut through to the new sleeping porch, so we had to crawl in and out Adlai's bedroom window.

That fall, carpenters were pounding on our roof, and

Mother went eagerly with Father to pre-election rallies, where Grandfather often spoke. When Wilson won over Taft, in the Bull Moose split, we were all jubilant. And even my young brother had to look at the telegram the new President sent to Grandfather:

> Your congratulations came to me like a benediction. I thank you for them with all my heart.
>
> Woodrow Wilson

We celebrated Grandmother's seventieth birthday with special gaiety, in their house on Franklin Square. Grandmother wore a low-cut black velvet gown, with her coral and pearl "set," and went radiantly in to dinner on the arm of her husband, "Mr. Stevenson."

Just after Christmas, a great tragedy came to our family. A friend from Charlevoix was visiting me, and I had a neighborhood party for a dozen boys and girls. One of the boys, home from a military academy, wanted to show us the manual of arms, so we asked Adlai, who was considered too young for the party, to get us a gun. He rushed excitedly to the attic and got Father's .22. After much parading up and down the drawing room, and the usual showing off by boys of that age, the gun was finally returned to my brother to put away. As he went into the hall he must have pulled the trigger a last time, and a bullet that had been stuck in the mechanism was dislodged. The gun went off, the bullet struck my friend Ruth Merwin in the forehead, and she died instantly.

Mother and Father came in a few minutes later, from a neighbor's. Adlai told Father what had happened, and then went up to Mother's room. Two days later, Mother took him and Dave Merwin to Chicago, and Father and I went to the funeral. It's a hard memory to look back on and one that only those who have shared such an experience can understand. It's impossible for me to evaluate or describe what the psychological, emotional reactions were after the period of shock.

Ruth Merwin was a cousin of our own cousins the Merwins, and Ruth's mother, Mrs. Clarence Merwin, was a tower of strength to our family, in those sorrowful days. She was a gentle, loving, deeply understanding woman, and she and Mother became very close. The strain on both families must have been heartbreaking, and it seems to me now that they faced it with courage and love and intelligence. I can't remember that the accident was ever referred to from that night on, until a reporter brought it up forty years later, in an interview with my brother.

Our parents' dear friend Julia Hodge said this year, "Your mother knew that tragedy and suffering can wreck a sensitive child for life, or it can deepen and strengthen him. She prayed—and anybody who knows Adlai knows that her prayers were answered."

Mother and Father took us south that spring. In the old Pine Forest Inn, in Summerville, South Carolina, Adlai taught me to bowl, and we sat restlessly through the genteel after-dinner musicales, clutching printed programs of the "selections." On the train, Father saw a lovely, dark haired woman walking through our car, followed by a distinguished-looking man, and exclaimed, "There goes Mrs. Cleveland with her new husband!" When we were introduced, I had a feeling Mr. Preston wasn't too pleased to have his bride's first husband's political friends popping up on their honeymoon.

Adlai and I were much more excited by a train encounter with John Hays Hammond. He took us into his compartment and told us wonderful stories of how he'd been captured in the Jameson Raid in South Africa, in the Boer War, and how Grandfather Stevenson had interceded to save his life.

Back home, we started weekly trips to Chicago, to have our teeth straightened by Dr. Noyes. As compensation for the dentist, we had matinées: Cyril Maude in *Grumpy,* Sothern and Marlowe in *Romeo and Juliet,* William Faversham's *Julius Caesar.* We also had good visits with our Hardin cousins, who lived in Chicago while Uncle Martin was pastor of the second Presbyterian church there.

In Bloomington, the Chatterton Theatre had a rousing performance of *Uncle Tom's Cabin with Ten Cuban and Russian Bloodhounds.* Father was charmed with a show called *Everybody's Doing It*—which was billed as "Direct from The Winter Garden Theatre, New York City, and also France and Germany."

That fall of 1913, both Adlai and I were in University High School in Normal. From my diary: "We think Adlai has a lot of literary ability, and he is doing so well in his studies. He seems to have quite a talent for Latin. I wish he might become a great minister. It is such fun but pretty sad to watch Ad grow up, he begins to try to train his hair now, to brush his clothes altho' he is very untidy about his room and hanging his clothes in his closet—I suppose most boys are—Father certainly is."

A photograph taken then shows him still in Eton collar

with his "trained" hair parted on the side, but he was trying more determinedly than ever to escape parental constraints. To Mother, visiting in the East, he wrote:

Please telegraph Father to let me play football as you said you would. I have been deprived of that pleasur for so long you ought to let me play this year, as I have been asked to.
. . . I have to write a theme for this afternoon on one of the following subjects, an hour in the assembly room an old bridge at sunset or an old fasianed school house. As I know nothing about these it will be pretty hard. . . .
With lots of love,
Adlai
P.S. Please don't forget about the football. *Please.*

Dear Mother: Buffie got your letter this morning in which you said you would not let me play football for another year, that is what you and Father have been telling me for so long, and anyway you promised me you would let me play this fall. If I wait another year I will not be able to play. All doctors say its a bad game but all doctors haven't played it, and more than that they did not play like we play at Normal. Everybody these days have such terrible conceptions of football when they know nothing about it, just because they have read of accidents in for instance a Harvard and Yale game—this is the third Normal team. . . . Lots of love, Adlai
P.S. All the games you mencioned in your letter are out of season.

In tackling the subject with Father, who was apt to answer with thunder and lightning, Adlai was as even-tempered as ever, but not to be cowed or sidetracked. He had a kind of unswerving reasonableness, in arguments, that made even parents think twice. He got permission to play on the third team—and I think he felt the way Yale feels when it scores the winning touchdown over Harvard.

Usually, our student-chauffeur drove us and a group of our friends the three miles to Normal every morning, but my brother balked at being picked up after school. (He said recently that the nightmare worry of his Freshman year was that somebody in his *family* would appear to collect him, at 3:30.) Football practice gave him a fine new reason to be on his own, and ride home on the streetcar with his fellow-players, bruised and muddy and happy.

We had a Halloween party, and according to my diary, "Ad was the ghost and played the part to a tee." At Normal, we went to a "Backwards Party": "A young lady played pieces backwards on the piano and we guessed what they were." The new song-rage was "Billy, Billy, Bounce Your Baby-doll." I was getting notes from boys in school, wittily signed, "Yours till the bench breaks."

Diary entry for February 5: "Adlai's 14th birthday—a beautiful cake. I'm reading *Macbeth* for the second time in two days."

My brother already preferred history. He was well into Markham's thirteen-volume work that took up a shelf of our bookcase: *The Real America in Romance.*

Our beloved Grandfather and Grandmother Stevenson, who meant so much to our growing America, died in 1914. Adlai wrote, many years later, that the most moving tribute to Grandmother was given by the colored coachman, George Meaderds, at her funeral. Weeping, he said, "She was a great lady."

Grandfather outlived his adored wife by five months. His funeral was like an affair of state, with dignitaries from all over the country, and a line of cars that seemed to stretch for miles. I was so put off by all this pomp that I had a sudden queer feeling of mourning for a stranger. At the Presbyterian church, Pathé newsreel men crowded around us. I'd never even seen a real movie, much less a movie camera, and the whole thing was so new an experience that my cousin Millie and I broke out in hysterical giggles, during the service. Aunt Julia had to tap us sharply with her black fan. Adlai sat solemn and sad.

The photograph which appeared in newspapers afterward showed Adlai and myself holding the American flag, at the door of the church. I pasted one of these clippings in a scrapbook, and am ashamed to say I scribbled on the margin: "This is my first newspaper picture, and I hope the first of many!"

That hot, eventful summer of 1914, the Archduke Ferdinand was assassinated, and Europe exploded into war.

In Springfield, sixty miles from home, the Secretary of State of Illinois suddenly committed suicide, and father was appointed to serve the remaining two years of his term. From that time on, politics swirled constantly in and out of our busy young lives. In with my excited diary accounts of this new world, I found time to jot casually, "Adlai made his first speech today—for the Boys' Anti-Cigarette League. And he's beginning to want to go out!"

Chapter 6

AFTER FATHER went to Springfield as secretary of state of Illinois, I announced in my diary—and to anyone who would listen—"I want to be a politician!" As far as I can remember, Adlai kept mum.

When we were invited to the Governor's Mansion for a Christmas dance, I felt terribly sorry for my fourteen-year-old brother because Mother and Father decided he was too young to have a dinner jacket and come along. I had my first real evening dress—yellow tulle with lethally pointed-toe satin slippers dyed to match, and I wore my hair up for the first time. White canvas was stretched over the carpeting of the Mansion that night, and it's the closest I've ever come to fox-trotting on a cloud. My diary reported: "Governor Dunne kissed mother under the mistletoe. Also me."

I longed to stay in this invigorating atmosphere, but right after the holidays I was sent back to the University School for Girls, on Lake Shore Drive in Chicago, and Adlai returned to Bloomington with Mother, to finish out his school term. Judging from my diary, I was trying to finish *my* school term prematurely: "I threw a pumpkin pie down out a window—on a man in the street. It made a great disturbance. I

didn't mean to hit the man. We were having a feast. . . .
Have been reading *My Past,* by Countess Marie Larisch. It
is fascinating. . . . All my privileges taken away for three
weeks because I went to the tearoom. Afterward we all cried.
I HATE Fraulein Schmidt."

I wrote Mother, "These cold icy nights make me think
of home, but when am I *not* thinking of home. So much
love to the three dearest beings in the hemisphere."

By spring, my parents agreed to let me stay with them in
Springfield. They had rented ex-Governor Richard Yates'
house, and Adlai had transferred to the Springfield high
school. I remember how impressed we were because he and
Sam, our houseman, drove the Locomobile to Springfield in
a record five hours. (It now takes an hour!) The only vehicle
I could drive was Mother's Rauch & Lang electric, a black
box of windows on wheels, that ambled along almost as fast
as we could walk, and was always running out of "juice."

Our next-door neighbors and close friends were the Medill
McCormicks, who lived in the state capital while the senate
was in session. Medill McCormick, publisher of the *Chicago
Tribune,* was a state senator; his wife, an ardent suffragette,
often let me sit in the gallery with her, and explained what
an important role women would play in politics. I could
hardly wait to begin. Father took Adlai and me to the House,
and according to my diary: "Today was very exciting—the
wet-dry issue. . . . Three senators and Lt. Governor Barrett
O'Hara came to dinner, and they were awfully nice to us. . . .
Mr. Mike Igoe and the two Sullivans came. They are all so
clever . . . I think Medill McCormick is fascinating. I am so
glad he flirts with Mother."

My parents were far from glad that I had developed a

full-blown girlish crush on the handsome Lt. Governor O'Hara. They thought my interest in politics had become entirely too personal, and when I look over my burbling diary entries, I think they were right: "I am reading *Way of an Eagle.* The hero makes me think of O'Hara. A man like him will be the only kind who will inspire me to do anything very great or good."

Vachel Lindsay, the poet, sometimes came to dinner, and Adlai and I were intrigued at the way he kept pushing the silverware around to make diagrams of whatever he was talking about. Later I noted sternly: "Vachel Lindsay is very sweet to young girls—Elizabeth & Christine Brown etc.—but I'm not attracted much. He's very boring after an hour's talk." Probably he didn't let *me* talk enough! I realize now how much Adlai was absorbing—from poets as well as politicians—sitting with his head slightly forward in what is still his typical "listening post" look.

That reminds me of the time a year or so ago when a young writer came to call on Adlai, who had just returned from the Far East. I was indignant because the young man spent all evening talking about *his* experiences and views and problems. After he'd gone, I said crossly to my brother, "Why did you encourage him to talk so much and stay so long? Why didn't you tell him about *your* trip?" Adlai said mildly, "But I wanted to hear him. How would I know what young people are thinking and doing if I listened to myself?"

Many's the night in Springfield I saw reporters and politicians come to the Executive Mansion to pump Governor Stevenson dry, but I noticed they ended up doing most of the talking themselves!

While Father was secretary of state, the Mansion was our favorite place, because we were so fond of Governor Dunne and his family. Mona, one of the daughters, was my ideal and I longed to be as gay and popular and unself-conscious as she was, at parties in the Mansion.

Father was working too hard to have time for many parties. (The *Springfield Journal* later said: "Lewis Green Stevenson brought new life to the Secretary of State office, reconstructed its system . . . to business efficiency.") He had two devoted, capable young assistants, Dewitt Montgomery and Amos Richardson, and when Amos went into the Army in 1915, Father had Adlai drive him to the train, saying "I want you to see Amos off on his great adventure."

As the Senate and House moved toward adjournment that spring, Mother and Adlai and I went to several night sessions. Father had presided over a seven-weeks-long bitterly deadlocked session of the state assembly, and we felt very proud the day it ended, when every member—Republicans as well as Democrats—rose to give him a moving vote of thanks for being so fair and impartial.

It's pleasant to remember how many Republican friends my parents had in Springfield, including the Oglesbys of nearby Elkhart and their beloved friend Logan Hay. What's even pleasanter is to remember that Logan Hay was an ardent admirer of Adlai's and foresaw his rise in the world. He had died before Adlai ran for Governor, but his widow, Mrs. Hay crossed party lines and supported my brother vigorously. It was during our Springfield stay that Adlai first met Logan Hay's daughter, Mary Douglas Hay. Now that he was interested in what he called, rather jeeringly, "the manly sport of dancing," "Dougie" Hay was his favorite partner in such new-fangled steps as the Lulu Fado and the Vernon Castle Walk.

One of Dougie Hay's family, John Hay, like our Great-grandfather Fell, had been closely associated with Mr. Lincoln, and Adlai loved to hear Logan Hay, one of the foremost Lincoln scholars, tell stories he'd heard of those early days in Springfield. Now that we were in the heart of the Lincoln country, and in the city where he still seems to live, my brother went out to the tomb, visited the old home, and quietly read and read about the young Abe, including anecdotes in Grandfather Stevenson's own book, *Something of Men I Have Known.*

I was much too busy having "crushes" on live politicians to look at Springfield history, just then. Probably to cool off my political fevers, Mother settled me that summer at Camp Wyonogonic in Maine. Adlai was at a boys' camp at Oxford, Maine, and for a while mother stayed at an inn near us. My brother had a boy's natural wariness of too many parental visits, and he wrote her:

Dear mother:
When you telephoned me you said you might come over tomorrow or soon but I advise you not to as the weather is pretty bad. Father wrote me and said that I should write him twice a week and if I did not he would write Prof. so I suppose I shall have to be real diligent and write him every Sunday and Wednesday.

I was very glad to hear that you had at last found a place that you like and was astonished to hear that Buff had gone to a camp and that she liked it. Our intermidate baseball team on which I play third base played Lake Pleasant Camp Friday and we beat them seven to five. I distinguished my self as a hitter and won considerable praze from the coach. I was chosen to play the singles in tennis against Camp Kohut the other day and was beaten only after three sets. The Keneo meet comes off in a few days and the swimming coach has me training for the plunge and high diving. I don't know whether I have told you all this before but I have to think of something to say.

With lots of love,
Adlai

Father, with warmhearted inconsistency, was writing:

My dear Old Boy:

I was delighted with your letter of July 21st. It shows me plainly you can construct a splendid letter, in addition to making it most interesting, if you will give yourself time to do it. With the exception of a few words which were somewhat shady in spelling, the letter was splendid.

I am so glad you are going in for athletics, and that you take the licking you got in such a manly way. The fact that you were chosen to represent the Camp, is in itself a great compliment, and you should consider it sufficient, even though you did lose.

I do not like your being in the swimming contests so much, especially the diving, and I wish you would tell me you will stay out of the diving contests hereafter. Playing ball is all right, and if I were you I would confine my efforts largely to that. . . .

Devotedly yours,
Pop

My dear boy:

Do not be afraid of not giving me sufficient news, for what you write about is exactly what I want, only I would rather you would tell me more about the boys. Who they are, where they come from, and what their different characteristics are. I want you to learn to observe people carefully; also to analyze them, and if you get into the practice of doing this early in life, it will be of immense value to you in later years. You may be very much deceived at first in your judgment, but you will soon be able to judge with more accuracy, and it will help you greatly.

I am delighted to know you are getting along so well in your athletics. Apparently you are doing splendidly. . . .

But in the next letter, he had switched again:

My dear Adlai:

I thank you again for another splendid letter, but my boy, I must urge you not to go in for so much athletics. I want you to stop this right away. The purpose of your being there and my spending so much money to keep you there, is not for you to take long hikes and overdo yourself in athletics, but to get you in good physical condition so you can have your tonsils removed without any harm. This is the one principal thing you should have in mind all the time, and not excelling in athletics.

Now I must insist upon your giving up some of these things and taking more rest; otherwise, I will telegraph direct to the instructor not to let you play tennis or take long walks. I want you to rest, lie around, read books, etc. for the balance of the summer, or come directly home. You simply shall not overdo, and come home all worn out, instead of in prime condition for the operation and your fall school work.

I want you to accept my statement, for I mean it, and do exactly as I say. Your mother and I both have enough trouble now, and we cannot afford to have you in anything but prime condition so please give up the little things that give you only temporary pleasure.

With a great deal of love,

Pop

Adlai's next letter to Mother proves he hadn't taken Father's impulsive ban on sports too literally.

Camp Oxford
Oxford, Maine

Sunday
August 16, 1915

Dear Mother:

When I got back yesterday afternoon I found your letters in which you did not want me to go on the White Mountain hike but I had already returned when I received them. I am certainly glad I went now.

We left Monday morning . . . walked four miles to the station where we caught the train to Bethel. The four of us left Bethel at half past eleven and got to Gorham that night a distance of twenty two miles. We slept in a railroad shop.

The next morning we walked to the Glen house and rested near there for about two hours before climbing the mountain. Mount Washington is 6,300 feet high and it is nine miles up the carriage road to the hilltop house. We reached there that afternoon after walking the last four miles in rain. The next day we waited until noon before we started down. We went down the Crawford trail and slept the night in a barn near the Canford House. The next morning after walking about six miles an auto picked us up and gave us a twenty mile lift. We walked on and reached Bridgeton that night covering a distance of fifty two miles in one day. We slept in a barn that night and believe me we slept well. We reached home about three o'clock. The scenery was beautiful the whole trip and some of the views were magnificent.

Please write and tell me how you would like to have me come home. I would rather wait until the Twenty fifth or sixth if possible.

With lots of love,
Adlai

P.S. Yesterday evening I swam the lake a distance of 2 miles in 1:16:21.

Adlai later gave me, in strictest confidence, some details of his adventure which he'd spared Mother. He and three other boys had eluded the camp counselor and had slept not "in a railroad shop" but in an empty boxcar. They woke in the middle of the night to find it moving, and they welcomed this chance to extend their travels! For two days, the young vagrants managed to live joyously and well "off the country."

I was thriving too, that summer: "Slept out on a platform down by the lake. It was wonderful to be off in the great world all night. This camp is so wholesome—I find I love it. I dived twice today. We turned the wigwam into a summer hotel to surprise the counselors. Admiral Peary came to lecture us on the North Pole. . . . Today the girls saw Adlai!! Tonight one of the girls fainted." (I'm sure there was no connection between these two exciting events.)

Soon after we got back to Bloomington, my diary continued: "Adlai had his tonsils out this morning. He was so strong they had to give him lots of ether. He is doing splendidly. Mother is worn out. Father is in bed with a headache. My sprained ankle is better."

I remember flouting doctor's orders to hobble off to Brokaw Hospital to see my brother, and in spite of all the ether, he seemed much the healthiest of all of us.

That fall, he was back in University High School at Normal, and taking mandolin lessons. My diary notes: "The nights are cold; Adlai and I sleep out on the balcony (sleeping porch). He's such a blessed, happy chap."

His mandolin stumbled along on "Has Anybody Here Seen Kelly," "Every Little Movement Has A Meaning of Its Own," and George M. Cohan's "I'm Awfully Strong For You." The last must have been done with special fervor because my brother had fallen in love. He and practically all the boys in his class were smitten by the ravishing Josephine Sanders, who was to become famous a few years later as a musical comedy star under the stage name of Irene Delroy.

Recently I asked several of the men who had been in high school with Adlai, "Can you remember what Josephine Sanders looked like?" and they were astonished that I could even ask such a foolish question! They all began their descriptions with a dreamy, faraway look, "Blonde, with dimples, and on the plumpish side." One of the men went on, "She was so *vivid*—a wonderful dancer, and the most glamorous girl in school. Her mother was hell-bent on her going on the stage and having a big career."

When my brother and Josephine got to the tender stage of exchanging notes in school, they signed them "ETA" for *ego te amo*! If the Latin was bad, at least there was nothing deficient about the sentiment. I was away at school and didn't have too many firsthand details of the romance (certainly not from my brother) but one of his school friends told me recently, "Ad got ahead of all of us. Josephine even went with him to the big winter dance in the gym. And now, forty years later, I'm still envious!"

While Adlai was struggling with beginner's Latin and romance, I was a reluctant and often rebellious pupil at Miss Wright's School for Young Ladies, in Bryn Mawr. Even before I went, the very thought of it had me exclaiming to my diary: "How ghastly it is to break up the home. I suppose we will never all live together again."

With Father working in Springfield, Mother was worried about leaving Adlai alone when she took me East to Miss Wright's, and she turned for help to Alverta Duff, as we've been turning to her for help ever since. I can't imagine life in Bloomington without Alverta's loving understanding and shrewd intuitive wisdom. Her grandparents had been slaves in Mississippi; her father came to Illinois right after the Civil War, as a boy of fourteen, and looked up Great-grand-father Fell, who had been noted for his active abolitionist beliefs and was always helpful to the newly freed Negroes. Great-grandfather agreed to let the boy live on his place if he would go to school; years later his daughter Alverta was also trained in that strict school of housekeeping practiced by the Quaker Fells. Her youngest brother played football at Normal and was one of Adlai's high school heroes.

Alverta remembers that while she was keeping house for him, "Adlai always phoned me ahead from school, if he wanted to ask one of his friends home for dinner. He was just naturally thoughtful."

When Mother left me at Miss Wright's, she tried to console me with one of her favorite sayings, "There is no parting," but I was inconsolable. I scribbled bitterly in my diary: "This seems to me so futile. We are balloons whirling in a world of indecision."

I wrote my brother:

Don't let the Blessed be too homesick for me. Oh, Adlai, she's too wonderful to be our Mother!

My roommate, Mary Hippie of Des Moines is a sweet creature, and we live in a bleak, bare spot called a room. Advantages: three windows & near the bathroom. Our beds are more uncomfortable than Allied Army cots.

Now that I have told the discomforts of life at the "annex" of Miss Wright's Fashionable Finishing School, I shall proceed by saying that the Swedish Gentleman, Mr. Oberge, who pays the taxes (we hope!) for this house, is a character. He is a scream. Mme. Oberge, a staunch Quaker, corners you every few minutes and tells you the most astounding facts concerning life, death, food, disease, and education. This noon after lunch she undertook to tell of the stupidity of the poor waitress right under her nose, then of how wildly wicked the "new dances" were, how shocking it was for President Wilson to marry (a theme she dotes on). I timed her and it took just 40 minutes to tell me all those things. . . .

Adlai, who hated to write letters, made a quick exception, to humor his homesick sister:

Dear *Friend* Buffie:

I received your epistle this morning, and was very glad to hear that you were still alive. On receiving this letter don't be surprised because I will not write you again for two (2) months.

I was glad to hear that your room-mate is sweet, and that all the people there are not like Oberge.

I just got through sending you a telegram regarding your cold about which Mother seems to be worried (although I am not).

I just wrote the "old man" asking for fifty seeds (dollars). I am expecting a hot reply.

I am going over to Decatur tomorrow with the football team. I hope your cold will improve as it gets older, I mean better.

Lots of love,
Adlai

P.S. I have been working extremely hard in school. This is what I will look like if I keep it up. ["This" was a doodled sketch of a bony, bespectacled professor, loaded with degrees, and labeled "Me 20 years hence."]

According to my diary, even *I* was beginning to study: "My French Literature is fascinating, and I will have to gather my rambling brains together and work. . . . Tonight some boys came to call and we nearly had a panic. Miss Wright was furious."

My closest school friend was Mary Wilson, who lived in Marion, a "Main Line" suburb of Philadelphia, and soon I was writing Adlai exuberantly:

> Friday I am going to the Wilsons' for the weekend—my first except with Mother. A little different from last year—n'est ce pas? I am going to wear my new yellow evening dress Sat. night to the Bok's for dinner. They are very rich & important & have a son at Williams who is home now with a guest. I hope that after that dinner you will hear something more of those young bucks from me! Wish me luck!
>
> I won't offer up any thanks at dinner tomorrow unless I get a letter from you in the morning post. Thanks for the telegram. You said "It is very warm and its snowing fast." What new kind of weather has Ill. manufactured?
>
> Loads of love,
Buff
>
> P.S. I hope I use the right fork at Bok's & don't mistake the butler for Bok Jr.!

My next diary entry: "Boks were fascinating. We had a dandy hockey match between the old and new girls. I cheered myself hoarse . . . I am so surprised to be on the Honor Roll! I got 90 in English Lit."

But by midterm, I was writing Adlai:

> I am *so* glad you are a student and have brains because I have not & will probably fail my exams. But my motto is "Love thy roommate—exams don't matter." (Such nonsense). Mrs. Julius Funk has invited Florence & Weldon [Funk], another boy & me to come down to New Orleans when school's out. Get Mother to let me go.
>
> The dance comes next week. I wish you might have come.
>
> One of the girls here has a fire rope! It's miles long & very strong. We will fasten it to the bed and climb down it out of the window to the ground. If we are discovered we will prob-

ably be canned. I'll pack my grip & take a trip to a good old Western town. Will you meet me in the Loco?

The farthest I went, at that point, was to New York for a weekend, where I jotted in my diary, "The suffragettes are out pleading with the populace."

Mother sent me the home news I was starved for: "My darling: Everything satisfactory here. Alverta happy. Adlai is well, but he had a bilious attack so you want to be prudent and when you are 'off your feed,' take calomel if you need it—10 gr. with soda or wintergreen. . . . Everybody is out cleaning up and making garden. Grass green and buds coming." (I could picture mother in her usual spring housecleaning frenzy, with a towel tied around her head like a turban. She was always so thorough, in those two-week-long cleaning bouts, that I used to think every piece of furniture in the house would be out airing on the lawn near the fresh-beaten rugs hanging on a line, before she finished.)

Her letter continued: "Adlai is so dear and getting so old. We have been practisting the mandolin and gossiping for three hours. The new car hasn't come. I was furious and Ad disappointed."

The new car was a Hudson Super-six; Adlai was flattered because Father had deferred to him as the mechanical expert in the family, and asked him to go to the automobile show in Chicago and recommend the model to buy. After it was delivered, I wrote my brother: "Wouldn't it be fun if Mother would let us put E.D.S. on one door and A.E.S. on the other!! Are you *sure* it makes 70? Don't you just *think* it does?"

He must have been too charmed with the new car to

leave it during spring vacation and go with Father to Washington, to see me unveil a portrait of Grandmother Stevenson in Continental Hall. Or maybe he was tired of such ceremonies, because as Grandfather's namesake, he had already pulled the cord to unveil his portrait in the Bloomington public library, and sat washed, brushed and uncomfortable at many a public affair. But I leaped at the chance to escape Miss Wright's confines and join Father. Cousin Letty Bromwell had invited us to stay at her beautiful house on Q Street, and after the unveiling ceremonies, I wrote home: "I wore my jabot waist and spats. Cousin Letty was too funny for words—she sat there hissing stories and laughing and telling her mother not to make faces at people. [We had sat in the box of the D.A.R. President General, Mrs. Storey—a rather conspicuous spot.] She is playing the ukalelli now. It's better than a vaudeville."

I should explain that Cousin Letty was noted in Washington for her high spirits, style, and original behavior, as well as for her extreme chic. My report to Mother and Adlai continues: "My new shoes were 5 AA which impressed Cousin Letty. They are all wild about my hair, they hate it so." (It was pulled back tightly in a knot.) A day or so later, I wrote, "After dinner Cousin Letty took me upstairs and tried all her hats on me—painted my lips and said I should always paint my lips."

I remember how impressed I was, sitting in that softly lighted bedroom like a French queen's boudoir, with Louis Quinze loveseats upholstered in jewel-colored velvets, and an exquisite bed with a Rosepoint lace spread. Cousin Letty, wearing sheer linen and lace underwear, paraded up and down before her mirror modeling her new hats. She had the most beautiful figure and carriage I've ever seen, and she gave her daughter Millie and me lectures on how to sit and walk. She also insisted on loaning me one of her hats—a white feather toque with an egret sticking up like an antenna. I was enchanted.

Father complained that I was acting affected, and mimicked me with devastating accuracy, but my taste of Washington "high life" must have gone to my head like Cousin Letty's hat. When he took me to the White House to meet the President, I was dumbfounded to find that Mr. Wilson, whom I'd pictured as an ascetic, thin-nostriled idealist, was so warmly magnetic and charming. He soon had me chattering on gaily, and that's when I rushed home to report to my diary: "Pres. Wilson is a dear!!!!"

I saw him again at Cousin Julia Vrooman's. Our gay Cousin Julia, Letty's sister, has been mentioned in memoirs as one of the wittiest, most entertaining women in official Washington of that period. (Adlai, who adores her, would stretch that to "one of the wittiest in the whole world.") Julia and her husband Carl, then Assistant Secretary of Agriculture, were so popular that everybody wanted to be asked to their house. Of all the guests I met there, the President still rated the best adjectives in my diary: "He is fascinating." When I added the bit about "His wife is fair, fat, and fortyish," I'm afraid I was doing the lovely Mrs. Wilson quite an injustice. I was so charmed with Mr. Wilson I wouldn't admit any woman was worthy of him!

I sent accounts to Mother and Adlai of a Sunday-At-Home of the Patten sisters, for years the most famous hostesses in the capital. Their house on Massachusetts Avenue was the international crossroads—and the gossip center for Washington society. I exclaimed over my first sight of footmen, and reported: "Andre Tardieu [special French envoy] made a

fuss over me at the Paton's. I talked French with him. Met
Walter Hines Page [Ambassador to Britain] who told me we
would be at war in three weeks." (His prophecy was almost
a year too soon.) "I've got to dress now and have my picture
taken in Letty's hat."

Mother's horrified opinion of the "hat" photographs is
obvious from this letter I wrote her after I'd returned to
school:

> I am *sick* you thought I looked so awful in the hat. I cer-
> tainly don't want to look *fast!* Oh dear! Why don't you like the
> photos. I have no idea of going back to Washington! . . . Got a
> vote for the kindest girl in school tonight! I didn't *pose* for
> any of those pictures—just sat naturally. I am *so* sorry.

In May, my diary notes: "Got a good mark in Economics,
to everyone's astonishment. Played Portia. I would love to
be an actress."

When I went home, "Dear old Ad met me. Heard him
speak at his banquet at Normal. VERY impressed."

The title of his speech was "To the Senior Celebrities,"
and although I can't remember a word of it now, I still recall the curiously strong impression I had that night as I
listened to the poised sixteen-year-old I'd always thought of
as my little brother. As a mark of my new respect, I asked
him if he'd teach me to drive the car!

He taught me, and I think he showed much more patience
and calm than most males do in that delicate situation, but
I must admit that when we go off in a car together now, he
still prefers to do the driving himself. And he drives much
too fast!

In June, Father wired Adlai and me to come to the Presidential conventions, and I exclaimed in my diary, "We are

much excited! . . . Adlai and I arrived this morning . . .
Chicago is aflutter with flags and politicians. Spent entire
day at G.O.P. convention. Sat in the Fred Uphams' box with
the nabobs and met everybody. . . . Mr. Ickes took us to
the Bull Moose convention. Heard a message from Teddy
Roosevelt read. It was much more fun than the Republican!"

When I got a cold, Adlai said I had caught G.O.P. germs.
Father, who was running for re-election for secretary of state,
covered us with badges that admitted us everywhere. He was
very eager to have Adlai begin to take an interest in politics,
and soon my brother was dashing around on his own. Suddenly Father missed his police badge, and started a frantic
search, with the help of the manager of the Hotel Sherman,
Frank Bering. When Adlai walked in jauntily wearing the
missing badge, which he'd "borrowed" to get him onto the
floor of the conventions, Father's face was a study. Having
urged his son to "learn about politics firsthand," he couldn't
explode.

We didn't go on with Father to the Democratic convention in St. Louis, because Adlai had to get home and tutor
in French for his entrance examinations for Choate. Afterward, he drove around the countryside tacking up posters
and handing out leaflets to help Father's campaign. Even
Hearst's Chicago paper, *The Herald,* and McCormick's *Chicago Tribune,* were for a Stevenson that year.

At home, we talked, ate and dreamed politics. Our whole
family was anxious about President Wilson's re-election, because we thought the country needed his vision and leadership more than ever. He was campaigning on the "Peace &
Preparedness" slogan, against the bewhiskered, distinguished
Charles Evans Hughes, and against Teddy Roosevelt, the Bull
Moose himself.

In September, my diary reported: "Mother and I are busy getting Wilson supporters together. Secretary of the Navy Daniels came this afternoon."

Josephus Daniels was staying at our house, and when he spoke that night at the Vote for Wilson rally, Adlai and I sat on the platform, and *that* time my brother stayed wide awake! I had spent all day decorating the old Coliseum with banners for the rally, and Mother had denuded her garden of late-blooming flowers to put around the speaker's podium. We thought nothing was too good for Secretary Daniels and a Wilson rally. The audience of cheering Democrats seemed to feel the same way.

A few weeks later, my diary noted, "Ad and I have been flying around getting his things ready" (for prep school). Mother was trying to ply him with a year's supply of nose drops, cascara, calomel, hair tonic, ointments and various medicaments which he patiently accepted and never opened. "We are sad to see him go, but he is excited and joyous."

Chapter 7

TOWARD THE END of Adlai's second year at the Connecticut preparatory school, he wrote us, "If I come back next year, it looks as tho' I'd be a pretty big dude."

He had just been elected vice-president of his class, captain of the tennis team, and had moved up from business manager to editor-in-chief of the *Choate News*. His letter also reported: "Last night there was an Athletic Association meeting to elect officers. The A.A. is the governing body of all the School's athletic questions and the officers are the big athletes of the School. However, by some freak that I can't understand, I was elected secretary."

Soon afterward, he wrote, "I have some good news for you, best yet, *I* think. I was elected president of St. Andrews" [the school's religious society for all denominations]. "You didn't know your son was a young evangelist, did you?"

Instead of returning to Choate to be a "pretty big dude" in what would have been his third and last year, he enlisted in the Navy, and he never again mentioned the honors he was passing up, but only wrote Mother, "Please don't worry so much about my going into the service. I am awfully anxious [to go]."

When he arrived at Choate as a "new boy" from the Midwest, the German submarine *Deutschland* had made a first ominous appearance on our Atlantic coast, and President Wilson was making his last movingly eloquent speeches before the 1916 election. The whole country, including schoolboys, was passionately aroused, rooting for Hughes or Wilson. Of the 200 students in Choate, Adlai was one of the three Democrats! His roommate, Harry Stearns, said recently, "We used to argue politics by the hour, but I never saw Ad lose his temper or act bitter."

It's probably just as well *I* wasn't at Choate that election week. I wrote in my diary, on November 7: "Hughes is winning! Oh, dear! I wonder what the future holds. . . . Mother and I waited impatiently for word from Father. He is leading his ticket but defeated. Wilson is gaining!! . . . Next day. Such a cheery letter from Father. It put Mother and me in fine spirits."

It was like my gallant Father to buoy us up in the midst of his own defeat. He had encouraged Mother and me to stay on in Lakewood, New Jersey, while he went through the last nerve-racking weeks of campaigning. Our dear friend Governor Dunne lost to Frank Lowden, but it's a gratifying proof of Father's popularity that he got more votes than the winning Lowden in Cook County, and even ran 60,000 ahead of Wilson.

My next diary entry: "I could dance with joy that Wilson has won!"

By a wry coincidence, who should turn up at our same Lakewood hotel, Laurel in the Pines, but Charles Evans Hughes and his frail little wife. Considering that he had been hailed as President for twenty-four hours, only to end up the loser, he must have been feeling even more let down than Mr. Dewey in 1948. I remember I kept staring at Mr. Hughes in the hotel dining room, to see how he was taking the defeat, and I had to admire his quiet dignity.

At Choate, the boys forgot politics for football, and were fiercely united in wanting their school to beat Kent school. Adlai was playing quarterback on one of the intramural teams. He was rooming alone that first semester, but later he shared a room with Harry Stearns and Jim Milholland, and he was so much happier with that arrangement he wrote mother, "I'll never room alone again. . . . After lights, the 9th floor had a very select feed in (Dick) Higgins' room. One of the fellows had received a box. We had chicken, meat loaf, crackers, jam, peanut butter, all sorts of candy and many other indigestible luxuries. Mr. Temple [House Master] was there and we had a great time."

Jim Milholland was noted for his prowess as a talker, and when his roommates insisted (occasionally!) on quiet to study, Jim would roam off to find other listeners. One night while he was out, Adlai and Harry rigged up a trap, balancing a glass of water, a hockey stick and a pair of skates on top of the door. When Jim walked into the room at midnight, the assorted objects clattered down with such a resounding, splashing din that all Hill House was aroused, and the Senior Master came rushing. The trappers got demerits, but they seemed to think the excitement was worth it.

The dormer windows of their top floor room overlooked the small campus that's surrounded by eight hundred acres of beautiful rolling Connecticut country around Wallingford. Choate has high scholastic standards, and Father had chosen the school partly because it would give the solid, relentless preparation Adlai needed, with his high school background, to pass the College Board examinations and get into Princeton.

During his first-year College Board exams, he reported in a letter: "I ought to pass Geometry as I got 85 in the final school exam, one of the best marks, however fellows have flunked in better condition than I am in. I got 63 in my final exam in English which was not bad as there were only 2 passes in my class. If my themes are good I will pass." (He passed!) "I have to take 3 Latin exams. Mr. Wheeler figures that I have a fighting chance to pass the Cicero as I know the speeches. . . . He says I ought to get the history question altogether correct."

One of Adlai's ex-teachers says now, "There was never any question he had the intelligence, but he was interested in so many things his studies often ran second or third."

My brother had inherited Grandfather Davis' love of newspapers, and he plunged happily into reporting school events and soliciting local merchants' ads for the *Choate News*. Harry Stearns, who was editor when Adlai was business manager, remembers the time Adlai persuaded the reluctant Italian proprietor of a newly opened store called Papa's Candy Kitchen to take space in the *News,* by describing how the Choate students would rush hungrily to Papa's to buy vast amounts of candy, as soon as they read the ad. Unfortunately, it didn't work out quite that way. When Adlai went back to Papa's several months later to collect the money owed the *News* for the ad, the proprietor, in a burst of Latin indignation, grabbed a large iron ladle and advanced on him shouting, "Nobody come buy. I don't pay!"

I don't think my brother has ever promised too much since.

While he was in that new-to-business stage on the *News,*
Mother wrote him:

I think it is splendid experience for you. You will learn
how to handle men etc. etc. and above all else I hope it will
show you how necessary it is to gauge your strength, to allot
your time, and not to give of both too ceaselessly. This is just
as important in becoming successful as talent—and another
thing, never be annoyed or anxious. *Worried* is the common
way of expressing it. It *never* helps and slowly and insidiously
it ruins your mind and body. "Sufficient unto the day is the
work thereof" the Bible says and you must learn never to go
to bed with a business thought in your mind! Just think, you
have already $500 worth of ads and you were a little anxious
about them. Now you see it was unnecessary to be the least
troubled. Please keep these things in mind and see if you can't
get steadier by the discipline this work affords.

To keep placid and cheerful, knowing all things come to
those who love the Lord and doeth His works. . . .

Did you get the express I sent you? I have some more things
which I will send you.

The shoes you don't need you can put away. Try to save
the good dancing pumps and use these old ones around school.
I don't believe these old high shoes will be comfortable. If
not, don't ruin your feet wearing them. You must buy a new
pair of hightop shoes soon for it will be getting cold.

We love you, my own dear good boy.

May God be with you always,
Mother

She kept close track of all his activities, and offered so
much good advice on each one that sometimes my brother
must have felt like Lord Chesterfield's son. When he was invited to a dance at a girls' school, Mother wrote him: ". . . I
suppose after a few days you should write Jane a little note
saying you had returned safely and thank her again for ask-

ing you, that you had greatly enjoyed the dance and the couple of days of freedom. Be careful that it is written well and properly spelled."

Adlai had joined the Dramatic Club and was selected to play one of the leading parts in Sheridan's *The Critic.* Mother's letter continues:

> The play will be of much benefit. I suppose the greatest thing for you, in the play, is to speak so you can be heard by all. Next try to be the part. Practise in your room aloud, and the gestures and movements. Try to keep well so nothing will hold you back. And to keep your throat in good order for the play, you must gargle daily.
>
> I am planning to get down to see you then, since you have to take part. I think it will be hard to have a girl over. However you can decide that later.
>
> I am overjoyed that Dr. Shortledge complimented your themes. I think you must be getting on to your work better. We all love you so, my dear, and long to see you. Buffie talks of you constantly and is tremendously thrilled over the play. Father and Buff leave next week.

Father and I were joining friends in New Orleans, to go to California with them, and the plan was that we'd go on to the Orient in our host's yacht. Mother had decided not to go because she was afraid she'd be too seasick.

Adlai wrote mother:

> . . . I was glad to hear that their trip had not fallen thru. But where will you be when they are floating around the world.
>
> I just got back from church a few minutes ago. It certainly was a long sermon, believe me. Last night we had moving pictures here at school. We are going to have them every Sat. from now on. We saw Marguerite Clark in Prince and The Pauper. It was very good. . . .

I go shooting almost every afternoon and am getting quite good at it.

Father was so proud of Adlai that he sometimes embarrassed him acutely. Adlai often protested against this parental pride and excess enthusiasm, but when Father *exaggerated,* it was intolerable. A stern postcard-warning from my brother at Princeton shows how desperate he somettimes felt about this:

Princeton, N. J.
Feb. 2, 1921

"Dear Father: Once more may I protest (as usual in vain I suppose) against your assumption of the duties of my publicity manager. As in the past, when I have strenuously objected, you have nevertheless gone ahead and with the apparent intent of pleasing a mere child, put things in papers which were altogether wrong in point of fact and most embarrassing to me. And now again: assailed from all sides with clippings from the *Chicago Tribune* to the effect that I am head of the Princetonian when as a matter of fact I am only second. Consequently many stories about how it got in, can't understand it, etc. Please desist and do me a real favor. . . . Adlai"

Even during prep school years, Father complained Adlai didn't tell him enough news, and while we were in California, that spring of 1917, he dashed off these two letters to his son—both written the same day:

Adlai: Why haven't you written me? Your not doing so has caused me an endless amount of annoyance. I am afraid my boy you often think if things just seem right they are, and you let it go at that. Don't, I beg you, believe this. Know you must do your duty. If I don't know all about you I am, of course, worried. . . . And not a word to me about your glory on the newspaper. Now, young man, you write me a note

weekly—every Wednesday as you said you would, or I shall
wire Dr. St. John [the Head Master] the first miss.

Second letter, later that day:

My dear Adlai: I received a letter from Mother enclosing
several good letters to her which I enjoyed very much. Evidently you were busy so I don't blame you so much for not
writing me. Am delighted to hear of your success in the play.
It will teach you the value of concentration and also that
every gesture and intonation is of value at all times & in every
walk of life. I wish you would remember this always. You
can't underestimate the value of expressing yourself correctly.
If you will take my advice you will learn it now. Form the
habit now & it will be of immeasurable value to you all your
life. . . .

"With a heartfull of love for you, Pop"

Soon after this, I wrote Mother: "You can't imagine what
a shock it was to hear that Ad had measles. There must be
an epidemic of them." There was. My brother remembers
that the school broke out in so many spots he was put into
an improvised overflow-infirmary, and was torn between feeling miserable and rejoicing that measles gave him a dandy
excuse to postpone cramming.

My letter to Mother bewailing his measles continues: "I
went over and took lunch with Cousin Bertha. She is such
a character. And admires *you*—thinks you're intellectual and
brilliant. She's so cute. Said she was tired of modern things
and would be glad to get to Heaven where there was no sex!

"Mr. O. said today I looked exactly like Madame de Pom-
padour when she was young. I don't believe the O's get along
very well together. . . . Some woman saw Mrs. K. smoking
at tea and said she would leave the hotel, it was no place
for *ladies* to stop!"

Soon I was writing:

> Precious one! I have something so fine to tell you I can't
> wait. This afternoon Father, Mrs. K. and I motored out to
> call on Mrs. Carrie Jacobs Bond, the famous song writer. We
> had a wonderful drive out—way back of San Diego and up
> into the hills—her house and that of Schumann-Heink are at
> the top—and oh, such a view. We found this fascinating little
> bungalow peeking out over the world. Carrie Jacobs Bond
> was wonderful, natural and frank and sweet—called me 'sweet
> enthusiasm' and kissed when I came and left. She sang and
> played a new song that hasn't been published yet—one called
> her Home Song. It was so enchanting and so appealingly ren-
> dered it brought tears to my eyes. Imagine listening to her—
> looking out of that huge window down over the valley and
> miles away to the mountains! It has been one of the great
> experiences of my life.

It was like Father to arrange such an enchanting day for
me. Our friend Mrs. Richard Yates of Springfield had helped
Carrie Jacobs Bond get her first songs published, so we were
made doubly welcome.

Our trip to the Orient was cancelled right after Congress
declared war on Germany that April of 1917, and Father,
in one of his docile humors, agreed that I could spend a
month with my brother at a Wyoming ranch. By the time
Adlai was writing Mother from school, "Well, in four more
days I will be traveling toward the best home in all the
world," I was back in Bloomington and happily awaiting his
coming so that we could make plans for our trip to Wyoming.

Mother thought we should have a chaperone, and as usual
she wanted to kill two birds with one stone, so our chaperone was the French teacher I'd had at Miss Wright's school,

Nora Caroe. The theory was that she would tutor Adlai—
probably on horseback.

My brother's letter described our settling in at the ranch:

H F BAR RANCH
Buffalo, Wyoming

Thursday

Dearest Maw.

Well we have arrived at our destination at last. It certainly
is a beautiful place. Buffie and Nora have a little cottage together and I have one all to myself. I expected that there
would probably be another man in with me, there are 2 or 3
in all the other cottages. Buffie's cottage is in or rather on the
edge of a little grove of cottonwoods which border a very
pretty and fast flowing mountain stream. Almost directly back
of us the ground rises into the first range of the Big Horns,
beautiful mountains. It is certainly a wonderful location. We
arrived in Clairemont about an hour and a half late. Clairemont consists of a water station and about 3 or 4 stores. We
waited there about an hour for the train to leave for Buffalo.
The ride from Clairemont to Buffalo on the little 2 car train
was lots of fun and the scenery beautiful. Buffalo is a very
pretty little town with paved streets and lots of autos. When
we arrived they were having a 4th of July celebration with
broncho busting, racing, etc. The ride out here (18 miles) in
the motor car was really very beautiful, it was an almost
steady ascent.

The people out here are awfully nice. Mr. Horton is a
dandy. The ranch is almost full. It only accommodates 100
and there are about 95 here all ready. There is a very nice
woman, Mrs. Goodwin, from Cleveland here with her husband, son and daughter. She took me out to the corral and
told me all about the place, (she has been here 4 years). Her
son is a very nice fellow (17) and goes to Thatcher, if that's
the way you spell it. There is also a girl here named Edith
Layman from St. Louis, whom I met in Charlevoix last summer. I have not spoken to her yet, but will soon. Our trunk

did not come from Chicago on the same train with us, however I suppose it will be here tonight. There's only 1 train a day from Clairemont to Buffalo. I think we will have a fine time out here. The horses are not very good, in fact quite rotten so tell Father he does not need to worry about any accidents from bucking bronchos, etc.

I haven't asked Mr. Horton about the typewriter yet, but will today. I think all the clothes I need is a pair of riding breeches in order not to wear any of my trousers out. Buffie did a very fine job of packing the grip. She put in about a dozen shirts for me and only 1 collar so I am washing that. Also only 1 necktie which will be worn out very soon.

Love,

Adlai

Nora Caroe did her best to corral him every day for a French lesson, but he had bought a pair of black bear chaps and was riding high, wide and handsome. At roundup time, he and his friend Ralph Goodwin were back guards for the cattle, racing their horses up and down the line. My diary mentions: "Frontier Day—wonderful bronco-busting by famous cowboys. I served in Red Cross booth. Adlai won a prize." I remember watching while he galloped by, leaning alarmingly far out of his saddle, to spear potatoes in the gymkhana contest.

Mother was adept at making Adlai and me feel responsible for each other. She'd say, "Do give Buffie advice," or, "Be sure to tell Adlai to do such-and-so." So I made the fatal mistake, at the ranch, of playing the older-sister role. We were all on horseback, and I rode up to my brother and gave him some command that must have infuriated him. He suddenly reached over, slapped my horse with his reins to make it start off, then galloped away in the opposite direction. *He* wasn't going to be dictated to! The few times I've ever been so foolish as to try it since, he gets that "Don't try to run my life or shove me around" look, and it always reminds me of that day when he left his sister in a cloud of dust.

The owner of the ranch, Frank Horton, took us off on a ten-day pack trip in the Big Horn mountains, and we fished in those icy rushing streams. At least the others fished, but my line got in such a hideous tangle I soon gave up casting. (Adlai not only caught a lot of trout, but learned to fry them in corn meal.) Once when we were all scrambling along the rocks beside a stream, I slipped and fell into a whirlpool. Our old-timer guide, Ed Powell, fished me out, but my rod was lost forever, and I can't say I've missed it.

Both Adlai and I loved the West, and often went back. When he graduated from college, he went west again and even made great plans to buy a ranch with Ralph Goodwin, but Father squashed that idea and shipped off his protesting son in the opposite direction—to law school.

When we got home that summer of 1917, the plan Father was currently against was Adlai's driving our car *all the way to Michigan*. We were to join Mother at Charlevoix, and I backed Adlai up so volubly that Father finally gave in. My brother and I set off in the Hudson, and got stuck in the mud that same evening. Adlai felt so responsible for our plight that he pushed and tugged and heaved for hours, before he tramped off to find help. We had to spend the night at the nearest farmhouse, and although I appreciated the hospitality, I nearly smothered, because the windows of the bedroom I slept in were nailed shut.

When we finally got to Charlevoix, my brother took all the blame on himself—and in fact, he often stood up for me in family scoldings that were all my fault. He'd say to

Father or Mother, "Don't keep on and on at Buff. She knows she was wrong and she's sorry, so don't be hard on her."

According to this letter written during his second year at Choate, he blew a sterner whistle on schoolmates, now that he was an "old boy."

> We beat Bridgeport High yesterday 18-0. I was timekeeper and also helped call the roll on the bleachers. You see we make everyone come to the games and if they don't, they get sat on. It certainly is nice to be one in authority, and believe me I exercise my authority. . . . I have been given a topic to speak on in St. Andrews in several weeks. I am afraid I'll make a fool of myself trying to tell the school about religion.
>
> This morning Harry Stearns and I led the whole school to church. Last night, Mr. Seymour, Mrs. St. John's brother, gave us a very interesting talk on the Kaiser.

He bought a Liberty Bond and asked if Father would send $50 to pay for it. "I will pay him back or some of it back next summer when I receive the money I hope to make out of the *News*." And he did. He made $130.

Father had been longing to do more for the war than buy an occasional Liberty Bond, so his friend Secretary of the Navy Daniels appointed him as special assistant to Admiral McGowan, investigating war contracts to prevent fraud, and helping speed up production. We joined him in Washington, and lived in the old La Fayette Hotel. In spite of the war the capital was feverishly social, as Adlai discovered when he came for the Christmas holidays. Our parents' friends, the Arthur Lees, had a daughter, Ellen Bruce, who was charmed with my brother, and when she was arranging to get him on sub-deb invitation lists, she'd say joyously, "I'll float you, Adlai." He went to some of the parties, and although my diary records that he "dances like a prince now," I think he spent most of his time just standing self-consciously in the stag line.

About the time Adlai returned to school after the holidays, a messenger arrived at our hotel with a neat, small envelope lettered in gold: "The White House," addressed to Mother and me, enclosing an invitation to tea. I have a pleasant recollection of a cozy upstairs sitting room with the tea table set beside a crackling fire. The lovely Mrs. Wilson (I finally admitted she was beautiful!) and the President's daughters completed the warm, relaxed family atmosphere, and ever since then, I've never been able to think of the White House as a coldly formal place. It seems to me official residences should have some rooms that reflect a little of the personality of their occupants, as the Wilsons' did. But I also feel strongly that the state rooms should be left in period, and not redone by each newcomer to suit their taste—or lack of it!

Our cousins the Vroomans had rented the charming Longworth house. I met Alice Roosevelt Longworth at a dance at the Joseph Leiters, but all I can remember is her long cigarette holder, and that I *didn't* hear any rasping wit. Congressman Bankhead's daughter, Tallulah, made a much more devastating impression, because whenever she appeared at a party, all the young men were so bowled over they went down like tenpins. While they crowded around her clamoring for a dance, or even a husky word, the rest of us were quite green-eyed. When I was invited to the Bankhead apartment, I was rather surprised to see the glamorous Tallulah in that antimacassar and ante-bellum setting.

Adlai, in letters, complained it was hard to get down to work after his wonderful vacation. "Tell Buff to write me often and give me all the dope on Washington Society."

It was Mother who sent him the "dope" when Cousin Letty Bromwell gave a dance for my friend Louise Thoron and me in her beautiful house—the nearest thing I ever had to a coming-out. I had my first black evening dress, with a floating skirt of chiffon petals, and as Mother reported to Adlai, "The Bromwell ball was a brilliant success. Many officers of all nations and three men to each girl. Buff is now about over her cold but not as well as she should be and I fear not as discreet as should be."

I remember one of my "indiscretions" was at a dance Mrs. George Vanderbilt gave for her daughter Cordelia. A Valentino-like attaché of the Argentine embassy gave me such a rush I danced with him all evening long and raised a good many eyebrows. But when the orchestra played "After the Ball Is Over," like all the other young ladies I collected my chaperone (a weazened Portuguese maid) with my evening coat, and rode demurely home with her in a carriage.

Many Chicago girls had come to Washington because their fathers, like mine, were "dollar-a-year" men. Of that group, Peg Cary, Courtney Letts and Edith Cummings were the great belles, and at Courtney's coming-out party I felt like quite a belle myself, because John Harlan, Allister McCormick and several Princeton men gave me such a rush.

Most of us worked for the Red Cross, knitting and rolling bandages (later I joined the Motor Corps) and then we dashed home to change into the elaborate long dresses we wore to "assist" at afternoon teas. I went off in broad daylight in an ankle-length creation of silver and gold lace over net, to assist at a tea of Mrs. Daniels'.

Senator J. Ham Lewis and his famous wife "Gypsy" were wonderful to me, and so were Speaker Joe Cannon of Illinois and his sister Helen, who often entertained for their nieces,

the Le Suere girls of Danville. Other friends from down-
state Illinois included Mrs. Gillette-Hill and her daughter,
Lemira, of Lincoln, and of course we saw a great deal of
the Vroomans, Cousin Letty, and her mother, our aunt Julia
Scott, who was a well-known figure in Washington society.
I also have affectionate memories of the Elkins-Davis clan
of West Virginia; Mrs. Warder, who had that beautiful K
Street house with its art gallery; and the Hamlins and Perry
Belmonts, the Henry Leonards, and Cecilia McCallum.

Secretary of State and Mrs. Lansing put me on their as-
sisting list for "at homes," and the amusing Vice-President
Tom Marshall (who said, "What this country needs is a good
five-cent cigar") took Mother and me to lunch at the Capitol.
At a dinner at some legation, I noticed a tall, arresting young
couple and asked who they were. It was Franklin D. Roosevelt, Assistant Secretary of the Navy, and his wife.

Adlai doesn't recall ever seeing Mr. Roosevelt until he
met him in 1932, when F.D.R. was touring the country during his first presidential campaign. Henry Horner, the Pro-
bate Judge of Cook County, was running for Governor that
year. Adlai had often appeared in his court and Judge Horner, who was something of an Illinois historian, had taken
a friendly interest in this last of the Stevensons of Bloomington. They had another mutual interest in Lincoln.
Horner was a Lincoln scholar and collector and frequently
talked to my brother about the famous three-page autobiography which Lincoln had written out and given to Great-
grandfather Fell in 1859. Cousin Emmet Richardson, as
executor of the estate of our great-aunt Fanny Fell, had the
disposition of this precious piece of Lincolniana, and Judge

Horner was determined to get it, through Adlai, for the State Historical Library in Springfield.

When Governor Roosevelt came to Chicago for a political rally, Judge Horner and a prominent Democrat and businessman, Robert Carr, took Adlai with them to call on F.D.R. in his campaign train. Adlai recalls that there was a line of political bigwigs passing through the car and shaking hands with "the candidate." When it was my brother's turn, Roosevelt, with his astonishing memory, immediately identified him and recalled his acquaintance with Father and also that his own father, James Roosevelt, had known our Grandfather Stevenson. F.D.R.'s grace and warmth at that first hurried meeting left Adlai stammering, surprised and devoted.

In the 1936 campaign, my brother, who was very busy practicing law in Chicago, worked on the Illinois Finance Committee for Roosevelt, but made only one really important political speech—at Carlton College in Minnesota. At least, that's what he *thought* he was doing! He said later that he never worked harder on a speech (and that's saying something) and that he had worked out what, to his judicial mind, seemed a balanced, reasoned presentation of the case of Democrats *versus* Republicans, from which one could only conclude that the Democratic case was overwhelming. The audience of students, faculty and townsfolk listened attentively, and Adlai sat down feeling satisfied that he had struck a solid, sober blow for Roosevelt. Walking with the president of the college through a darkened corridor to a side entrance, he overheard two students discussing his speech. One said, "That was the best political speech I ever heard." The other nodded enthusiastically. "It certainly was." He added in a puzzled tone, "But could you figure out which side he was for?"

The next time Adlai actually talked with Roosevelt was in 1941, and now that I've skipped this far ahead of my story, I want to include a funny account Adlai gave us years ago of the frenzied adventures that led to that second meeting with F.D.R. The President had appointed Frank Knox, the Republican publisher of *The Chicago Daily News,* as Secretary of the Navy, and Knox had asked Adlai to come to Washington as his special assistant and personal lawyer. My brother's first big assignment, when he arrived in the summer of 1941, was to prepare the groundwork and legal papers in case the Navy had to take over the strike-bound Kearney shipyards to keep up production on essential warships. It was a tense time, mid-August 1941; the German armies were knifing into Russia and marching on Moscow. Adlai worked around the clock to get everything ready, but the first big government plant seizure could not become effective until an Executive Order was signed by the President, and he was somewhere on a warship off the coast of Maine, returning from the Atlantic Charter meeting with Churchill. Secretary Knox and his advisers decided Adlai should make a quick flight, or rather, a series of flights, board the cruiser at sea, get the President's signature, and fly back at once, thus saving a day or so. That was the start of a frenzied adventure.

Just as Adlai was about to take off, with the papers, Knox called him back to his office again. A very senior admiral was there, and no one else. The room was heavy with solemnity. Knox said, "The admiral has a message he wants you to take to the President and deliver to him in person. Go ahead, Admiral."

"You are to deliver this message to the President and to
no one else," the admiral said. "Tell him I have learned
today, from a heretofore reliable source, that Stalin has
opened negotiations with Hitler."

This was startling news indeed, because if Stalin was ne-
gotiating with Hitler, it must mean that the Russians were
capitulating and all the power of the German armies would
be turned against the West.

"Can I write the message down, sir?" he asked.

"No, nothing on paper!" the admiral said sternly.

"Can I repeat it to you, to make sure I have it right?"

After Adlai had repeated the message, to be sure he'd
got it straight, the admiral and Knox cautioned him again
that he must deliver it to the President *alone*, and as fast
as possible. Then Adlai took off in the Secretary's big plane
for the Naval station at Quonset, Rhode Island, where he
was to change to a small seaplane.

At Quonset, the weather was so bad all planes were
grounded. Adlai explained to the admiral in command that
he *had* to get to the President's ship immediately. The admiral had seen too many panting civilians on "missions" to
be much moved and he took quite a lot of persuading, but
finally hours later, he told an aide, "Let Stevenson have a
small plane to fly to Rockland, Maine. Maybe he can get
there by the time the President docks."

After all that delay, by the time the plane reached Rockland, my brother could look down and see the President's
ship at the dock, huge crowds around and the special train
in the station. The pilot landed in a field and Adlai ran to
the highway and flagged down a passing car. The old lady
driving it was startled, but she rose to the emergency nobly,
and stepped on the gas to rush Adlai to town, where they

quickly got caught in a traffic jam. Adlai leaped out and
ran toward the station clutching his brief case. But he was
too late. The President's train had started and the crowd
was rolling back from the dock. He hitchhiked back to the
airport and they flew off to Portland, where the special train
would make its first stop hours later.

In Portland, Adlai went to the movies, bit his nails, and
went to the station in plenty of time, but alas, so had thousands of citizens—all hoping to see the President. All ap-
proaches to the station were blocked by solid crowds. In
desperation Adlai explained to the police that he had come
from Washington with an important message for President
Roosevelt, but it probably sounded just a little more elaborate than the other demands for special consideration, and
all they said was "Stand back, buddy." Adlai burrowed his
way forward through the crowd and spied Senator Pepper
of Florida whom he knew slightly, with some other gentlemen and a police escort. He told Pepper about his Kearney
shipyard mission (he didn't dare mention the "top-secret"
message) and the senator said to come along and he'd see
what he could do. When the train pulled in, the senator and
the others promptly boarded, but the Secret Service men
had never seen Adlai, so he waited on the station platform,
and for fifteen agonizing minutes he stood there expecting
the train would pull out any minute. Finally General "Pa"
Watson poked his head out of the door of the Presidential
car, and he was very nice and sympathetic, but he couldn't
understand why Adlai wouldn't just hand the papers over.
My brother obstinately insisted, to the amusement of everyone around, that he *had* to see Roosevelt personally. Pa
Watson went away, and the next five minutes seemed to
Adlai, who had become something of a public spectacle on

the crowded platform, like five years, before the aide came
back and said the President would see him.

"I got into the car," Adlai said later, "and what do you
think I found? There was F.D.R. sitting at the dinner table
as relaxed as you please, just as though five thousand people
weren't shouting for him on the platform, and just as though
he hadn't just settled the world's future with Churchill—
and just as though I wasn't loaded with bad news! There
were several other people at the table—Marvin McIntyre,
Harry Hopkins, Mrs. Roosevelt and one of the secretaries,
Miss Tully, I think, as well as Pa Watson. F.D.R. looked
up when I burst in.

" 'Well, Adlai, how are you?' he asked. 'Glad to hear
you're working with Frank Knox.'

"I mumbled something incoherent and rushed on to say
I had some emergency papers for his signature.

" 'That's fine, Adlai,' he said, 'let's have a look at them.' "
As Adlai tells it,

"I opened up my brief case clumsily and fished out the
Kearney shipyard papers. I explained the situation as best
I could and pointed out where he was supposed to sign. He
looked it over for a minute and then said:

" 'Well now, Adlai, you just leave all these papers in your
folder with me, and I'll read them over tonight. We'll have
a meeting at the White House in the morning. You fly
back to Washington and arrange it. Tell Secretary Knox I'd
also like to see Myron Taylor and the Attorney General at
nine o'clock—and you be there too.'

" 'But, Mr. President,' I said, 'these are supposed to be
signed right now!'

" 'I think it will work out all right this way,' said the
President.

" 'Well,' I said, 'if you say so I guess it will be O.K.' I marvel that I could have talked like such a fool but I was so nervous I hardly knew what I was saying—mostly, I suppose, because I hadn't yet said the really important thing— the message—and I didn't know how to deliver it with all those people sitting around. I could see he was waiting for me to leave, and I had to come out with something. The talk went about like this:

" 'I have something else to tell you, Mr. President.'

" 'Do you, Adlai? What is it?'

" 'Well, Mr. President, it's a message from Admiral ——. He said to tell you . . . alone.'

" 'Oh, I think you could tell me here, Adlai.'

" 'Can I write it down for you to read?'

" 'Why certainly, Adlai.'

"He gave me a menu and I wrote on the back of it. 'Admiral —— has heard from a heretofore reliable source that Stalin today started negotiations with Hitler.'

"Then I gave him back the menu. He read it carefully and then looked up at me.

" 'Adlai,' he said, 'do you believe this?'

"That was too much! I didn't know what I thought. 'Why, I don't know, Mr. President,' I stammered.

" 'I don't believe it,' said F.D.R. 'I'm not worried at all. Are you worried, Adlai?'

"I said I guessed I wasn't as much worried after all. Then, mission completed after a fashion, I took my departure, and in my embarrassed confusion, I wheeled around and crashed right into a closed door, thus bending my crooked nose some more. I flew back to Washington, woke Secretary Knox to tell him about the meeting at the White House and we all went over there at nine o'clock. My crowning mortification was that the President hadn't even opened my precious Kearney shipyard papers. He pulled them out and settled the whole business in fifteen minutes and signed the Executive Order. As for the negotiations between Stalin and Hitler, the President was, of course, right again, and the Admiral's source was unreliable that time. We never heard another word about it."

But that wasn't the last Adlai saw of President Roosevelt during wartime. Two years later, he asked Adlai to head up an important economic mission to Italy to devise means of immediate relief and rehabilitation for the Italian people behind the battle lines. Meanwhile, Adlai had accomplished so many successful assignments for the Navy—among them, helping to improve labor and race relations—that he was awarded the Distinguished Service Award in 1945, after he had left the Navy.

To go back now to World War I, while Father was working for the Navy, and we were still living in Washington, I went up to Choate to a dance. Adlai had also invited Mother and Dougie Hay, but neither one could go, and my diary sounds as if I went under duress: "It is snowing. Went to Adlai's dance. Liked the school. Bored. How blasé I feel. Love to be doing something for Adlai."

He was probably wishing to goodness that Dougie Hay was there instead of his oh-so-blasé twenty-year-old sister. At a concert before the dance, the Mandolin Club played "Wait Till the Cows Come Home," and the Glee Club sang "The Elf Man." As the *Choate News* reported, "A harmless punch was served in the Study Hall during Intermission."

It was impossible to keep up a blasé Society manner

around anyone who gets as much fun out of things as my brother, so I ended up having a fine time, and was flattered when Adlai wrote to Mother afterward, "Tell Buff lots of the fellows have been asking for her."

By late Spring, he was writing us:

> I had to work pretty hard last week getting out my first *News* as Editor-in-Chief. When you receive it look at the picture on the right side of the front page and see if it resembles any one you ever saw before. Also read the article about the 1918 board as I wrote most of it. Also read the editorial which is another product of my pen. Furthermore notice my name in the headlines on the Loomis Tennis match. . . .
>
> I am thinking seriously of going to Blairstown after college exams. That is the prep. schools religious conference and an awfully good thing. I will write you more fully about it later.

As his honors piled up, Mother wrote him:

> My darling Laddie,
>   . . . How you keep your equilibrium with so much glory being thrust upon you, I do not see. Perhaps this is the reason why your grades this month were not quite so good in French! However if this is all the effect it is having, I think you are to be congratulated.

Adlai wrote her how hard he was studying: "I sincerely believe that you will not recognize me in my present intellectual disguise when next we meet."

From my diary that spring: "This has been the most depressing day. I think we feel the war in Europe. The big German offensive began yesterday. I think I could cry for joy if the war stopped."

Instead, the war brought a tragedy to our own family. Uncle Bert's son, our cousin Louis Davis, had been a cadet pilot in the Air Force, training at Ellington Field in Texas.

On the day he was to get his wings, Uncle Bert and Louis' young bride stood watching the flight maneuvers proudly, when Louis' plane crashed and he was killed before their eyes. Adlai and I had adored him; my brother wrote Mother: "It is the first time that the seriousness of the situation has struck home so closely and it seems unfair that we have to lose one so dear to us. . . . He sacrificed his life for a cause that should inspire in us all the spirit of sacrifice which alone can unite us."

I think that's when Adlai decided to enlist, now that he was eighteen. By the end of that summer, he was writing:

Dearest Maw: I passed the medical exam alright. My chest expansion was 4" and I weighed 137 stripped. Height 5'9". . . .
I have taken the oath of allegiance for 4 years service anywhere in the world and am now a real "gob" in the U.S. Navy. Believe me, I am certainly one hot looking little "Jack" and you will just about split when you see me.

He was an apprentice seaman in the naval training unit at Princeton, New Jersey.

Chapter 8

MOTHER, like all mothers of sons in the service, could hardly wait for the postman that fall of 1918. The terrible scourge of Spanish influenza had struck, and she sent her Navy son anxious if somewhat impractical advice: "Keep out of crowds."

Adlai and the other boys in the naval training unit were living in a Princeton dormitory—Little Hall—and they rowed whaleboats on Lake Carnegie, drilled on the athletic fields and marched up and down Nassau Street. He was rooming with his old Wyoming friend Ralph Goodwin, William Hale of California, and Hendrik Terry of New York, and he soon reported, "Terry has gone to the infirmary with a bad cold. There are several cases of influenza in the Army here and a few in the Navy, however I don't think Terry has it."

Mother was convinced Terry *did* have it. She had planned to take me down to Princeton for a visit, and I wrote my brother:

> We are very keen to get down to you but the flu epidemic is quite horrible. The country club has 64 patients now, in Aunt Julia's house 29, and the Bloomington club is a convalescents' home. Father is very nervous about things. We

sent all the spare beds in the place (none on the sleeping porch now) and soup each day. Cousin Letty says in Washington they have the funerals at night and there aren't enough coffins for the numbers of dead.

Adlai mentioned in a letter that he was smoking cigarettes, and Mother reacted like a Victorian; she was almost more alarmed about that than flu germs:

My Laddie Boy:

Your good letter of last Sunday was received today and I am hastening to reply because I hope I can show you the futility of getting the tobacco habit.

It seems to me you should at once, before it is too late, put the matter squarely to yourself and see honestly if the one advantage (that of being companionable, one of the crowd) will offset the disadvantages!

The latter are legion but above all, in the matter of health alone, it should never be considered by you, for your throat is your most delicate organ and tobacco one of the worst things for it. Then your eyes and above all your nerves.

These are only a few of the physical disadvantages but they are, of course, secondary to the moral side. What is your desire after all in life? Wouldn't you have me believe that you had but one big object in life and that is to lead it as decently, uprightly as is possible, and be an example of every moral virtue to your fellow men?

The one advantage, that of companionship or fun, is a dangerous gauge and if applied to other temptations, like whiskey, gambling, etc. would soon lead you far astray.

Please remember you had two grandfathers who never found it necessary to smoke and they were held in the highest esteem. Uncle Berte said tell Adlai "you expect always fine things of him," and when I told him you thought of smoking, he was so surprised and said "Well, he can't afford to do that."

Please, my dear boy, try to resist if only till you have your growth. It will stunt you physically and mentally.

I must leave you to decide all things for yourself but I shall pray that you be led into the light in this matter.

God help you.

Mother

She urged me to "give Adlai good advice" (meaning "convince him he *mustn't!*") and I wrote him piously: "I am awfully sorry you find you have to smoke. It's not alone the smoking because I feel utterly sure you would never let it become a habit, but the fact you have to do it because the other fellows do. But then the time has come for you to be the judge and arrange your life according to what you would have it be."

Manlike, Adlai seems to have blandly ignored the subject from then on, in his letters home.

. . . John Harlan, whom you remember I told you was in charge of the battalion here, came to see me this afternoon. Needless to say I felt very much honored. He is certainly a fine fellow and I like him very much. He is in naval aviation. You can't get in Naval aviation until you are 19 and 6 months so I guess I'll go out for the line, although I am awfully anxious to get into aviation.

We marched to the University chapel this morning and heard President Hibben speak. I don't think he is an especially forceful speaker but his ideas etc. are fine. [As an apprentice seaman, my brother seems to have retained the family's traditional freedom of opinion!]

We had a big smoker to which a bunch of Army fellows were invited. Each company put on a stunt. It was a lot of fun and lasted until about 10 o'clock. John Harlan was in charge of it all and certainly is wonderful at putting thru anything he undertakes.

One of the projects John Harlan undertook, with my brother as co-partner, was to get up a brass band for the

Naval unit, on the theory that this would bring them to the admiral's attention. Neither of them could play an instrument, but they got around this neatly by making John the conductor, and Adlai assistant conductor. As I heard later, the band they assembled actually learned to play two whole pieces, and was even invited to parade down Fifth Avenue. This they did, in great style, alternating their two pieces as they went. When they reached Thirty-second Street, where they were scheduled to turn, the band was playing "Smiles," and by then had worked up to such a crescendo that the crowds along the curb cheered. John and Adlai, delighted with this success, executed a smart turn and marched down the side street. It took them awhile to realize that the sounds of the band were becoming oddly faint and far away. When they finally took a quick look over their shoulders, they were dumbfounded to find the band had vanished entirely, and they were marching alone. They had turned left, and the band had gone right, still playing "Smiles."

I remembered John romantically from Washington (where he's now a justice of the Supreme Court), and I was thrilled when Adlai wrote Mother, "Harlan inquired very particularly for you and Buff—when you were coming, etc." My eagerness to get to Princeton wasn't entirely because of my brother!

Mother decided we could risk the flu germs on trains, and when we arrived at the old Peacock Inn she was reassured to see Adlai looking very pert and healthy, in his gob's uniform. He already loved Princeton, and he took great pride in showing us around that beautiful campus, where ivy and serene old traditions seem entwined. Our Great-grandfather Lewis Warner Green had studied at the Theological Seminary in 1831, and Adlai Osborne had been in the Princeton

Class of 1764. My 18-year-old brother's loyalties were a mix-
ture of Old Nassau and Navy. During dinner at the Inn, he
reeled off nautical terms, but he'd only gone to sea in a
whaleboat! He talked a lot about Admiral Goodrich, the
commandant, whom he admired enormously not only as a
distinguished old naval officer, but because the admiral told
such good stories of his experiences at student smokers.

My brother seemed astonished but pleased that his other
hero, John Harlan, should want to take *me* to the Army-
Navy promenade. I remember the Peacock Inn was so
crowded with servicemen that John and I couldn't even find
a corner to be alone in, and took long walks to find privacy.
It was a difficult place for love-smitten youth, but we managed. With my new beau a Navy man, I had all the more
personal reasons for wanting the war to be over soon.

On November 11, my diary records: "This morning we
were awakened by the chimes singing out the national an-
them & all the bells in Princeton ringing the news that the
Germans had signed the peace and the Kaiser abdicated. Ad
brought the boys to dinner—and we go to bed with bells
still ringing."

When Adlai was discharged from the Navy, in January,
he was accepted as a Freshman and his college life began in
earnest. He wrote us that he was heeling the campus newspaper, the *Daily Princetonian*—"I have to write a story a
day from now on"—and gave a lively account of his initia-
tion into the debating society, Whig Hall:

> Took about two hours to go thru it. They put black bags over
> our heads and we had to go thru the whole thing crawling
> on our stomachs. They certainly did paddle us and we had to
> crawl thru a long winding passage under the foundations of
> the hall. After the initiation was over we were led upstairs

and the blindfolds were removed. Pres. Hibben, who is a member of the Whig, made a speech and told us all about the society. Pres. Wilson and Pres. Madison were members of it. The society meets every Friday and listens to a debate etc. . . . You can either be an active or an inactive member. I have to be an active member as I am taking Hall English which is a course you can take in place of regular Freshman English. It is mostly the science of oratory, argument, etc. I think it will prove very worth while. [I think he's made quite good use of it!] I am going to have to work pretty hard with Latin (we are reading Pliny) Chemistry and Math. (Coordinate Geometry). I have the same Prof in French as last term and I have a big drag with him so that won't be so hard. . . .

He mentioned meeting Paula Van Dyke at a *thé dansant:* "She is the daughter of a professor and a corking good dancer." (It shows what a green new Freshman he was, to refer to the famous Henry Van Dyke in such anonymous terms as "a professor.") What interested *me* much more was a social note in another letter: "John (Harlan) asked me if Buff was going to be here at the time of the Junior Prom (March 15). I think he is going to ask her."

Adlai approved of my coming for proms, but when Mother decided in the fall of his sophomore year that she would rent a house for us in Princeton, my brother thought that was really too much. He did his tactful best to discourage our coming, but he was *too* tactful—or probably Mother was too determined. I remember his saying he'd be too busy to see us often, but I was so charmed at the prospect of spending eight months in Princeton I was blind to his qualms. It wasn't until recently that he told me how apprehensive he'd been. He said, "I thought it was the cruelest thing a parent could do—coming to live at a son's school." He admitted it hadn't been nearly as bad as he'd expected.

From my diary, October, 1919: "First day in the new house, Adlai has been with us & helping." We were in Dean Fine's charming house in Library Place, a beam-and-brick building in the style of a seventeenth-century English manor, with mullioned windows overlooking old apple trees and giant pines. I always think of that lovely living room as a place mellowed by wood fires and books and laughter, and groups of boys around the grand piano after a Welsh-rarebit supper, singing "K-k-k-katy," "Limehouse Blues," and "Poor Butterfly." I could play in key, even if I couldn't sing, and my brother bayed joyfully.

The peal of chimes, boys singing through the streets, and the occasional whir of a car were sounds that blended with the lovely tranquility of Princeton in our day. We're so used to students now in T-shirts and blue jeans that it's odd to recall what "correct attire" the boys wore then, even on the campus. Most of them looked like young businessmen on the way to an office. Or they wore knickerbocker suits with camels' hair stockings, button-down Brooks Brothers shirts and brogue shoes. I don't believe they would have dreamed of sitting down to dinner in their eating clubs without coats and ties, and probably vests, too.

Adlai usually carried a brief case loaded with books and work—assignments for classes or the *Princetonian*. (He had made the editorial staff his Freshman year.) Some of his roommates gave him the nickname of "Rabbit," and Adlai says it was because of his taste for raw carrots and salad. Several classmates have told *me* that they called him Rabbit because he moved so fast—and he still does.

It's always interested me to watch how eagerly Adlai enters into things and absorbs new experiences, with a quickness and direct concentration, and an intense curiosity. I think

I realized this all the more sharply at Princeton because I was uncertain about what I wanted to do. I was going into New York every week to stay with my friend Louise Thoron in her apartment and attend lectures on religion at the Union Theological Seminary. I envied Louise her talent as a painter, and I admired my brother for what I described to him in a letter as "your special God-given gift—a wonderful & practical philosophy of life. You are full of constructive thought and hold it! You seem to know when to hold on and when to let go, and your ease is a gift."

I remember once when I was bemoaning my own lack of talents and direction, McMonies, the sculptor, who did the World War I Monument for Princeton, told me, "The most lasting work of art is the example set by a good life. And if you keep your own individuality and standards, you can have a real influence on others. Sometimes I think the most important thing in life is to be able to grow old and still smile at yourself in the mirror."

That sane bit of advice comforted me, and I tried to look at myself with more humor—another gift my brother was born with.

We had our old Hudson car at Princeton, and I remember Adlai's giving me a funny account of the night the car broke down on a country road, on the way home from a party. He said, "There I was swinging a monkey wrench and trying to be nonchalant in a dinner jacket with a girl I hardly knew and a car I knew all too well!"

Another incident he told on himself later, when his attempt at nonchalance boomeranged, happened at a Vassar prom. He and his girl were sitting out a dance, and Adlai said he felt he'd convinced her he was rather a clever fellow and a man of the world to boot. While the two were sitting talking, a dignified gentleman came by carrying dishes of ice cream on a tray.

"Waiter," Adlai called, "may we have some?" His girl reeled, and looked as if she were going to faint. When she'd recovered her voice, she said, "That was no waiter. He happens to be President McCracken."

From my diary: "Mother and Ad and I drove out in the country and picked leaves. . . . Gave Ad dinner here and we all went to the Vreelands for charades. . . . Adlai's girl [Harriet Cowles] came today—also Norman Davis from Harvard. Jolly dinner here and all went to prom. . . . Princeton beat Yale, 3 to 6!!! Big bonfire celebration of football victory. . . . Out walking in snow with Ad, then to singing at Butlers."

Adlai usually came for Sunday dinner, and he often brought his friends, among them Bill Hale, Monk Hackney, Chas Denby, Winchester Jones and Doug Ward. Jim Douglas of Chicago was more my age than Ad's, and like Adlai, he sometimes parked his pretty girls at our house over week ends. Weldon Funk visited us several times, and there were many others. Mother had engaged an efficient Negro couple, and she enjoyed entertaining the students and their girls as much as they seemed to enjoy coming. Our friend Francis Comstock, now a professor of architecture at Princeton, remembers how "serenely charming" Mother was to all the boys. "Franny" also remembers how miffed he was when he strained his budget to send me roses before a dance and then I told him I was allergic to roses and couldn't wear them. But Mother admired his flowers so tactfully he felt mollified.

Adlai stayed with us at Library Place over the Christmas holidays, Father joined us, and my diary reports: "December 25th—One of the happiest days I've ever spent. First, not a single family row." (Father was so delighted to see us again he must have been angelically good-tempered.) My clearest recollection of my brother is sitting on his spine at blissful ease, before the fire, while Mother and I read aloud. I varied the family entertainment by doing imitations; Adlai liked my take-off of Irene Bordoni singing with an oo-la-la accent, "Why Do You Make Zose Eyes At Me?"

There were wonderful parties that season; the Laflins of Lake Forest had taken a house, and entertained for the young people. Paula Van Dyke, the three Marquand girls, Caroline Owsley and Alice Eno were surrounded by beaux at the dances. Dick Cleveland was staying with his beautiful mother, Mrs. Preston, and dented feminine hearts at a great rate. He was what we called a "fusser"—a dashing man with the ladies. Allison Armour ran him a close second!

For all his debonair ways, Dick had a deeply serious side, and was carrying on a courageous one-man campaign against the snobberies of the Princeton eating-club system, as Woodrow Wilson had done when he was head of the college. I think Dick wanted to abolish the clubs altogether, but Wilson had wanted them remodeled on a more democratic basis.

By February of 1920, President Wilson was returning from the Paris peace conference—I think to make his heartbreakingly futile pleas to his countrymen to join the League of Nations—and my diary reflected the somber world news: "Horrible in Europe. Clemenceau shot at, minister of Germany killed, Russia starving. . . . Poor Mr. Wilson!"

But the arrival of spring in Princeton made the woes of the world seem very far away. John Harlan was to go to Oxford as a Rhodes scholar after his graduation, and that lent a special poignance to our walks on the campus. I thought I'd never seen any pattern of shadows and sunlight so lovely, and the fragrance of white lilacs and tulip magnolias completed the spell, but perhaps only part of that magic was Princeton.

I haven't the faintest notion of what Adlai was doing then, because I was too concerned with my own life, but I think my brother had already lost his heart at Vassar, or a small segment thereof—a vividly lovely, dark-haired girl from the Far West.

My diary mentions: "Reading Shelley—'Spirit of Solitude,' " but it's followed by a cheerier extrovert note: "Saw our baseball team beat Harvard! . . . Went to a club dance with Adlai. Mother was chaperone." During the week end of spring house parties I recorded tersely, "Chapel and Dickinson Hall burned to ground."

In Princeton, students always turned out for a fire as if it were a social event (once they dragged a piano out of a burning building and sat down to play "Keep The Home Fires Burning"), but that 1920 blaze was the most spectacular of all, because everybody came in evening clothes. The night of the big club dances, sirens suddenly shrieked above the blare of orchestras' saxophones, and students and their girls rushed off to see the fire. A lot of chaperones were conveniently lost in the rush! Exuberant undergraduates also took advantage of the confusion to grab a hose and turn it full stream on the Dean of students, a severe disciplinarian who was known as The Hanging Judge.

After that fire and the hosing down of the Dean, exams were an anticlimax. In June, Adlai sailed for Europe with Bill Tucker, Tom Matthews, Monk Hackney and some other classmates. Reading over old letters now, it seems to me that his writing style matured a great deal during that trip. When I was in Switzerland with him later that summer, I wrote Mother: "Darling: After great effort, Ad has gotten a letter written to you—he simply *works* when he writes! He would say much more than he does if it weren't such an effort!"

What amused me even more was to find a note Mother had written to Adlai when she was passing along some of my travel letters to him: "You mustn't read these letters of Elizabeth's critically for they have been dashed off between trains, so to speak, as Elizabeth is in the habit of writing, but this spontaneity and entire frankness is what makes them interesting."

I went abroad with Father, who was going on to Berlin on business. I think it's a fascinating note on his ahead-of-the-times ideas that he had organized a syndicate to acquire American rights on basic patents of German lighter-than-air craft. He had interested Dr. Johann Schuette, the German engineer-inventor who had built twenty-two dirigibles—and I see from an old newspaper clipping that among the men lined up as potential investors in the proposed Zeppelin line between Chicago and New York were: Marshall Field, William Wrigley Jr., Owen D. Young, R. B. Mellon, David Goodrich, and Franklin D. Roosevelt.

Father was postponing our trip until after the 1920 Democratic convention in San Francisco, at which James Cox was nominated with F.D.R. as his Vice-Presidential running mate. In the meantime, Adlai was writing:

On S.S. New York
8th day out

Dear Mother:

We will reach Southampton sometime Friday—Hoo-Ray! Until then we'll all continue to brace ourselves for the next roll—woop—there it is. I am writing this illegible epistle perched up in a bunk listening to Harry and Tom compose poetry on some of the many queer passengers on the boat. There is certainly sufficient material to inspire some remarkably satirical poetry.

However, I better tell you about the trip and not dwell at too great length on the peculiarities of some of my fellow passengers. On getting on the boat at N.Y. I was not surprised to find that our cabin was down somewhere in the depths of the ship at the end of a very complicated system of passageways, stairs, etc. But it appeared perfectly comfortable and really quite clean so Bill and I decided that as an economical measure it had been a very good one and we were quite satisfied. Everything was delightful that first day out. We discovered that there were in all some 15 Princeton men aboard— three of them, including Bob Campbell and Jake Waxter, were and still are stoking. . . . There are also quite a lot of Yale fellows and three or four of them are stewards in the steerage. We hear some wonderful stories when the stokers and stewards etc. are off duty. In fact we're getting quite intimate with the entire crew and needless to say there are some very interesting characters. One in particular—a Jugo Slav— is most entertaining. He has been all over the globe which is not strange as most of the crew have, however, the remarkable thing about him is that he has a really beautiful baritone voice and can sing offhand any selection from any opera in the correct language.

Well, as I said, the first day was fine. We all got chairs together on deck and Harry, Tom, Bill, Rummie, Marvin and I eat together with Bishop Matthews [Tom's father] and two other clerical celebrities—the Bishop of California and the Bishop of Ohio. There are about a dozen Bishops on the boat all going to the Lambeth conference and they are, for the most part, quite a venerable-looking body of men. The first couple of meals were rather a disappointment but we have since discovered that the food is really exceptionally good and one just lives from meal to meal—that is, of course, providing you are not suffering from that horrible malady—Mal de Mer—and, strange to say, thus far I have not had a qualm. In fact I think that I must be becoming a very good sailor. Tom hasn't been sick either, but he says there is something wrong and is beginning to get suspicious.

. . . A couple of days ago the wind freshened up and the boat has been pitching unmercifully ever since. Last night it was so bad that the racks for the dishes in the galley broke loose and $500 worth of crockery was broken. Yet the seamen say that the boat has not really begun to roll yet. Its lots of fun to lie in your bunk and hear bottles etc. go crashing to the floor in the cabins around you—hear women scream etc. But in spite of it all I remain undaunted and eat ravenously. It is, however, extremely difficult to write as you have probably observed, so I'll continue later.

Love,

Adlai

When they got to England, Adlai, Tom, Bill, Jake Waxter and Jack Wainwright set off from Oxford on a walking tour, but I think they must have spent a good bit of time lying under "great and ancient trees." Adlai wrote mother, "Everything was glorious—except my feet!" After a hike of twenty-four miles the first day, to Banbury, they rode trains and buses most of the time. My brother had outgrown his early passion for knights' armor, but he still made a beeline for old castles. As a devoté of Sir Walter Scott, he had to see Kenilworth, and he reported in a letter:

That famous ruin lived up to my fondest expectations and it was impressive to sit there and look at those massive walls and towers—the last relics of what was one of the most magnificent and powerful castles in all England. We stayed there quite a while and I read the history of the castle.

He was still reading Scott when they got to Stratford-on-Avon:

. . . Perhaps you have heard of the annual Summer Festival that is held at Stratford in honor of Shakespeare. All his plays are produced by an excellent company under the direction of Forbes Robertson. Well anyway the festival was beginning that day and Cymbeline was to be given at the Memorial Theatre that evening. So we secured tickets and had lunch. In the afternoon we walked out into the country and reclined on the banks of the Avon and read. It was really most delightful and it was quite an inspiring atmosphere. I read the Lay of the Last Minstrel by Scott and Bill read Cymbeline and consequently was able to refresh our memories as regards the play. We stayed out there until almost time for the play to begin and then hastened back. The theatre was well filled and I was surprised to see how many Americans there were there.

. . . [Back in London] We went to the tailors and had the final fitting on our suits. That night we went to the opening of a new comedy—I'll Leave It To You. It was awfully clever but apparently a first night isn't a very important event to London theatre-goers.

The next morning Bill and I left for Paris by *Airplane!* . . . The passage cost us $42—about 2½ times as much as it would have cost on the train. It sounds pretty extravagant but it was, I think, altogether worth it for the experience was wonderful.

. . . At the field it was quite thrilling for there were a large number of the enormous Handly-Page planes already to leave and their motors were running to warm up. We showed our passports in the office and a customs man asked us if we had any dutiable goods & thats all there was to it. We then proceeded to enter the plane, which carries 10 people and is fitted up with windows, wicker chairs, etc. There was even a lavatory in it. We happened to be the only two passengers in the cabin as the one other passenger was out in front with the pilot. As it was my first time up everything was, of course, most interesting. . . . You could observe clearly the different methods of cultivation employed by the French and how they differed from the English—the ground in France looked like a vast puzzle composed of pieces of wood and in straight geometrical figures and painted all shades of browns & greens.

I've run out of paper & will have to finish this letter later.

Love

Ad

Hotel und Weinhaus
"Trabue"

Coblenz
Friday, July 30, 1920

Dearest Mother:

You may be surprised to be getting a letter from me from Coblenz, but don't worry for we are having a wonderful time and not getting into trouble. On the other hand, the Germans are most effusively polite to all Americans; especially here where one might say that the Americans were "on top."

Frank Murray, Bill Tucker and I got military passes into the occupied territory from a colonel that Frank knew at the American military legation in Paris and here we are at Coblenz on our way to *Berlin*. We left Paris last night at 9 and arrived here, via Chateau Thierry, Epernay, Challons-sur-Marne etc., at noon today. The American captain met us at the train in a Cadillac limousine and brought us to this hotel where he had billeted us. Not bad, eh?

We went out to Ehrenbreitstein this afternoon and have been looking the town over since. It is indeed very pretty but we haven't much time to spend on this trip as we all want to get back to Paris by the 7th—I especially, to meet Buff & Father.

. . . Last night while riding on the train just out of Chateau Thierry I saw a sight that is indeed hard to describe. You will remember that last night, the 29th, was the sixth anniversary of the first declaration of war between Serbia & Austria and that the moon was full and—here anyway—very brilliant. Well, anyway, when a couple of miles out of Chateau Thierry I could [see] the ruins of walls and houses on the surrounding hills standing out against the sky and bathed in the brilliant white of the moon. A little further down the track we passed a great field of neat little white crosses arranged in symmetrical rows and stretching away over the hills—the final resting place of some 30,000 American soldiers and marines. It also occurred to me that it was almost exactly 2 years and 1 week ago that the Chateau Thierry offensive was begun, which lent a kind of subconsciously sad & romantic air to the scene. . . . In the next compartment to me a girl started to play a violin— this was the middle of the night—and before long the whole car had assembled to hear, and how she could play! Some man, who had heard her before said that she was rapidly becoming the most promising violinist in France. A remarkable night.

Love,
Adlai

Hotel Excelsior
Berlin

Sunday
Aug 1, 1920

Dearest Maw:

Here we are in Berlin! There are very few Americans here or other foreigners and the Germans don't seem to be too anxious to have foreigners around. However, although Americans are about as popular here as the proverbial snake at a lawn party, they treat us nevertheless with considerable respect and we are having a wonderful time.

. . . The trip to Berlin which we had determined to take during the day in order to see the country was frightful and the train was horribly crowded. There was, however, in our compartment a young German about 23 years old who informed us that he was a comedian and was just returning from an engagement in Baden. He fulfilled all the requirements of a comedian and kept us in an uproar all the way to Berlin.

We arrived last night and got rooms here. It is an excellent hotel and, were it not that there is a 50% tax on all Americans in the Berlin hotels, would be very cheap. As it is we are paying about $1.50 a day for a luxurious room and breakfast. We had an enormous breakfast in our room and then determined to go and see the horse races which started today. We hired a car for about $2.00 each to take us out to the track and back. On the way out he took us all over the city and around the principle buildings. The city is beautiful and I was especially surprised to see how happy everyone appeared to be and how the entire city apparently turned out for the races.

The track, which is quite a long ways from the center of the city, was huge and very beautifully laid out. It was all turf and covered with jumps, etc. More like a steeple chase than a race course. All the races, there were seven of them, started from different places and wound around over the course, according to the distance, finishing at the same place. We had seats in the grandstand, and making little pools of our own, managed to get quite excited over the races.

There was an enormous crowd of people there and it appeared an excellent opportunity to study the German people and their characteristics. In the first place, the language, in my opinion, is a very disagreeable one to hear. As for the people, individual ones that I have met have, as a rule, impressed me very favorably, in fact I like them very much. The women to me are quite unattractive and dress badly but that, I suppose, is due to the exorbitant prices of clothes etc. in Germany.

. . . We are leaving Thursday for Brussels where we will met George Piper and go to Rheims, Verdun and some of the

140   *MY BROTHER ADLAI*

other battlefields. We should get back to Paris on about the
6th or 7th where I will meet father & Buffie and bum around
with them. . . .

The way Father "found" Adlai in Paris was quite funny.

Chapter 9

FATHER AND I arrived in Paris a day earlier than we'd planned. He had reserved rooms for us at Claridges, and after we'd settled that evening, Father said he was going to take a stroll and stop by Adlai's (much cheaper!) hotel.

My brother, who hadn't expected us till the next day, was out having a gay evening with a party of friends, and naturally they had wound up at the Folies-Bergère. As Adlai told me later, "There we were, watching the seductive ladies in the chorus, and imagine my astonishment to see *Father* walk in! And he had the nerve to claim he had just come there to look for me!"

When I met my brother for lunch the day after he'd been "found"—or found out—I was amused to see him twirling a cane and being very much the sophisticated *boulevardier*. After lunch we sat on the banks of the Seine and talked our heads off, getting caught up on travel news. I remember telling him how shocked I was when Henry Wellcome, the great English chemist who had visited Grandfather Stevenson, took me to his London museum to show me historical medical exhibits, and one was George Washington's false teeth.

Adlai laughed and said, "Even great men have to chew."

Father chose the Café de la Paix for our first dinner, but later Adlai introduced us to all his favorite little restaurants in Montmartre. He knew that section like a book. In fact, I think he'd explored, on foot, almost every inch of Paris, and we used to have amiable arguments because he said it was the most beautiful city of all, and I held out for London (and still do).

Adlai admired the Parisiennes' chic, and he had become very clothes-conscious; he'd look me over with a critical eye and tell me a dress was "nice," or he'd say, "That's too fussy. The simplest clothes are best." Judging from my diary, I doubt if I took that to heart: "Wore my blue satin dress and large brown hat. My pearls grow more beautiful by the minute." The pearls, which Father and I picked out in Paris, were a gift from my parents. Adlai thought they were "nice and simple"!

When Father went off on his business trip to Germany, Adlai and I started for Switzerland, and sat up all night in the train. I tried to snatch cat naps between showing our passports six times, but my brother stayed out in the corridor most of the night, talking eagerly with strangers.

It was odd to stop off at Lausanne, where we'd lived as children. We made a kind of pilgrimage to the scenes of our "lost youth," with tea at Niffenegers, and a look into the old Savoy Hotel and Adlai's former school. It was hard to believe we'd gotten so old. Adlai was now twenty and Mother was already worrying for fear he'd get bald. She had given him a scalp tonic which she knew he'd never bother to use, so she told me to rub it on him, in Switzerland!

Our destination was Zermatt, then a charming unspoiled Swiss village with a scattering of chalets and hotels, and a magnificent backdrop of snow-covered mountains crowned by the Matterhorn. Adlai and I had rooms with a connecting balcony, and I remember one day when I was standing admiring the view, I turned and saw Adlai in his room preening before the mirror in his new English tweed knickerbocker golf suit. Both of us were so dressy that summer that when we wanted to go climbing, our dear family friend "Aunt May" de Lapalud, who was a real mountain climber and lived near Geneva, had to lend us heavy sweaters and spiked shoes.

The highest climb I made was done out of sheer stubbornness. Adlai, his friend Harry Hart and I had started out in the morning, and after an hour of uphill work, Adlai told me in a brotherly tone that this was as far as I could go. After the boys left me, I started dutifully back to the hotel, but I changed my mind in midmountain. Four hours later, my brother, Harry and the guide were eating their lunch in a high *cabane* (way station), when suddenly I walked in. (Well, maybe I staggered in.) Adlai was so dumbfounded his jaw sagged. He said in a hoarse, unbelieving tone, "Buffie!" as if he thought I might be a cloud formation. He and Harry and the guide made such a gratifying fuss over me I felt as if I'd just run up the Matterhorn. Several times that afternoon, my brother would remark in a pleased voice to the others, "I've certainly got to hand it to Buff. Who would have thought she could do it?"

After Harry left, Adlai and I did a lot of walking in the

pine forests where the cold pungent scent goes right through you. We spent several afternoons on a mountainside near a huge cataract, reading French aloud, with the tinkling bells of the goats and cows, and the yodeling of their owners, for sound effects. In the village, we thought it was very funny to watch the daily promenade down the cobblestone street— of tourists and goats.

We found Mrs. James Stillman chaperoning her daughter and a group of our friends, including Elizabeth Keays, Joe Werner and Fowler McCormick, in another hotel. There was a pleasant English family staying at our hotel, and my brother was enormously entertained at the way they chased butterflies all day. At meals, he and I laughed as gaily as we had together as children. The only time I can remember his being cross was the day a batch of copies of the Bloomington *Pantagraph* arrived, in which some of Adlai's travel letters were published—a parental "surprise" that nearly gave him a fit. He was very angry and said the letters were abominably done, and that if he had known they were going to be published, he'd have at least tried to write well!

We had some long, serious talks about our "careers," and I was interested to come across a long-forgotten fragment of those conversations, in a letter to Mother from Zermatt:

> Ad told me a few nights ago he wanted to go to law school one year and then Oxford one year & then work on a London paper one year—& if in the end he chose to join the reorganizers of the Diplomatic Corps, would Father be very mad?! He is so wise and wonderful! [I guess I didn't see the humor in Adlai's proposal to live off "the old man" indefinitely.]
>
> . . . He is going off for a day & night mountain trip with the Figaro boys and their Swiss tutor to climb the Breithorn, after which they are entitled to join the Alpine Club.

This is Adlai's account of his climb. (He didn't know it was going to be published thirty-five years later!)

Montreux
Sept. 5, 1920

Dear Mother:

. . . The guides entertained us with stories of people who had fallen in crevasses and issued from the foot of the glacier as much as 30 years later—their bodies perfectly preserved. I couldn't help but think what an efficient preservative cold storage was.

Despite the harrowing details I found the glacier most interesting and the ice formations were intensely beautiful. While we were crossing the second glacier in the afternoon I saw something sticking out of the ice that looked rather peculiar and discovered that it was the pick of an alpine stalk. We finally chopped it out and also a hat and a pair of snow goggles. As these things had obviously been in the glacier sometime, the guides concluded that they had probably belonged to a party that had been lost on the Theadule during a snow storm last fall. I am bringing the ax home and shall keep it for further trips to Switzerland as a reminder of the dangers of the mountains. We reached the cabane in the late afternoon, had supper and, after witnessing a glorious sunset, went to bed, for those of us that were going on up had to get up at 4.

I shall never forget that night. It was intensely cold, the moon full and brilliant and not a cloud in the sky. I found it quite impossible to sleep and actually sat or rather lay spellbound looking out of the window until time to get up. My window faced the Matterhorn which rose like a jagged column of granite out of a sea of sparkling white. Down below me, glittering in the moonlight, lay a vast glacier which occasionally uttered a reverberating groan as the ice cracked or moved slightly.

In every direction great jagged peaks shot up and stood out black against the unearthly blue of the sky, and over all was a choking, maddening silence. The intense cold and clearness of the atmosphere made the stars unbelievably brilliant and everything seemed magnified and brought closer while the real vastness of the scene was unconceivable. It was a sight that I shall never forget and I know hardly whether to call it beautiful or horrible for there was something about it that was awe inspiring and at the same time fascinating, frightful and supernatural. I could not determine whether it was nature —whether I should thank God or Satan and in fact I feel sure there was more of the latter in it—an awful grandeur that was really not beautiful but magnetic and fear-inspiring. Anyway, I lay there enthralled and at last got up and went out to look some more—it fascinated me and I stood there stiff from cold and unable to realize that this was merely a "clear night in the high Alps."

After breakfast, and it was before the sun had risen, we all started off, roped to our respective guides. As we climbed higher & higher across the snow I could see the ultramarine of the sky between the mountains toward the east begin to fade. However, the sun did not rise for a long while—not until all the stars had disappeared and the clouds beneath us in the valleys looked like the burning crater of a volcano. The sun did at last jump up over the top of one of the mountains. And then we had to put on our snow goggles for the endless snow in an instant became dazzling brilliant and sparkled like a floor of diamonds. The guide kept me moving steadily and I was convinced that I should die several times before reaching the top, but *tant mieux* for me if we had ever stopped to rest, I doubt I would have ever gotten under way again.

We reached the summit long before the others and the guide said we had made the ascent in as fast time as he ever believed it had been done. Some consolation anyway. I won't attempt to describe the view—suffice it to say that we could see into 4 countries and had an excellent view of Monte Rosa which is within 10 miles of Marseilles on the Mediterranean.

. . . It was a great experience and I enjoyed it immensely. We left Zermatt the following day and met Father down here and since then a life of luxury in this beautiful hotel. Mrs.

Stanley McCormick of Chicago, Washington, New York, etc. is here and most attractive. We see a great deal of her and are going out in her car soon.

Best love
Adlai

I wrote Mother from Montreux:

A wonderful thing has happened! Mrs. McCormick, with whom I have been talking all evening, is greatly interested in psychology and its practical application. When she found that I was, she fairly shouted and said the place for me to go to study, which you know I am so keen to do, was at Zurich, where there is a university and an opportunity to have special work with some famous psychologist. [It was Dr. Carl Jung.] She invited me to motor to Zurich with her the day after tomorrow. . . . I gasp to think that perhaps the course of my life has at last turned into its intended channel!

Only one day more and Adlai will be gone. It is going to be so hard to say goodbye to him, but it will bring you very near, knowing that so soon he will be talking to you!

My first report on Jung, in a letter to Adlai, is sandwiched between chitchat on friends:

Hotel Baur au Lac
Zurich, Sept. 18, 1920

Dearest Ad:

You are out at sea by now and it certainly is hard to think that you have gone! I am wondering millions of things about you and all you have done since you have left. We had a glorious trip over here in Mrs. McCormicks heavenly Rolls Royce; we wound up above Vevey, and thence thru the mountains to Bern. There we had lunch with the American Minister Mr. Gerry, his wife and Marie Sims, and two third secretarys. Mrs. McC. wasn't greatly thrilled but she rallied. Marie said she was engaged.

We had a difficult time getting on here, we got lost in each little hamlet, the winding streets were confusing. As we approached Zurich a huge motor whirled past us with a lady swathed in leopard coat and purple veils streaming, she shouted and waved to Mrs. McC. who said it was Mary Garden on her way from Monte Carlo here to see Harold McCormick. We all drove up to this hotel together. The McCs have really been so kind and sweet. He looks Irish and has a most breezy Chicago manner, she is pale, not smartly dressed. The girls are plain, speak English a bit brokenly, seemed more Swiss than American. The oldest one is coming to America and wants to be a singer. Fowler [McCormick] is so nice, he seems a bit nervous. He wants to stay on here and study; he thinks the club system is rotten from start to finish, especially the bicker week (so did Dick Cleveland).

. . . Dr. Jung was a wonderful person, wonderful personality, quiet humor, knows his business. Mrs. Stanley and Harold McCormick took Father and me out to Kusnacht to call. All the time we talked Jung was analysing me, I suppose. He said I had an honest, frank, independent mind and that I am very sensitive. That is no fault of mine, I was born that way, but that I must learn to get along with myself. He says I don't know anything about balancing Feeling and Thinking. I have good moral strength but I must get my energy in control and directed. He is going to London for three weeks and I can start with his assistant or maybe with Mrs. Edith Rockefeller McCormick. You [had] best tell people I am studying psychology as few understand psycho-analysis, they don't know what it is.

I don't know what hall you live in so send me the name. Please take exercise of some kind each day and sleep and don't waste time. Fowler says he is willing to go back to Princeton next year when his friends are all gone! One wastes so much time! No real study—I think he has a good angle.

Father has a new leg doctor who says the Paris doctor did the wrong thing, I think he is pulling both legs now!?

Be a good goopher and don't forget your sister.

Buff

In those three short months in Zurich, I learned more, lived more, actually, than I had in all my twenty-three years put together. If I went there to "find myself," I did just that. What I found may not have been much, but what Jung gave me, or rather made me see of myself, awakened me. Psychoanalysis was new, it was dangerous and it still is, if it's not in the hands of true doctors—honest, kind and good physicians of the human soul. I wasn't analyzed, I was given some education, and it has stood me in good stead; it has saved me many hours of suffering and misunderstanding.

From my diary I've picked out several remarks of Jung's that seem especially interesting in retrospect:

"Dr. Jung felt that the American psychology confused him but he finally found we were orientals—and said that our next war would be with Japan."

"Jung spoke of the wave of sensuality in the world and said that it was especially bad in Germany."

"Dr. Jung has me reading the New Testament. He says it is an expression of the Christian mind. As we are all Christians, it is time I read it."

Mother wrote me:

Belvedere Hotel
Charlevoix—September

. . . You could study architecture a little too. But forgive me, I *do* want to let you be free! To do as you please & be your own veritable self—I always resent people comparing us because I have always wanted you to be yourself and ever dreaded lest your schools would change the natural currents—however schools didn't have nearly as great an influence as I had imagined!

The weather makes me long for our open fire on the family hearth. The hard maple tree back of Pecks is turning to gold already and the people are thinning out very fast. It carries me back to our life here when you and precious little lad climbed the sheds, played golf, pressed autumn leaves and spent the long cool evenings in Daddy's room, when we had the famous little stove that burned upon suggestion.

. . . Be very careful of the money I have sent you—remembering that the $1000 in French money should be used *first*. You can pay for your return passage in francs in Paris and then you will want to be in Paris, I suppose a couple of weeks or so, before sailing—for shopping, theatre, opera, friends, etc. This will take some money. If you haven't paid for your *"psy"* you can send a check on Morgan Harjes for it.

Some one told me that pulling out eyebrows would make the brows only coarse and curly in time, so be careful. Keep them brushed & smooth. Also do not burn your skin, it ruins it, or your upper lip especially. Also, are you careful to use your lovely mouth artistically? The English are such good examples of decorous manners.

. . . You are attaining to great health, happiness and wisdom, my beautiful one, I know. How I love you!"

Zurich, September 25th

Dearest of all mothers: I am established in my permanent quarters in this hotel—one large sunny pretty room with bath & charming balcony. The situation of the hotel makes me think of Venice. It is built along the canal and from my window I look into the river at one end of the garden and the lake at the other end. [I also enjoyed watching some of the amazing guests there, including the lovely Queen of Roumania. I remember she turned the whole place upside down when the Crown Prince didn't come home one night, but he sauntered in the next morning, still a prince!]

The next few months will fly by and I will have gotten a lot of new ideas, friends and a knowledge of myself—you can imagine how much I enjoy the languages. Don't worry about Adlai and me, just use your splendid mind for something more profitable! There is everything waiting for us, but with our straining modern American life, we lost sight of what it is we

do want out of life. I think we are all confused. Professor Jung
says "America has a big problem coming with her women."
. . . I neglected to tell you that Mr. Gerry told me that
"Switzerland is the whispering area of the world." It is full
of spies and intriguers, especially now because of the meeting
of the League of Nations here the 15th of November. The
Russian Refugee population is 15,000. The Austrian King
who now lives at Morges, he says, will be recalled to the
throne.

Father is in Germany. It is quite delicious to feel entirely
alone, to breathe the air of freedom!

> Baur au Lac
> Zurich, Nov. 1920

Dearest Old Ad: You are a dear to write a good newsy letter
in the middle of so much college activity. . . . How interesting
that you are "doing politics" too.

As for the "politics," Adlai was one of the founders of
the Cox-Roosevelt Club at Princeton, and on the committee
that brought Cox to speak at Alexander Hall that fall, before
the 1920 election. He was also writing a good many articles
for the *Princetonian,* which was strongly pro-Cox and pro-
League of Nations, and he was an usher at the rally when
Governor Cox spoke to the students.

I had gathered from his letters (lost, alas) how hard he'd
been working in that campaign, and I suppose that's what
prompted a stern sisterly query in the same letter that mentions his "doing politics": "How about your lessons? Remember this is a good time to learn!"

. . . Dr. Jung is a remarkable psychologist, to see him tear
me to pieces with one stroke is too fascinating. He explains
his break with Freud this way: Freud believes that one's sex
instinct controls, and F.'s first pupil Adler believed one's power
instinct controlled one's actions, and Jung says both control

us, and more too—the Soul. He is a wonder and I am getting full of dope just listening to him talk on any subject.

I go to concerts and opera. L. takes me to dine in the old restaurant where Wagner (he lived here ten yrs.) dined with Keller. Also I have a German girl three afternoons a week and am learning lots of German. It's a lusty language!

Father is in London, pleased with his German affairs. He wants to spend half his time in Europe.

Don't exhaust yourself helping make the Philadelphia debs belles. You have too much that is useful to do at college. Be an influence for GOOD—this soggy old world needs it bad!

Heaps of love

Buff

I must have been getting very wise indeed, because I told Adlai just how to understand himself:

Zurich
Baur au Lac
Oct. 24, 1920

My dearest Ad:

I want to write you a few things (if you don't object to read-ing them!) I have been noticing & thinking of in the last few days. First & last, learn young to be true to yourself. You know your persona, Adlai Stevenson dressed in a brown golf suit, but you probably have not much idea who it is that is prompt-ing you to say that you want to go to Oxford & be a writer, or a diplomat or whatever you want to be. The person who says all this is YOU—your soul or the bit of God in you or whatever you want to call it. You have to encourage the acquaintance of this unconscious you & learn to listen to it. You have to find out just what you are & you have to know that what is good & right for *you* may not be right for the next fellow & may not even be to his approval.

Stand back sometime & look at the collection—the great troupe of people around you—& see how they are all trying to forget themselves, & they imagine they must do what the other fellow does or some one may misunderstand them. Have the courage to face yourself & do what you want, & KNOW that what you can do best because you BELIEVE, it is the best. Of course you must face the facts of reality, but facing them squarely and your*self* at the *same time*—you can't be at a loss.

I say all this now especially because I go out to dine some with the consul here, Mr. L——, & he doesn't understand why he doesn't *prove* anything in life. It's because he doesn't honestly know what he *wants* to prove.

. . . Isn't there just too much to do in one life time! I do want to get to Egypt someday, & to Palestine & the east.

A great deal of love
Buff.

Baur au Lac,
Thanksgiving Day 1920
Dearest Ad:

This will be the last letter I write from Zurich. It is very difficult for me to realize that my freedom will be over so soon. Two weeks from today will find me in Paris, and four weeks in the N.Y. harbor. . . .

Mother talks about peoples plans in her letters. I am glad to do anything at all for the holidays that is pleasant for you all, Bloomington or the Equator, its all the same to me. . . . I have had a wonderful feast of freedom, just what I wanted and needed, so now you take what you want, and I will enjoy it.

. . . It has been a great feast, going to the opera. I drink in the singing, I understand the German and the music much better. Some times I hear things we have played on victor records at home, and you can imagine how swiftly I am carried back to our little gray home in the west. I usually see it just before Mother was giving a party—everything shining— a breathless hush and waiting—oil lamps burning—Katie and Sam in the kitchen, and I standing on tip toe all eyes and ears for the feeling of beauty about me. That house a glowing jewel, Mother has true creative ability.

Did I tell you that L. has asked me to marry him? I appre-

ciated his generosity but I enjoy my freedom. He and I will
have our Thanksgiving dinner in our favorite restaurant at
the end of a winding little dark passage way lit by a rusty
lantern and a moon!

I am so proud of you and think of you often—and I am so
jealous of all you do that is valuable and of all you learn
that is useful!

Heaps of love

Buff.

On the ship going home, I was in a cabin with Ruth
Draper, the famous monologist, and she must have been
amused at my prattling on about the libido and the unconscious, because when I went to see her in a theater the next
year, she was doing a very funny monologue of "A Young
Girl Who Has Just Discovered Psychoanalysis." I went backstage afterward and told her how much I'd enjoyed it.

I'm sure Adlai would have enjoyed it even more, because
he used to get crimson with embarrassment when I babbled
on at Princeton parties about psychoanalysis. In those days,
it was considered a very wacky fad!

Two months after my return from Zurich, he had his
twenty-first birthday, and Mother wrote him:

> 21 years old, 21 years young, 21 years wise, 21 years beloved!
> Your babyhood, boyhood, and young-manhood have been a
> natural sweet unfolding and gradual development! Round
> upon round. There are no dark, muddy spots thus far in your
> career. Since you have become a reasoning being, you have
> made always an earnest, honest effort towards high living. This
> effort is character-building. The rewards are secondary in im-
> portance. . . .
>
> You have never wanted something for nothing, nor anything
> that was not rightfuly yours. And so whatever in rewards come
> to you, you can rejoice over Right for the sake of Right! These,
> my dear, are the only principals that make for permanent

success or happiness, and better never be rewarded or successful than to allow these to be forgotten for one moment. Character is better than all success and it will bring success more certainly than friends, fortune or talents.

She wanted him to keep his hair, too! She kept urging him to have scalp treatments from a woman she had gone to when we were living in Princeton. Adlai wrote:

"I have found Miss Green and have weekly treatments from her. She has a nice room on Bank St. and I think I shall continue to go to her for the rest of the spring in order to get my hair in good shape. . . . The baseball team looks awfully good. . . . House parties begin on the 14th of May and I am having Harriet Cowles down. Bill Hale will have a girl from Vassar also and so we can have them stay together.

. . . In my estimation, Princeton is almost supreme at this particular time of year. It is difficult for me to conceive of anything more beautiful than the view out towards the Junction in the early morning when the grass is still damp and mist envelops everything. . . . I play tennis on the club courts every afternoon. At present I am working on a committee which is drawing up, with a member of the faculty, the constitution for a new organization which is to have entire control over all matters pertaining to the clubs; administration, methods of election, etc. The Prince. manages to get out every day and continues to interest me.

He had become Managing Editor that spring, which meant he was in charge of make-up and production. One of the men who worked under Adlai on the *"Prince,"* Byron Dexter, told me recently about an incident he thought was typical of my brother: Byron was on the editorial board, and when it was his turn as Make-Up Editor he worked one night till 3 A.M., then went in the next day, exhausted but proud, to hear what the Managing Editor had to say about the issue of the paper. This is his account: "Ad smiled and said, 'It's very good—but there's one little thing,' and he pointed to the headline I had written for a story about Professor Henry Norris Russell, who had just come back after a year as visiting lecturer at Cambridge or Oxford: WORLD FAMOUS ASTROLOGER RETURNS TO PRINCETON.

" 'The word is astronomer,' Ad said gently. And that was all. No lecture on my awful boner. Naturally, I became your brother's devoted slave, from then on!"

Another colleague on the paper, Fritz Dashiell, has told me how generous Adlai always was with praise, and says he never saw my brother rattled. The foreman of the press, an old German named "Duke" Eberlein, would shout: "I keep telling you boys—these forms are not made of rubber. They have to *fit*." Duke would also tell the staff fiercely they couldn't hold a candle to last year's editors—a needling my brother took with great good humor, because he had no faster friend than Duke.

Mother and I were back in Europe in the spring when Adlai sent us a clipping from the *Princetonian*, with the modest explanation:

> It was a great surprise to me to be one of the first 12 men nominated by the present Senior Council. The Council ordinarily nominates the 12 most prominent men in the coming Senior Class and that I could be considered in that category was quite unexpected. Only five men out of this number are elected by the class this spring and then the remaining ten, making a total of 15 which composes the Senior Council, are elected next fall. Of course I will not be elected among the five taken on this spring but now I at least have hopes of making it next year.
>
> . . . I think I told you that I am going to Europe with Bob Brooke, Ev Case, and Ogden West of Chicago. We have se-

cured passage on the *Finland* sailing from New York on June 25, which will give us just a few days here after commencement. The *Princetonian* is to play the *Yale News* in baseball on June 18th and the event promises to be most amusing. The Prince played the Tiger yesterday and we were victorious 5 to 4. I played short stop.

By the time we met him abroad, I could report on my first close look at British royalty.

Mother and I had been in Paris when I began getting exciting accounts from my cousin Mildred Bromwell and friends staying in London about the parties planned with an eye to the young Prince of Wales. When he'd visited in the U.S., Millie, Geraldine Graham and Millicent Rogers had been among the girls invited to meet him, and they wanted to see him again! Mrs. Graham was already installed in a charming little mews and with her perfectly beautiful daughter was "doing the season." Mrs. Rogers had a very elegant house from which to launch her fascinating Millicent. My cousin Millie and her mother were at Claridge's. I don't know how many other leading ladies were menacing His Royal Highness, but I longed to get in his path at least once, so over to London we went. The city was terribly crowded, but dear Mrs. Stanley McCormick put me up on a sofa in her sitting room, until we finally got settled at Claridge's.

Lanier Winslow was secretary of our Embassy, and his exquisite wife Eileen was wonderful to me. The Prince of Wales often went to their house, and it was thanks to her that I was the only one of the American girls even to speak to H.R.H. at the great ball in Lansdowne House. While the others assembled eagerly in the ballroom, Eileen took me into a small anteroom and murmured, "We'll just sit here.

He's bound to come this way." And he did! He walked with
quick strides, followed by an aide, and when he recognized
Eileen, he smiled charmingly and came right over. She curt-
sied deeply, but when I was introduced, I was so breathless
I don't know to this day if I bent my knee. [When I was
presented at court to the King and Queen years later, I had
time to practice.] The Prince of Wales took Eileen off to
dance, and the aide sat with me. I didn't think the Prince
looked like a very good dancer!

The dance I went to with John Harlan, at Balliol College, Oxford, was more to my taste. I had thought Cambridge was beautiful, but after I saw the curving streets and
crumbling walls and glorious gardens of Oxford, I longed
to be a scholar there myself.

Adlai and Monk Hackney went to Spain in July, where
Ed Hackney and John Harlan were studying at the University of Madrid, and when Adlai joined Mother and me in
Lausanne, he was full of excitement about his Spanish adventures. He and Monk had traveled all over the country in
spite of the torrid heat that summer, and had climaxed their
adventures by a brush with Spanish police in Burgos. They
had gone to Burgos unexpectedly, after their train broke
down on the way from San Sebastián to Madrid. While they
were sitting beside the tracks waiting for the train crew to
finish repairs, a priest came down the road in that Spanish
countryside setting and rather surprised them by saying, "Hi,
fellows, my name is Simpson. I'm from Cincinnati." He was
studying at a Catholic seminary near there, and he told them
that the most exciting event of the summer was to take place
the next day in Burgos—the reburial of the Cid, and a procession headed by King Alfonso, re-enacting the medieval

pageantry of the fourteenth century. He also mentioned that the most famous of the bullfighters, Belmonte, was to perform the same day. So off Adlai and Monk went to Burgos, and found it so crowded they couldn't get a hotel room and had to sleep on a park bench. The next morning early, unshaven and uncombed, they rushed off to the Plaza de Toros, to get tickets for the bullfight. The line of people waiting to buy tickets was already blocks long, so Adlai and Monk decided to speed up the process by edging into line near the head. The Spaniards who had been waiting patiently in line since dawn were understandably indignant at this trick. In fact, they expressed their wrath so loudly that the police joined in, and told the two unshaven *Americanos* to wait their turn or they'd end up in a cell. Adlai and Monk never did see that bullfight, but they saw several others, before and after Burgos, and Adlai wasn't too keen on the sport, because he thought it was mighty unfair to the horses. He was much more enthusiastic about the Spanish painters—Velázquez, El Greco, Murillo.

His first day at Lausanne, he stayed out on the lake in a boat so long that he puffed up with a mean case of sunburn, and was in bed several days swathed in bandages, with a high fever. My diary reports: "Practised tennis in Ad's room this afternoon. He's giving me lessons in how to serve better. We read Swiss history and played checkers."

When he'd stopped looking like a boiled lobster, he and I went off to Venice with three of his college friends. I felt very risqué to be traveling with *men,* and I was humiliated to break out in big red lumps, from eating fish.

Except for the lumps, it was a marvelous week. The Venetians were celebrating the Prince Royal's visit extravagantly; they had hung brilliant tapestries and banners from every balcony along the Grand Canal, and the Prince went about in an ancient style barge of crimson and gold, rowed by twenty boatmen in livery. Flags floated from all the gondolas, and fireworks blazed over the Lagoon every night.

I'd have been content just to sit and gaze dreamily, but Adlai, as usual, wanted to get out and see everything. He rushed me off with his friends to Murano and watched the glass blowers with such concentration I think he could almost have blown a few goblets himself. He also had to go through every dungeon in the Doge's Palace (what grim places they were) and take in the art galleries as well as the required tourist run from St. Mark's to the Lido beach. Much as I adore Italy, I was exhausted trying to keep up with my brother's appalling standards of sight-seeing.

I was reminded of that a year or so ago when a friend who'd accompanied Adlai on his trip around the world told me, "After a killing day of receptions and interviews, I'd mutter, 'Well, at last we can rest,' but Adlai would look surprised and say, 'Why, this is our first chance to walk around the town and do some sight-seeing.' That guy *never* rests."

I felt like saying, "You're telling *me!*"

When my brother started his Senior year at Princeton that fall, he was busier than ever as managing editor of the *Daily Princetonian,* and with other extracurricular activities, besides a fairly stiff schedule of class work. He was studying European Economic Policy in the Nineteenth and Twentieth Centuries, the History of the Renaissance, Shakespeare, Geology, and also taking one of the toughest senior courses: Dr. Corwin's Constitutional Interpretation. This last one in-

terested Adlai so much that he even crowed jubilantly to
Father when he got a high mark in a test! Father refrained
from announcing this in the home-town paper, but he
"leaked" the news that his son had been elected by his classmates to the Senior Council, the student governing body—to
Adlai's discomfiture as usual.

Mother and I lived in Princeton again from February
until Adlai's graduation. It was the spring that "Ah, Sweet
Mystery of Life" first reared its silly head, as a tremolo
menace to June weddings. At parties, we sang "Chicago,
Chicago, That Toddlin' Town," and came out resoundingly
on, "Positively, Mr. Gallagher? Absolutely, Mr. Shean!" I
can't remember which girl of Adlai's stayed with us the
week end of spring house parties—and neither can he!

I had a new, happy feeling of doing something useful,
working with Paula Van Dyke as a captain of Girl Scouts
in the Italian section in Princeton. I rode horseback with
my friend Helen Russell, and the time galloped by until
June.

I'm ashamed to say the only thing I remember about that
Commencement Week is wandering around in the garden at
President Hibben's reception with Allison Armour. Adlai
must remember some of the graduation speeches all too
clearly. In 1954, when he went back to receive an honorary
degree from Princeton, he spoke at the Senior Class Banquet,
and I'll quote a few excerpts that show his views on graduation oratory and himself at twenty-two:

> I feel as though I were opening the hunting season on col-
> lege seniors. From now until mid-June, college seniors are fair
> game for all of us uplifters, viewers with alarm, Chautauqua-
> style orators, even for occasional unemployed politicians. From
> now until mid-June college seniors are to be repeatedly re-

minded how fortunate they are and what they should do with
their hard-won educational disciplines.

. . . Thirty-two years ago (and I might say quite a number
of pounds and a good many inches around the waist ago)
when I graduated I believe I listened to these same challenges
flung down by orators whose names I have completely forgotten. Now it is my turn to be forgotten. In doing my homework
this morning on this evening's oration, I not only let my mind
run back to the state of the world 32 years ago when I graduated from Princeton but I also glanced at the *Nassau Herald*
of 1922 in the hope that I could find something about myself
that would impress you. Well, I must say, in the long corridor
of retrospect, I don't look as important as I thought I was. I discovered that when my senior class voted to bestow the sobriquet
of "biggest politician" upon one of its members I received only
eight votes—but when it voted on *"thinks* he is biggest politician" I won second place, and that was due to a conspiracy
among my roommates. For the title of "most likely to succeed," I received the impressive total of two votes (I don't
know yet who the other fellow was).

Thirty-two years ago my classmates and I graduated into a
world that was quite different from the one you enter in 1954.
. . . Nor do I need to enumerate for you in sepulchral tones
the problems that you face. You know them only too well. Perhaps you can solve them. I would not presume to tell you how
to do it. This University has given you the tools with which to
try. Moreover, even if I would guide you, I could not. What a
man knows at fifty that he did not know at twenty is, for the
most part, incommunicable.

. . . What he knows at fifty that he did not know at twenty
boils down to something like this: The knowledge he has
acquired with age is not the knowledge of formulas, or forms
of words, but of people, places, actions—a knowledge not
gained by words but by touch, sight, sound, victories, failures,
sleeplessness, devotion, love—the human experiences and emo-
tions of this earth and of oneself and other men; and perhaps,

too, a little faith, and a little reverence for things you cannot see.

Nonetheless, I would speak to you not of the past, when my generation held its hopes so high—a time when even I received two votes as the most likely to succeed—but rather I would speak to you of the future, of your future. . . .

In 1922, Adlai's future—and mine—were roads we were eager to explore. I remember thinking that college had matured my brother, and hadn't given him what I was glibly calling "complexes."

Chapter 10

GRANDFATHER STEVENSON, like Great-grandfather Fell, had started out as a lawyer, and I think perhaps Father regretted his own lack of legal training. At any rate, he wanted Adlai to have a good knowledge of law because he said it would be useful "no matter what you do later."

Although Adlai probably still dreamed of the West and ranching, he must have decided Father was right; he was much too independent-minded to let anybody run his life, and I remember an instance of this, after he had passed the bar examination and was ready to look for a job. Father, with the spirit of a born promoter plus the instincts of a very proud parent, was eager to fix things up. He wanted to alert all his friends and political connections (which would have embraced a large section of forty-eight states) but my brother insisted he wanted to get a job entirely on his own. Father felt rather wistful and frustrated, but he had the good sense to keep hands off. When Adlai quickly got a job with Chicago's oldest law firm—then called Cutting, Moore and Sidley—Father must have been a little startled to discover that they were all *Republicans*. But somehow that made him prouder of his son than ever. After all, if a Stevenson was hired by Republicans, he must have been hired on merit alone!

To go back to the fall of 1922, Adlai's confidence in himself as a lawyer-to-be was still unhatched, and I suspect his heart was at the *Pantagraph* or on a Western ranch. He had arranged to room with Bill McIlvaine and Chas Denby at Harvard Law School, and after they'd settled in, Adlai wrote an account of the horror stories the newcomers had been greeted with:

> Claverly Hall
> Cambridge
>
> Tuesday night
> Sept. 26, 1922
>
> Dearest Mother:
>
> We have just finished abstracting some cases in property! Doesn't that sound formidable? And maybe its not! This Harvard Law school is the most feverish place I've ever seen—everyone works *all* the time and still about 25-35% get dropped every year. All we've heard since we arrived were gruesome tales of disaster from our friends and staggering stories of astonishing hours of work when the big reviews begin in March. Until then it is a comparative loaf. Just do your work from day to day—and it can be done easily in about 8 hrs. Oh the news is certainly encouraging and I'm looking forward to a very delightful winter. Everyone around here insists that the Harvard Law school is the hardest graduate school of any kind in America. It certainly is a charming prospect and attendance at a total of 4 classes so far substantiates the worst I've heard.
>
> . . . Am quite happy but we all will have to get adjusted to an entirely different standard of work and life in fact. The law school is sort of like being in business, not college. We have so many enormous books and notebooks that we have to

carry them back and forth to class in satchels. More bad news later.

> Best love
> Adlai

When he mentioned in a letter, "I have to argue a law club case on Nov. 7th and am getting worried about it already," Mother wrote him her usual loving and ample advice:

> Dearest Laddie:
> As the time draws near for your argument, I wonder if you are in doubt about your success? Success as regards your equanimity? I hope you will let this be an opportunity to prove to yourself that if you have done all that was necessary in preparation, nothing is worth getting nervous over, and that you are going to let your will take a back seat and allow your unconscious, imagination, or God, work through you without any strain or fear or doubt. "Let go your hold," as Wm. James says, resign your destiny to higher powers and you will get a perfect inward relief.
> . . . I want you to get plenty of sleep and relaxation for the few days before. Rest and sleep have always been your best medicine and please take my advice and get it now. Be perfectly sincere, serious and natural. Show that you are doing the best you can and everybody respects that. Each experience will be a milestone in showing you how foolish it is to be afraid to do the best you can and how really simple it is. Forget there is anybody there. Just talk to yourself or rather let your subconscious come forth. I am so proud of you and want you to do your work honestly and faithfully.

Judging from his next letter, my brother had already stopped worrying:

> . . . I have almost finished my law brief but will have to do some more work polishing it up before the actual argument takes place in Nov. Its hard but interesting work preparing

them and gives you some idea of what a practicing lawyer has
to do when he has a case before a superior court that involves
a nice distinction or problem.

If you have a little rug somewhere around the house you
might send it for my bedroom. It's nice to have something to
step on instead of the cold floor in the mornings. If you
haven't one don't worry because I can get a bath rug here
for a couple of dollars.

Soon afterwards, he wrote:

Chas, Bill, Irv. Harris, a Harvard boy named Bob Finley,
and myself study together most every night. Talking over
cases is about the best way to study so we're going to make a
practise of doing it as much as possible.

I still find it hard to reconcile myself to Cambridge. As for
the University the thing that impresses me particularly is that
nobody seems to know or care to know *anyone* else. It's an
entirely different atmosphere from Princeton. . . .

When I went up to Cambridge for the Harvard-Princeton
football game, I was amused because Adlai, the Harvard law
student, cheered wildly for the Princeton team. and was beside himself with joy when Old Nassau won. So was I! He
and Dale Warren took me over to a tea dance at the Hasty
Pudding Club, and Adlai's comment on that affair was,
"What a polite battle." Boston and environs still left him
rather lukewarm. (Later letters show how enthusiastically he
changed his mind.)

I think he envied me because I was going to Bloomington
for Thanksgiving, and this letter from Mother must have
made him rather homesick:

Tomorrow is the first Thanksgiving day since you went off
to boarding school, six years ago, that we have not been together—at least you and I. I hope you are not as lonesome

for us as we are for you. And yet I know you are thinking of us and wishing we were all together. History has never attempted to prove that the home is not the foundation of civilization, which is the best argument that it is true—but we "home lovers" do not need an argument to prove to us that with the home begins and depends the salvation of the race and its evolution.

Without this *love of home* and our desire to get together—to love and protect one another—where would be the use of living? But although we three are here at the old home it is not entirely home because one of our little family is absent. Last year we didn't have Buffie, now we haven't you, but we are so happy in the thought that you are well and doing so splendidly that we shall cheer up and make a "day" of it. . . .

We were all at "home" in the nicest sense of the word over Christmas. Adlai had just won his second case in class, by a point score of 25 to 15, and he and Father had a fine time discussing legal problems. (From then on, he often sent Father the *Law Review* with pages marked on some particular case.) My brother had been doing extracurricular reading in snatches; I remember he was interested in Sir Arthur Quiller-Couch's new book, *Literary Studies,* and wanted me to read the famous lecture on Byron. I had just "discovered" Emerson (this must have pleased Mother, who was an ardent Emersonian) and he was featured in our reading-aloud sessions. It seems to me we had Eugene O'Neill's *Anna Christie,* too.

Adlai left just before New Years to join a house party of Eastern friends at Lake Placid, where he wrote Mother, "If there is a heaven on earth, I've found it at last. . . . Skiing is the most delightful sport I've ever indulged in."

A month or so later, he wrote about a week end at Jaffrey, New Hampshire, where a group of fourteen boys, girls (and chaperones!) had what sounds like a very invigorating romp in the snow. His letter mentions cross-country ski runs, tobogganing, an impromptu hockey game, a sleigh ride "accompanied with much good cheer and rough housing" and ends up exultantly, "The girls were a great bunch—not an unattractive one among them, in fact all knockouts. . . . We were all weak with laughter from beginning to end. Incidentally the whole thing, my fare and all, cost only $32 for 4 whole days."

Mother answered:

> Your Sunday letter written Monday after a weekend's debauch, just rec'd. It was good for you to get a change and from the tone of your letter it must have been a success.
>
> I shall now expect you to go to Jaffrey for several weekends for rest & recreation. Please do so. I'll send you money if you need it—please tip me off if you do!
>
> Father writes glowingly of your health, spirits and poise. [He had visited Harvard and Adlai had taken him to some of his classes.] Glad indeed to know you are well and enjoying a rare opportunity—that of really *learning*. As much as possible, seek the association of wise people. Mr. James H. Robinson says that the best way to be educated is to live with educated people. Don't waste much time on mediocres. Better be alone, thinking for yourself. And have some fun out of it—encourage and nourish your sense of humor. Life is dull, even stupid, without it. . . .

This reminds me of the night in 1952 when Adlai heard a funereal-voiced radio commentator criticize him for making "jokes" in his speeches. My brother said to us suddenly, "What's the line about 'A merry heart is like a medicine but a broken spirit drieth up the bones?' Is it Shakespeare?" He found it, in *Proverbs,* and used it in a speech to answer his sour-faced (or sour-grapes?) critics. Another time, he said, "I refuse to conform to the Republican law of gravity!"

Boston and what he called "The case of Blackstone versus Stevenson" hadn't dampened Adlai's humor. He was in fine spirits when he came down to New York to see me off on a visit to our cousin Millie in England, the spring of 1923. Millie had married Sidney Bailey, the British naval attaché, in a lovely simple wedding in Charlevoix the summer before. (She's now Lady Bailey.) I had been her only attendant, and I was eager to see her in her new home. The night before I sailed, Adlai took Aunt Letitia and me to dinner in New York, and we laughed over our forthright aunt's description of her own return from a trip around the world. A friend asked her if she'd had a good time, and Aunt Letitia said, "Do you want my advice? Just plan your trip down to the final detail—and then cancel your ticket."

Much as I enjoyed that story, I didn't cancel my passage. At the boat, Adlai arranged for my deck chair while Dale Warren plied me with flowers and sentiment, so I went off feeling very pampered and gay. From the Baileys' house in Essex, I wrote my brother about my first brush with "county" living:

> Rickling House,
> Quendon, Essex
> May 10, 1923

Adlai Dear:

. . . This house is small (plain English house) unpretentious but full of atmosphere and charm. It is in parts 300 years old. The walls of the hall & library are covered with the most curious and ferocious heads of the animals Sid had killed.

The great fat pompous old butler gives us our orders and we mind our manners when he is around. At table if I refuse a dish he continues to stand there until I explain I don't want it and then he tells me in a commanding tone that I must eat it—everyone that comes to Rickling eats it!

The garden is charming—gay with flowers. The gardener has been here 30 years and the asparagus bed is 90 years old. There is a tennis court, many apple trees—a large lawn and very ancient trees where the nightingales sing at night. I have learned to drive the Stutz and have run to Cambridge twice (18 miles) and go for golf at Golf-Magog 14 miles away. It takes about a half hour to get there; each time we've gone, we have got caught in a driving English rain and had to seek shelter in a lodge of a great estate. Then today we managed to play and between drives clouds opened up on us and we went into little huts for protection. The view there is a great one, all over Cambridgeshire and to Ely Cathedral, 16 miles distant.

The Fiat is broken down—it's a bum motor and has gone to C. to be overhauled, so no trips for a time.

Some English ladies called today to ask me for "tennis on Sunday afternoon!" I'm *scared*. Going over to Kings Chapel for Church on Sunday and will perhaps lunch with the "lads."

You would be amused with the police dog, Rex, who has already become my companion and slave. He sleeps by my bed even. Also a large and terrifying black cat—the dog and he play together. Rex takes the cat's head in his mouth and drops him all over the place!

I can understand now why the English are such sports—they live so much in the country they are lonesome and have to exercise for amusement, and to keep warm! Gad, it's cold! Little fires in all the rooms but the maids run about opening the windows as fast as we close them. I'd be a whiskey drinker if I lived in England, I guess.

. . . We went thru' "Short Grove"—the estate of Sir Joshua Bailey (let for 12 years) and found it a *huge* house with 30 bedrooms and 1100 acres. Also to Quendon Hall which was once a monastery! In the park they had 100 head of deer that had always been living there, and in one field the hunters [horses] were frisking about deep in buttercups. They came over to the fence and talked to me!

While I was renewing my love affair with England, my brother's letters sounded as if he were falling in love with *New* England:

. . . Last night Francis [Plimpton], Chas. and I staged a novel party. Our companions were Lorna Underwood, Cornelia Hallowell and Pauline Ames. Lorna as usual had the original idea—we wandered down into the foreign quarter of Boston below Scully Square. It was quite an experience and gave us a glimpse of the old world. The open air market stretches for blocks along a narrow and crooked old street. Saturday night is the big night when all the people do their marketing and the street echoed with the vendors' shouts, snatches of laughter and song. It was a warm, balmy evening with a promise of spring in the air—the lurid gas flares and the hurdy gurdys lent a very South European atmosphere to the whole enchanting scene. And there we boldly entered an old and villanous oyster bar and ate a tremendous sea food dinner in little alcoves on hard and narrow benches. Then followed the usual visit to the Brunswick for dancing. It was a most entertaining evening and the girls got a tremendous kick out of it.
. . . We rode all morning—a soft warm spring day; it was too good! I'm afraid the love of the saddle & the open country has found an easy and willing victim in me. Another extravagant inclination to overcome! But I can say with becoming modesty that I am beginning to cut a not unpleasant figure on a horse and find myself able to keep at the front of the field over hedges and brooks and thus far not a fall this year. What bravado! I'm knocking loudly on my "chamber door."
I went to the Underwoods for Sunday dinner & a mighty fine dinner it was. As always in the bosom of that most natural of families we had a riotous time. After lunch we spread rugs on the terrace and drank our coffee and bathed in the sun. Thus went the whole afternoon; a few neighbors dropped in

and as tea time approached the usual delegation came out from Cambridge to pay homage to the Underwood girls. . . .

Lewis Farm

A.D. 1742

Walpole, Massachusetts

Sunday

Dear Mother:

Chas., Bill & I came out here for the weekend with Francis Plimpton, a fellow law student, the boy who is going to room with us next year. This is his ancestral manor and an exceedingly interesting place—filled with pre-revolutionary family relics, autographs of George Washington and other celebrities ad infinitum. The family spend most of their time in New York & Bermuda but were up here overnight to arrange things for the summer. The farm comprises some 800 acres, principally of woodland and is primarily a dairy farm.

Mr. Plimpton is an interesting straight-laced old Puritan with many hobbys, of which the farm is one. He is chairman of the Board of Trustees of Amherst College, President of Ginn & Co. the publishers and quite a well known gent. He and Mrs. Plimpton, the second, returned to New York this morning leaving us in complete control of the manor.

Yesterday we played golf at the Norfolk Country Club and are going riding this afternoon. The schedule ends up with work tonight and back to Cambridge—about 20 miles—in time for classes tomorrow.

. . . The native and imported wonders in this old house have left me simply spell-bound and I've had a delightful & enlightening time examining them all. The dining room table is from the house Washington lived in at Germantown.

Claverly Hall

Cambridge

Dear Father:

Things are going fine with the beautiful weather making it progressively harder to keep to the books and their appalling contents of undigested knowledge. Its only about 3 weeks now until the first exam and I certainly have some few things to learn.

. . . I wish you would send me 2 or 3 hundred dollars for I'm getting pretty short. Also I had to pay my Univ. bill for the 4th quarter in tuition & second half in rent which was $215. So a little "separations" would go big just now with your profligate offspring.

My best to the office—i.e. Fred

Adlai

Poor Father—both his offspring were profligate that spring. I had gone to Paris with Cousin Letty Bromwell, and under her chic wing had splurged on clothes. I also wrote my brother expansively, "Is there anything you want me to bring you? I bought you some golf socks, what color is your tweed suit?"

When I docked in New York and had paid duty on my Paris finery, I was so broke I didn't even have railroad fare home. I turned to one of my fellow-passengers, who knew Father, and asked nervously if I might borrow some money from him. Fortunately, it was Thomas Lamont! That kindly capitalist reached for his wallet and said, "Are you sure you only need fifty dollars?"

Two other passengers I'd met on that homeward voyage— Adolph Ochs, the brilliant publisher of the *New York Times,* and his wife—made my next winter in New York especially delightful. I had taken over Louise Thoron's little apartment on East Thirty-sixth Street after she and Ewen Mac-Veagh were married, and the Ochses asked me to dinner parties whenever they needed an extra woman. Two of the people I met there have been my friends ever since—Arthur Hays Sulzberger and his wonderful wife Iphigene, the Ochses' daughter. The Ochses' guests ranged from talented young writers to international financiers, famous actors, conductors and statesmen, and the talk at those dinners was stimulating. Mr. Ochs had the warm, searching kind of curiosity that reminded me of Grandfather Davis and my own brother, although the publisher had quite a different way of drawing people out. Toward the end of dinner, he'd tap on his glass with a spoon to get attention, and then he'd go around the table asking each guest's opinion on some current subject. Usually, it was something controversial enough to arouse some awfully lively talk.

I went to opening nights and art exhibits and concerts all that winter, and sent back reports to the *Pantagraph*—book reviews too—but I didn't presume to call myself a critic. Several attentive young men made life all the pleasanter in that bewilderingly beautiful city, where the sky seems so far away. I saw a lot of Anne Stillman and Constance Binney, and my friend Connie Russell Winant was often in town. Dr. Joseph Collins and the brilliant journalist Isaac Marcosson were very kind to me. When Adlai came down to spend a few days with me, he listened with great delight to Marcosson.

The night my brother arrived at my apartment, he looked dead tired and he even *admitted* he had a sore throat and felt "lousy." This was so unusual for Adlai that I made him go to bed for a fourteen-hour sleep (I slept on the living-room couch) and by the next day he was as fit as ever, when Doug Ward, Morrison Ulman and several other Princeton friends came in, for what they called "a good bicker." He spent all one morning shopping around for a gift to take back to his favorite family in Cambridge, the Underwoods, and finally settled on a beautiful eighteenth-century book on riding. When we went to the studio of a sculptor friend of mine, Bryant Baker, the piece that interested Adlai most was a fine bust of Woodrow Wilson. I provided a pretty companion and two theater tickets for *Outward Bound,* and my brother reported he'd never enjoyed anything more.

He had seen Pavlova recently, and he was very funny describing old Bostonians' reactions—a lot of genteel headshaking and sighs over the dancer's "not being what she was ten or twenty years ago." Adlai said that never having seen Pavlova before, *he'd* had to be unfashionable and show how much he was enjoying "her 1923 form."

My brother was in his second year of law school, and working very hard, but I'm not sure how interested he was and I suspect he sometimes felt a little guilty because he was enjoying the life in Cambridge so much, especially the week ends. Mother, with her intuitive wisdom and loving good sense, wrote him:

> Dear One:
> Your optimism and faith are contagious and have given me a boost. Naturally, I had courage, my father used to call it, but with low physical status, I am liable to slumps. [She hadn't been well that spring.] I needed your letter!
> Now, my dear, you must not feel guilty unless there is reason and the only reason for guilt is wrong-doing. I do not believe we can have too much happiness unless it interferes with the happiness of others. Then it is selfishness. I believe God wants His children to be happy.
> So, hop along to all the best that is going on and do not become an ascetic and imagine you ought to mortify the flesh.
> I, too, wish and believe we could all be as happy and peaceful as you are just now. Of course, there are ugly things to be met all along the road and in ourselves. But if we are fortified with optimism, good health, and faith, we can meet these demonstrations and go unscathed rejoicing.
> I believe in realities and seeing clearly and making right

deductions in thinking and we should not declare a thing or person beautiful or good when it is not so. If we would get in this habit of seeing clearly, we will, in the long run, be much freer, wiser, truer and, above all, of more service to the world. After all, it is true beauty, greatness, we are after and you must not confuse falsehood with truth. You must not worship the shadow for the substance. "Having eyes, see."

You say, "Laddie is getting his eyes open." They can't see too much or too far. "Know thyself." Know the world, know values, know what you want—above all, know God, universal Good. Stand for that, whatever befalls.

It does me good to hear you say it has been the happiest year yet. Work and play. That is what all good life should be and be guilty only when you are not getting the balance. . . . We all have so much to be grateful for and happy over. Buff— so full of the beauty and possibilities of life and you, my precious boy, so happy and wise. Father is in his political stream and I see no reason for our not all being just the happiest, healthiest people in the world. "THE GREAT SOUL OF THE WORLD IS JUST."

All love of the fullest and tenderest.

Mother

P.S. Remember that I know you couldn't be so happy and grateful if you were not trusting God and so consider how happy you are making me.

She didn't hesitate to mix in homilies and reprimands when she thought they were needed. I've picked these few samples from her letters to Adlai:

Early hours are most important, to live by artificial light is *unnatural,* and Nature is a perfect guide.

. . . By the way, I have had it in mind to scold you about the small courtesies of life. Never neglect to acknowledge a favor, promptly and adequately. Never let any debt of honor from a postage stamp to a fortune go without proper, prompt acknowledgement and courtesy. It is easy and unpardonable to neglect, forget and evade, and so form the habit now of not so doing.

Sometimes I send you things and you do not mention them, especially money, and naturally I am wanting to know if they landed. This latter is a business matter and only business methods are permissible, so there! Courtesy, without emotion or effusion, kindness, great appreciation, sympathy are fine attributes and you have them deeply engrained and must never neglect to use them.

. . . Have you grown much since I saw you! Would I recognize my 24-year-older. Please keep on growing up and out and through, remembering that in drawing yourself up to a high level, you draw others with you.

If you can only go through life, taking the bitter with the sweet without complaint or resentment, you will have conquered much of life's frustration. However, do not misunderstand me—one must also not hesitate to fight for the right and have courage to see justice done.

In these days of moral relaxation, the spirit of love and righteousness are most necessary. I would rather have you sound physically and morally than president.

Adlai and I were both in New York for that long Democratic convention in June of 1924. Father was honorary secretary of the convention, and he arranged for Adlai, B. Davis and Francis Plimpton to be assistant sergeants of arms. Adlai was staying at the Plimptons, and I was visiting the Charles R. Cranes and their beautiful daughter Frances, who later married Jan Masaryk. Mr. Crane was a wealthy philanthropist and internationalist, and often had students from all over the world visit him. I loved staying at the Cranes' because it was like a gathering of the League of Nations.

Mr. Crane was backing David F. Houston for President. The Houston headquarters were in the Hotel Saville, and Father was the guiding spirit. The day before the convention opened, Adlai wrote Mother, "Father has a mighty good but very dark horse in Houston. Frankly, I don't think he has much chance of getting the nomination and it looks more and more as if John W. Davis was the man." John Davis was—but it took the deadlocked delegates 103 ballots to decide. "Alabama casts 24 votes for Oscar W. Underwood," rang out day after day. I wasn't sorry over the McAdoo-Smith deadlock because I was having such a good time from June 24 to July 9. When F.D.R. as Al Smith's manager failed to get him nominated, John W. Davis got the candidacy on the hundred and third ballot. Adlai's job was to carry messages to delegates on the floor and back to the "smoke-filled rooms," so he had a good long look at politics behind the scenes.

Father made the nominating speech for Houston, and Franklin D. Roosevelt for Al Smith. I thought theirs and Newton Baker's were much the best speeches, but I may have been a little prejudiced! Father very nearly didn't get there in time to make his speech. His taxi was caught in a traffic snarl, and he got more and more frantic, as the minutes ticked on, until suddenly he thought of a way out. He called to a cop, "Officer, I've got to be at Madison Square Garden in five minutes to make the nominating speech for Al Smith." At the mention of that adored name, the cop's whistle blew frenziedly, he jumped on the running board and cleared the taxi's path crosstown to the convention, where Father rushed in and spoke—for Houston. He atoned for this trick a few years later, in 1928, when he organized the Smith Independent Organization Committee, with

George Peek and Chester Davis (the latter Republicans) and worked valiantly throughout that campaign, in Midwest farm areas, for the "Happy Warrior."

Two young men I saw during the convention were Briton Hadden and Harry Luce, who were just launching *Time* magazine on a shoestring. I remember how worried and amused I was one night when a party of us went to the Astor Roof, and Dick Crane, the only wealthy man of the lot, whispered to me that he was tired of always footing the bill, and he was going to fool the others this time by leaving before the waiter brought the check. He vanished five minutes later, and I felt pangs for those poor young publishers Hadden and Luce—stuck with that check.

If my memory is right, Adlai had flirted with the idea of investing some of his earnings from the *Daily Princetonian* in the *Time* magazine project, and even working for them. Instead he cautiously put his profits into an invention of a garage mechanic down the street in Bloomington who was going to revolutionize the gasoline engine. All that Adlai and some of his friends got out of that "investment" was experience!

In the spring of 1924, Adlai's second year at law school, Uncle Bert Davis died in California. Uncle Bert was publisher and the active manager of the *Pantagraph,* and many complications immediately arose in connection with his estate which took much of Adlai's time and changed his plans, at least temporarily. Due to various deaths, and ambiguities in Grandfather Davis' will, there was a question as to whether the ownership of the newspaper passed to Aunt Jessie Merwin and Mother in equal shares, or three-fifths to them and two-fifths to us, because there were three Merwin cousins and only two of us. It was all straightened out after a long lawsuit, but until the outcome was decided (giving equal shares to both sisters) Adlai and Davis Merwin both went to work on the *Pantagraph,* Adlai on the editorial end, and his cousin in the business department. That way, both families were represented in the management.

My brother deplored the family feud, but he enjoyed the chance to do some writing and reporting again. His loved friend Lloyd Lewis, the author, editor and humorist, once told me before his untimely death that Adlai was "the best natural-born reporter he'd ever known." One of the stories Adlai covered that year was a terrible tornado around Murphysboro, Illinois; almost a thousand people were killed, and several towns were devastated. In "human interest" stories from the scene he described survivors in "a bleeding, smoking world":

> I saw a farmer dressed in his best blue suit, pale but dry-eyed and composed, push his way through a crowd in front of a morgue and emerge a moment later carrying a tiny white casket not three feet long. He placed the casket tenderly beside him in his Ford and drove away. That was Mary, aged two. Baby Jane is still inside; he will come back for her.
> . . . A little girl sits quietly weeping on a pile of rubbish, hugging a shattered doll. A cow wanders aimlessly and hungrily among the smouldering ruins. An old lady was sitting with her aged husband. She was unharmed; of him, there remained to her two limbs and a watch with the crystal intact. . . . The few available hearses in Murphysboro are racing back and forth to the cemetery, carrying two caskets at a time. Of formal funerals there are none, but of heroic fortitude there is much.

He also did a series of thoughtful editorials on the famous Scopes trial in Dayton, Tennessee, where a teacher was being tried for teaching the story of evolution. William Jennings Bryan and Clarence Darrow were pitted against each other. Bryan, the Great Commoner, and Grandfather's running mate in 1900, had been an heroic figure to Adlai from childhood, and I think he was a little saddened by Bryan in his old age and his extreme fundamentalist views. Adlai's editorials left no doubt that Bryan or no Bryan, he was against religious bigotry and censorship through ignorance.

While my brother was getting a taste of professional journalism, I was facing my first real audience—as an actress at the Pasadena Playhouse. Father, with his finger in as many projects as ever, had started the Community Players in Bloomington, and after I'd played with them in *Captain Applejack,* my appetite was so whetted that I took off for California. The brilliant director of the Playhouse, Gilmore Brown, was putting on our friend Rachel Crothers' *Expressing Willie,* and he let me play a vivacious society type who waved her arms and talked constantly about expressing herself. For this role, I wore an elaborate borrowed tea gown with fur-banded sleeves that were very effective for gestures!

I took my work very seriously, and ruffled my feathers (or fur bands) a bit belligerently to ward off family advice. I wrote Mother:

> I am sorry Adlai wishes I were "married and settled" because I've no one to marry & it is quite apparent that I won't be ever settled, leading a theatre life, & whats more, I doubt if its in my nature to settle. I suppose it would lessen your problems to "settle" me but after all, I'm my own problem, & as long as you can & will support me, let me work out my own salvation & don't fret over me. . . .
> "The strongest man upon earth is he who stands most alone"
> Ibsen

I also quoted a long passage from Ecclesiastes to back up my argument, and wound up my letter:

My heart is full of love for you on this warm, smiling day, & I wish I could see you both.

P.S. Am rather glad Ad didn't go back to Princeton although it must have been very hard to turn one's back on such a job in that lovely place! [He had been offered a job at Lawrenceville School, near Princeton, teaching History or English, but he wanted to stay with the *Pantagraph*.]

Father came out to Pasadena to take a look at his emancipated daughter, and wrote Mother a reassuring report. I think his letter is the best review I ever got:

Buff is certainly happy in her new surroundings. We had Gilmore Brown (the director) with us at dinner last night. I had satisfactory talk with him later. Thinks Buff has talent but needs experience which I'm sure is the case. Witnessed the dress rehearsal [I think we were doing *To the Ladies*]. Buff played her small part—that of middle-aged mother—very well. Wore gray wig & had to line her face for age effect. Wore all white in first & all black in second act & looked stunning. Had good poise & presence & used her sweet voice well. Rest assured I'll be patient & do everything possible. She has been so sweet to me I'm very happy.

Much love, Lewis

Father's idea of "doing everything possible" was very potent. He learned that his friend Charles Wagner was going to produce Sabatini's *The Carolinian,* and a month or so later, I was on my way to New York to start rehearsals. (Father had somehow persuaded Wagner and his star, Sidney Blackmer, to come to Pasadena to look me over.) I played the part of Lady something-or-other, and I still have fond memories of another member of that cast, Reginald Owen, because he told me frankly he didn't think much of me as an actress, but he was wonderful about giving me tips on make-up. To show how incredibly wide-eyed I still was—when I went to a party at Rachel Crothers' and met Katherine Cornell there, I was shocked to the core because Miss Cornell had on a *suit,* and not the glamorous gold lamé or whatever I'd expected all great actresses wore.

The Carolinian opened its tryout run at the Bonstelle Theater in Detroit. Mother and father came to the opening night—and I got laryngitis and lost my voice. They begged me to give up the whole thing, and probably the director would have agreed! When we moved on to Boston, I was up at the Women's Republican Club, and it never occurred to me then it was a strange place for me to be.

The show's press agent got pictures of me in all the Boston papers—with some such headline as *Granddaughter of Vice-President Goes Legit*—and a story saying I was an heiress, which was certainly news to me. Right after that, I had a call from Morris Gest asking if I'd understudy the nun (played by Lady Diana Manners) in *The Miracle.* He said he thought I might have publicity value on tour. Nothing was said about histrionic ability. I appealed to my wise friend Adolph Ochs, and he said stoutly to stick to my guns and come into New York with *The Carolinian.*

On opening night in New York, my tiny dressing room was massed with huge baskets of flowers—more than the leading lady's! In the audience sat Father, Rachel Crothers, Major Bowes and his wife Margaret Illington, Mrs. Henry Breckenridge and several other friends Father had assembled for my Broadway debut. I appeared early in the first act just long enough to mouth a few words, and imagine my distinguished claque's surprise when they waited all through the rest of the play for my next scene—but there wasn't any more. *The Carolinian* closed two weeks later, but I refuse to take *all* the blame for that.

I worked next with a stock company in Trenton, playing in several plays including *Flaming Youth,* and commuting from an apartment on East Sixty-third Street. Adlai was smitten with a very attractive girl he had known for a long time who lived across the street from me, so he'd sandwich me in whenever he came to New York to see her. He was taking his final year of law school at Northwestern University in Chicago, and traveling back and forth to Bloomington week ends so as to keep in touch with things on the *Pantagraph.* I didn't urge him to come see me in *Flaming Youth,* so he missed that doubtful pleasure.

In the spring of 1926, I got a job with Gilbert Miller's stock company in Rochester, at $50 a week. George Cukor was our director, Rosamund Pinchot was the ingénue, and the talented Glenn Hunter starred in several plays. Ilka Chase and Louis Calhern, two other members of the company, supplied the off-stage romance by suddenly getting married. They invited all the cast to a wedding reception in their little hotel sitting room, and we drank a toast from paper cups. Calhern seemed to me very handsome and very sulky.

Elsie Ferguson joined us to play the lead in *The Outcast,* but she didn't look or act the way I'd remembered her as a child, when Mother pointed her out in the Paris hotel and told me to use that beautiful lady as a model of decorum. In rehearsals at Rochester, Miss Ferguson was rather inclined to talk back to the director—in a loud tone.

Most of that very hot summer, I worked happily in very small roles. We did a new play each week, and I always marveled at the transformation when jerky small scenes suddenly flowed together, and the performance would come alive. Meanwhile, Mother and Father must have been plotting anxiously how to pry me loose from a career they were convinced would come to nothing, and finally they dispatched Adlai as emissary. They wrote me that he had *Pantagraph* business to attend to in New York, and would go by way of Rochester.

It was the only time my brother ever saw me act, and when he took me out to supper afterwards, he tried to be tactful, but I remember he said, "All you did was come in and sit on a bench long enough to say one line."

His tempting counterproposal to this bench-warming was a trip to Italy with Mother. Adlai would accompany us part way, but he pointed out that Mother needed me along because he intended to go off to the Balkans and Russia. This idea of going to Russia had been cooked up at a convivial bachelor dinner after a friend's wedding earlier that summer. His friends George Norton and Bob Page wanted to go along, so George got credentials as a foreign correspondent for his home-town paper, the Louisville *Courier-Journal,* Adlai got his from Hearst's INS, with some help from Father, and Bob just took a chance.

My brother had just received his law degree from Northwestern, taken the bar exam, and wanted one more travel fling before he settled down to practice law. He wanted to see something of Eastern Europe, where he had never been, and have a firsthand look at the Soviet experiment. Besides, he said he might get a scoop. Russia was closed to foreigners in those days, and it was hard to get in. And since negotiations had broken down over the Czarist debts and expropriated American properties, Chicherin, the Foreign Min-

ister, had refused to see any of the few correspondents stationed in Moscow. Adlai's rosy idea was that if a naive young
man showed up full of bright ideas about liquidating the
debts, trade, student exchange and so on, Chicherin just
might be intrigued enough to talk a bit—and what a story
that would be! I remember my brother saying eagerly, "I
think that's a new approach to breaking the log jam, and
of course I'll tell Chicherin that I've come with an open
mind."

I was sure the Russian Foreign Minister would be happy
to hear that Adlai had come with an open mind all the way
from Chicago, and I thought that together they would work
things out very nicely. I must have had an open mind too,
because I couldn't resist Adlai's urging to come along to
Italy. I did say firmly that I'd go back to my theater career
in the fall, little knowing that my "career" awaited me in
Europe, in the guise of a handsome Virginian.

When mother, Adlai and I sailed on the *Conte Bianca-
mano* in early August, there was a great crowd at the pier
providing a spectacular send-off for Generale Umberto Nobile, who had just flown over the North Pole in a dirigible.
He was a small, dark, gentle man who stood patiently with
his little dog, Titina, while newsreel cameramen and VIP's
swarmed around. Even Rudolph Valentino was there to see
him off.

I thought Nobile was fascinating, and was pleased that he
seemed to like being with me. We talked together a great
deal on the ship, and I remember his telling me sadly, in
his broken English, that he rather dreaded the return to
Italy, because he feared Mussolini. When our ship stopped
at Gibraltar, an Italian newsman who interviewed the gen-

eral told me I looked like Duse as a young girl, and I was
so overcome I couldn't even say thank you.

Even before we docked in Naples, planes and dirigibles
were buzzing overhead and naval craft were firing welcome
salutes in honor of the returned hero. Nobile asked me to
stand beside him on the bridge as the ship sailed into the
beautiful Naples harbor.

The first day Adlai, Mother and I were on a train in Italy
(Il Duce had them "running on time," all right) we felt the
ugly influence of fascism. I had tucked my feet up under me
on the seat, trying to sleep, and a Fascist guard came in and
screamed that I was under arrest—for defiling the upholstery.
Adlai was so furious he got white, but he kept his head and
got me unarrested. The more changes we saw in our beloved
Italy, the more my brother despised the new regime. In
articles he wrote for the *Pantagraph,* he said:

> Fascism has adopted the same tactics that Communism has
> in Russia. Historically, suppression leads to violence. Taking
> away free speech is taking away the safety valve. . . . Imagine
> being liable to imprisonment for the mere expression of an
> antipathetic point of view, no matter how sincere! . . . It is
> evident that order has come out of chaos, but the "beneficent
> tyrant" has conferred these benefits by locking the lazy, quar-
> relsome boy [Italy] in a straight jacket, stuffing a handkerchief
> in his mouth, and then hypnotizing him with juggling feats
> performed with sticks of dynamite.

Adlai had applied for his Russian visa in New York
months before, but when he left us in Italy to join his
friends in Berlin, he still hadn't got it. George Norton and
Bob Page were no better off. After a week in Vienna of
haunting the Soviet consulate, Bob gave up in disgust. In
Budapest, when no visa was forthcoming, George announced

that he was going back to Poland or somewhere and join a delegation from the Southern Baptist Church which was going to Russia, and that way he would be *sure* to get in. (The delegation was turned back at the Polish-Russian border.)

My brother was still stubbornly determined to get into Russia and get that story. From Budapest he went on alone to Belgrade. Still no visa. Then to Bucharest, with the same result. This stalling—or trip tease—continued on through Sofia to Istanbul. In Istanbul, after sitting on the consulate for a couple of days, Adlai got fed up and went out to see the sights. Thus refreshed, he went back to the consulate a day or so later and was stunned by cordial cries of "Where *were* you yesterday? Don't you want this visa?"

The consul couldn't offer any suggestions as to how my brother might get to Russia from Turkey, even with a visa, so Adlai hired a boatman to row him out into the Bosporus to a little Italian freighter, the *Diana*, that was bound for Batum. Somehow, in spite of very little Italian he talked the captain into taking him aboard. In this he traveled five days, putting in at the ancient ports along the south shore of the Black Sea, sharing a cabin with an old Italian diplomat headed for Persia and participating without relish in the officers' sport of shooting sea gulls from the bridge with a rifle. When they got to the Russian port of Batum, all my brother's books and papers (including Pares' *History of Russia* and a French-Russian dictionary) were confiscated.

By stages, and with difficulties of all kinds, lingual, financial and nutritional, this strange apparition in the Caucasus of 1926, an American, got himself to Tiflis and then to Baku on the Caspian. Then for days he was locked up in a railway compartment under a carpet of dust with a heavily bearded cartoonist's model of a Bolshevik bomb thrower who never uttered a word in any language. Adlai knew the Russian words for "tea" and "eggs," but his accent couldn't have been very good, because the first time he asked for them, what he got was beer, bread and cheese.

He didn't get much more when he finally arrived in Moscow. It was before the homeless children, the spawn of war and revolution, had been gathered up, and the first thing he saw outside the station was a pack of these ragged little wolves frantically scraping the cobblestones where someone had dropped a jar of jam, and licking their fingers. He found refuge with two kind Quaker ladies who had been working in the famine relief organization. But he rushed right off, before he'd unpacked, to call at the Foreign Office to explain his mission. He was told to come back the next day. Each afternoon he presented himself, and each day he was put off "till tomorrow." Chicherin's press secretary sat with his back to folding doors, and my eager young brother persuaded himself that right behind those doors sat Chicherin, listening to him and every foreign visitor. Day after day, Adlai would launch into long eloquent speeches to the press secretary explaining what Russia should do about the Czarist debts and everything else, and why he should have a talk with Chicherin. He told me later that while he hardly expected Chicherin suddenly to burst through the door crying, "Ah, my boy, how right you are!" still, he lived in hopes.

Those interviews at the Foreign Office took only a little of his time, and he tramped miles seeing the famous city and talked endless hours with the few American and British correspondents stationed there, who usually came to eat at the house of the Quakers. Colonel Voevodsky, Nicholas Galitzene, Prince Rastislav, Ilya Tolstoy and other Russian refugees in America had asked him to look up their relatives caught behind the iron curtain, if he could, discreetly. Countess Tolstoy, who as curator of the Tolstoy Museum was tolerated by the regime, became Adlai's guide in Moscow. But it was a good thing that my brother has a phenomenal memory because of course he didn't dare carry any list of names which might have been seriously embarrassing to people who still lived in dread of "the terror" and the knock at the door. The few he located, in Moscow and Leningrad, seemed happy to take a chance on at least one surreptitious meeting with an American, to get news of their relatives and give Adlai messages to carry back.

After a month in Moscow, when he still hadn't seen Chicherin, even Adlai's patience was exhausted, and he asked for his passport, bid good-by to his friends in need in Moscow, and left for Leningrad. If his dream of the "big story" had come to nothing, at least he'd had a firsthand look at the Communists, their methods, and a bit of their country, that was enormously valuable in later encounters with the Russian diplomats after the war. (It was especially useful when he headed the U.N. Preparatory Commission in London nineteen years later and negotiated with the Russians day and night.) After a week in Leningrad, he left for home by way of Finland and Sweden, in October of 1926, while Mother was saying to me in Switzerland, "Oh, if only I could get hold of Adlai to ask his advice about this."

"This" was my falling in love! Mother and I had gone from Italy to Valmont, above the lake of Geneva near Montreux, to spend a few peaceful weeks. Mother was taking a "cure" for a digestive upset and stayed in bed, so I roamed around alone. In the dining room, I soon noticed a very handsome young man who kept looking at me. A day or so later, in the lounge, we both reached at the same moment for the Paris *Herald* in the newspaper rack.

"Are you an American?" I asked.

"No, a Swede," he said, in a drawl straight out of Virginia. He introduced himself—Ernest Ives, secretary at the American embassy in Constantinople, in Valmont to take a cure for neuritis in his shoulder.

We went walking that afternoon to the Château de Chillon, and that night I wrote in my diary: "This is a terrific attraction!!! Guess Adlai's in Russia by now."

The next morning I told mother I'd met *such* an attractive man. She laughed and said, "Oh, Buffie, you're always meeting such an attractive man."

Something must have made her realize this one was different, because she asked me to bring him up for tea on her balcony. Ernest was his usual easy, charming self. He told my dieting mother, "You shouldn't live on that gruel and weak tea. What you need is a cold bird and a bottle!" I think she decided that what *we* needed was a chaperone, because she came down to every meal from then on. Not that it made any difference! Three days after we'd met, Ernest and I were engaged. On the fourth day, I borrowed a huge tome from him—I think it was Satow's *Diplomatic Practice*—because I wanted to show an interest in his work. I never did get beyond the first chapter, but by then it didn't seem to matter.

Ernest had been consul in Alexandria, and when he discovered I wanted to see Egypt, he suggested we go there on our honeymoon. Next he decided we should marry right away, while he was on leave. And *that's* when Mother wished she could get hold of Adlai.

She persuaded Ernest and me that a few months' separation was only reasonable. Ernest saw us off on the train for Paris, and after he'd left our compartment, I flung my hat in the rack and wept. He wrote me saying he'd watched me through the train window, and I was horrified that he'd seen me looking such a red-eyed disheveled mess. I'd had some fancy photographs taken to use for my theatrical job hunting, so I hurriedly dispatched one of those "seen through a retouched mist" poses to my fiancé. I was glad it found a better use than being on file in an agent's office.

In Paris, Ernest's ex-chief, Mr. Thackara, the consul general, came to tea and told me jovially, "Oh, lots of girls have thought they were going to marry Ernest Ives." Clearly, he thought I was another of those over-optimistic maidens. On the ship going home, pretty Mrs. James Duke had the deck chair next to mine and regaled me with warnings about the difficulties of marrying into the diplomatic service, and all the moving from post to post. She forgave me for not heeding a single warning, and was a dear about helping me pick up last-minute trousseau packages three months later.

Mother had agreed that I could go back to Europe to meet Ernest (also his mother and sister) early the following year, and to be married in Naples. Then we'd have our coveted honeymoon in Egypt before reporting back to the embassy in Constantinople. But when Father heard of all this, he simply exploded. There I was, planning to marry a stranger he hadn't even seen. (He certainly couldn't have missed seeing *pictures* of Ernest, because I had them propped up all over the house.) Mother assured Father she approved of my choice, and Adlai backed me up all the way. He was already working a fifty-hour-week in the law office but he took the time to do all kinds of thoughtful things for me. Father calmed down somewhat, and Adlai handled the an-

nouncement of my engagement in the papers and also persuaded my parents to establish a trust fund for me, because
he thought when I was going to live so far away I should
feel I had some money of my own.

Father had decided he would go over to "give me away"—
or snatch me back; I wasn't sure which. He kept saying,
"Now Buffie, I want it understood that if I don't like your
young man when I meet him in Naples, you'll call off the
wedding at once and come right back home with me."
Naturally, that made me more nervous than ever. Adlai not
only talked to Father but, as I found out later, wrote him
a long letter which must have been very persuasive indeed,
judging by Father's sudden shift from roaring lion to lamb.

The night I sailed, two still faithful beaux took me to the
boat and acted very sad and doubtful, as if I were about to
jump off a cliff. If Father still felt doubtful, he was hiding
his feelings nobly.

In my cabin, I found a bon-voyage note from Mother:

> My blessed child:
>   . . . I am in such a happy state of rejoicing and gratitude
> that you are to have one of life's best experiences that I can't
> be sad a moment. And when I realize, and you must, that your
> father has dropped everything to be your companion, I can't
> be humble enough in grateful thanksgiving.
>   . . . Just know that Nature has her rights and adhere to your
> rules for good health of Mind and body. Be of good cheer, for
> Life is wonderful and love is its greatest blessing.
>   Farewell, my own precious child
>   Mother

There were cheering telegrams from friends too, and I
remember being amused because the Ochses wired something about "Sailing the matrimonial seas."

The one that meant most was from my brother:

THERE IS NO PARTING. BON VOYAGE.
BEST LOVE TO YOU BOTH. ADLAI.

A few days later I wrote him from midocean:

Dearest Adlai:

You can't imagine what an effect your splendid letter had on Father. He has done everything possible to help me and not fret me, and I do appreciate your tact and understanding in writing to him as you did.

Your letter (to me) was wonderful, and it is so good that we can express the nearness we feel. I love you more than anyone in the world and revere you more. . . . We are destined to have long times together and we may know how to value them more then, and get more from one another. I am thinking now of our trip last summer, and how near you and Mother and I are. Remember that no duty will ever be more sacred to me than my sisterhood to you, and I shall rejoice to cross lands and seas for you.

. . . We enjoyed Madeira today, quaint and lovely, a nice place to hide! I am terribly impatient to get to Naples and to be on our way to Egypt.

You should hear OLD PAPA tell me he thinks you have a "master mind, and altho' a boy, one of the great men he has ever known." He has utter awe of you, as I have love and confidence.

Buffie

Chapter 11

T HE FIRST TIME I had the odd feeling that our lives were thrust under a floodlight for strangers to examine, was a cold day in February of 1948, when Adlai launched his campaign for Governor of Illinois, at a reception in our old home in Bloomington.

My brother had been practicing law in Chicago for twenty years, broken by long intervals of government service in Washington and abroad. In 1928, he had married Ellen Borden, and they were living with their three sons on a little farm near Libertyville, forty miles north of Chicago. I had spent most of my married life in six different countries, wherever my husband was stationed in the Foreign Service. (I think it's an amusing coincidence that the villa we lived in while Ernest was consul general in Algiers later became Eisenhower's headquarters.) Adlai had visited us during our assignments to Copenhagen and Belfast, and we had had occasional reunions in Bloomington. Twice he had the full responsibility and anguish when our parents died, Father in 1929 and Mother in 1935, when I was far away across the sea with my husband and baby.

After thirty years of foreign service, Ernest retired and

we came back to America for keeps. With our son Tim we spent part of the summers in Bloomington in the old family home, and the winters on a 115-acre farm we'd bought in North Carolina, near Southern Pines. My husband and I were sitting peacefully in our lovely log cabin at the farm, before a crackling pine fire, when I opened Adlai's letter that was to change our lives, written on New Year's night, 1948.

In the letter, he said the Democratic State Central Committee had asked him to run for Governor of Illinois, and that he had accepted, although he wondered if he'd be "thick enough skinned" to take the slings and arrows of politics. (What a long time ago that seems!) He asked if I'd come to Illinois in midwinter to open up the Bloomington house, so that he might launch his campaign in the place that still was home to us. Ernest and I forgot all about being "retired." I was very much stirred at the thought of another Adlai Stevenson running for Governor, to serve the state our forebears had helped settle. I wrote my brother that we'd come up early in February.

It still warms my heart to think of the way our friends in Bloomington responded with offers of help, as soon as they heard the news. Republicans and Democrats alike—their pride and affection for Adlai cut through any political mists. They even called me in North Carolina to ask if they could get the plumbers in to turn on the water, and order the invitations for the reception so they'd be ready by the time we arrived.

Ernest and I took off from the farm in the midst of a freak Southern ice and snowstorm; the roads were so icy that our tractor had to cut a path for the car across the fields. Our cook, Ola McLaurin, had sportingly accepted the

challenge too, so there were the three of us making the
rugged trip, through snows and floods. It was good to reach
Bloomington and have our housekeeper, dear Alverta Duff,
standing at the door as usual, to welcome us. Thirty-two
years before, when Father was running for secretary of state
of Illinois, he had asked her, "Alverta, are you going to vote
for me?"

"Certainly not, Mr. Stevenson," she'd said. "I'm a Republican. The only time I'll ever vote Democrat will be the day
Adlai's running."

Now that the day had come, Alverta made a terrible face
and muttered, "Bah, don't know why Adlai wants to have
anything to do with politics."

I knew she was as proud and excited as I was, and so I
didn't take her remark seriously, but the sad truth is that
too many Americans say "politics" as if it were a dirty word,
forgetting that some of the greatest men in our country, including Jefferson and Lincoln, were politicians. I get indignant whenever I encounter that attitude, because my brother
and I were brought up in the tradition that politics and public service should be high and honorable callings in a democracy.

It's rather embarrassing to admit that although we'd been
born into a "political" family, I was incredibly ignorant of
the practical side of politics. As one small sample of my
naïveté, when Adlai had mentioned a reception, I pictured
it as a small gathering for our friends and relatives! As the
invitation list grew longer and longer, I had my first lesson
in the intricate network or groundwork of politics: local,
county and state Democratic committees, chairmen and
workers, candidates, and so on. Soon the list added up to
four hundred people, not including the press and radio.

By noon of that day, technicians were dashing around laying wires and setting up "mikes" in our drawing room—the room that my brother and I had entered practically on tiptoe, as children. Reporters and photographers were everywhere; at one point, I remember seeing a pile of used flash-bulbs in the seat of a wing-backed Queen Anne chair, as if a strange bird had nested and laid eggs in that unlikely spot, and I hoped distractedly that nobody would sit on them. The reporter from *Time* asked me something or other, and I thought with surprise, Why, that's a *personal* question.

All the press wanted Adlai, and he was up on our old sleeping-porch writing-room finishing the speech he was to give that afternoon. I knew enough to say, "He can't be disturbed now," but later, when a photographer asked again, I said innocently and truthfully, "He's shaving." Instantly, several of the men asked if they could "take a few shots of your brother shaving," and I was so anxious to be helpful and adaptable in this strange new situation that I said, "Well, I'll see." I slipped up the backstairs to ask Adlai, not realizing that two enterprising photographers were right at my heels. My brother was standing in the bathroom with the door open, razor in hand. When I said, "May they photograph you shaving?" he looked astonished and said, "Certainly not." Then he saw the photographers behind me, cameras already raised, and managed to shut the bathroom door with his foot, just in time. I was to learn that there's seldom a closed season on "shooting" a candidate. Adlai had worked closely with the press during his wartime assignments for the Navy, and his peace-building assignments to the United Nations. But that day of his debut into politics started a glare and blare of publicity, and for my reticent and modest brother, it was not an easy kind of relationship for him to get used to.

But he adapted himself to all the uncomfortable exposures with high good humor, and I am sure it meant a lot to have his oldest friends around him. Even his first-grade teacher, Miss Kitty Cowles, had come to wish him well. I could tell by looking at him how happy he was to be "home." And he seemed to have a kind of cheerful confidence and strength that came from believing in what he was doing.

In his brief speech that afternoon, he said:

> . . . I think the efficiency, the simple honesty—the quality, in short—of government by the people must improve all along the line; at the city level, at the state level, as well as the national, if it is going to compete successfully for allegiance; if it is even going to hold our own faith and respect. Already too many people think of state elections as merely the quadrennial struggle to decide which set of politicians will dispense the patronage for the next four years.
>
> I think that government must be the efficient, effective agent of a responsible citizenry, not the shelter of the incompetent and the corrupt. It must be the positive business of all of us, and beneath the dignity of none of us. It must be the honorable calling the founders of a government by the governed meant it to be.
>
> Few people express any pride in the quality of the government of Illinois; many, Republicans, Democrats and Independents alike, are indignant about it. So am I. And that's why I've undertaken to run for Governor.

I should mention right now that my brother would never attack a political opponent without a good, strong, honest reason. In fact, he bends almost too far backward trying to be fair, but once he sees something really wrong, he comes out fighting. Many well-meaning friends and supporters who were outraged by the spoils system and stories of corruption in the state at that time still advised Adlai not to say anything against the opposition. But in the face of the serious charges of kickbacks, padded payrolls, shakedowns, gambling alliances and so on, to have kept quiet would have been pussy-footing and tantamount to condoning practices altogether too prevalent. In his second speech that opening day of the campaign, at a dinner given by the McLean County Democratic organization, he spoke emphatically and spared neither party.

> This machine [Republican] which has degraded, corrupted and corroded the public service in Illinois must be destroyed. Its foundations must be uprooted and the earth scorched so that another can't rise in its place—whether it bears the trademark of the overfed elephant or the lean donkey.

Perhaps the reason I've never gotten tired of hearing my brother speak is that his words are never canned oratory, mouthed automatically. From the outset I found interesting indicators of his sincerity and his impact on others in the faces of hard-boiled reporters in the audience. At the start of a speech, they so often looked bored or skeptical; back in 1948, they even looked a little pitying, waiting to hear a man they considered a political amateur—a man they felt had been flung to the wolves as a political sacrifice. Soon they were listening to him intently, and by the end they were applauding. As one Chicago newsman wrote wryly afterward, "Put away your handkerchiefs. Don't cry for Stevie. He was a smash hit."

Another said, "A clean shirt, good grammar and the manners of a gentleman don't mean that a fellow can't put up a tough fight. Stevenson is punching the ears off the opposi-

202 *MY BROTHER ADLAI*

tion in his campaign, and the Republican machine mob is
going to have to learn some new tricks. . . . He is putting
up the sort of fight that pleases the honest American. He
has brought to light shameful larceny, deliberate neglect of
duty, and unpardonable extravagance."

Of course, I was delighted to see how quickly the newsmen recognized my brother's qualities, but I'm a little mystified about where the idea ever got started that Adlai was an
idealistic amateur and could think but not act. I've never
known him when he wasn't in action. As Arthur Krock of
The New York Times wrote, Adlai was "one of the archi-
tects of the United Nations," and in negotiations in London
and New York he had shown such top Russians as Vishinsky
and Gromyko that he could take care of himself and his
country. On the business side, my brother was a successful
lawyer, the director of a Chicago bank and business com-
panies, and the careful manager of the farms we'd inherited
in Illinois, Indiana and Iowa. I also knew him as a man you
could go to when you were worried by a problem, and when
you came away, you wondered why you'd ever been so
worried.

People who had worked with him in Chicago on civic
projects had told me the same thing. For years, he'd been
an officer of the Illinois Children's Home and Aid Society,
a trustee of Hull House, President of the Legislative Voters'
League, a director of International House at the University
of Chicago and of the Immigrants Protective League, and
an active champion of civil rights for all. As head of the
Chicago Council of Foreign Relations, he had fought against
isolationism for years before Pearl Harbor proved how right
he was.

Archibald MacLeish, who was Assistant Secretary of State

during World War II, once told me, "Adlai was doing far more responsible war work than was generally recognized. Everyone who had to do with him in Washington in the days when he was assistant to Secretary Knox soon learned that the best way to get action in some places in the Navy Department was through Adlai. I had a mean chore in the fall of 1941 and '42 trying to develop a government information policy and program. The only way I could act was through an inter-departmental committee which met once a week and tried to fashion consistent policies for all the agencies of government in order to keep the people properly informed in those dramatic, early days of the war. Jack McCloy represented the Army, Francis Biddle the Justice Department, Ben Cohen for the White House, Jimmy Dunn for State, and so on. Adlai represented the Navy. He said little but did a lot to increase the flow of information. It was then I began to realize how effective he could be and so, I think, did a lot of others."

Now that Adlai was in politics, it wasn't just newsmen who saw that he knew what he was about. When the long entrenched opposition became alarmed at the way listeners were responding to the force and honesty of his refreshing eloquence, they tried to discredit Adlai by labeling him "a cookie-pusher striped-pants diplomat." So far as I know, my brother had never even owned a pair of striped pants. In fact, he had such a dogged fondness for old clothes that friends had already taken me aside to beg, "See if you can get him to give up wearing that battered raincoat when he's campaigning."

I tackled Adlai, and he said indignantly, "What's wrong with this coat? It's perfectly good." He was equally loyal to an old hat that was really only fit to stick fishhooks into, and several suits he'd worn for years. His attitude reminded me of that sturdy line of Thoreau's: "Beware of all enterprises that require new clothes." We were enormously amused by these assaults of his opponent and *The Chicago Tribune*. Then some long-memoried reporter on the *Chicago Daily News* dug into the files and came up chortling, with a photograph of the Republican candidate dapperly attired in top hat, cutaway, and striped pants. When this appeared in the paper, readers roared with laughter, and the opposition dropped that nonsense in a hurry.

Adlai, unheard of in most of the state, was running his campaign on a shoestring, against the richest, most deeply entrenched machine in Illinois history. Once he phoned me to ask if I had enough in my bank account to pay for some billboards that had been ordered. Luckily, I did. It was several thousand dollars (which he later repaid), and that was only one of the many basic costs of campaigning I'd never given a thought to, till then.

I think the best kind of campaign fund would be for every registered voter to contribute one dollar to the candidate or party of his preference. All too often, special interest groups are large contributors in exchange for favors promised or expected, and my brother's orders were to refuse or return all such money. Moreover he wasn't given much chance of election in what looked like an overwhelming Republican year—1948. So his campaign fund was "poor but honest," and we all had to scramble to keep it alive. I had never before contributed a cent to a political campaign, and the idea of asking other people for money seemed to me like begging alms. But our wise and dear friend Mrs. Florence Fifer Bohrer of Bloomington, a Republican, who had been the first woman senator in the Illinois legislature, said to me, "If people want good government, then they must spend their time or their money or both, to support a good candidate and help him get into office."

She made me realize how foolish I'd been; I sat right down and wrote to all our relatives and friends, asking for contributions. Some of them gave and some of them didn't. I'll admit that I felt rather bitter when people who had said over and over how much it would mean to have a man of Adlai's integrity and ability in office, failed to support him in any way. But not once did my brother act resentful. He'd say, "You must remember they have their reasons."

When a candidate never loses his sense of justice, his humor or his ideals, and is willing to work himself like a dray horse, there's an unselfishness of spirit that sparks everybody around him. Jim Mulroy, a well known newspaper man in Chicago, was Adlai's "manager". His old friends Hermon Dunlap Smith and Mrs. Edison Dick, both Republicans, headed the Independents-for-Stevenson group, and did a brilliant job. ("Dutch" Smith, Ed McDougal, Louis Kohn and Steve Mitchell were the ones who had first urged my brother to get into the 1948 campaign, and Colonel Jacob Arvey, who was chairman of the Democratic Cook County Committee, was their early and powerful ally.) I want to say right now that I learned a great deal from seasoned party workers, and I came to have a humble respect for people who take citizenship seriously enough to ring doorbells in their own precinct and get out the vote. Those veteran campaigners and many eager new volunteers teamed up and accomplished miracles, all over the state. Some of our volunteers were youngsters, and how they worked, doing everything from addressing envelopes to distributing thousands of leaflets. One boy in blue jeans said to me earnestly, "Your brother says the things about government we've been waiting to hear. He's *got* to win."

My husband was one of the hardest workers in Bloomington, although he has the Virginian's charming trait of being so calm and easy and quiet-voiced that you don't realize till later all he's accomplishing. He found one-room headquarters in the Klemm Building for our Volunteers-for-Stevenson group, and helped get contributions and even went around putting up signs. Our son Tim, when he came home from the University of Virginia for his summer vacation, sometimes drove his uncle on speech-making trips, in his Chevrolet.

In the Chevvy, Adlai would prop his brief case on his knees and work on a speech. Occasionally he'd glance out at the country, and his face would light up, and he'd say, "The corn looks fine this year." Then he'd go back to making pencil corrections on his script. Newsmen who covered his campaign were soon commenting that he not only wrote his own speeches, but that he even knew what he was talking about. When he spoke to farmers at the Dewitt County Fair, the *Joliet Herald* reported, "He discussed problems like an agricultural expert, and not like so many spell-binders."

I never could understand why there was any surprise about his knowledge of agriculture. After all that was his father's business, he had been raised in the heart of the Corn Belt, much of his inheritance was in farm land and his very first job in government was in the Department of Agriculture in the depths of the depression. I'd also been rather amused at the people who told Adlai he mustn't mention Grandfather but "stand on his own two feet." I think only timid, watered-down descendants of great men are afraid to acknowledge their heritage. Adlai was proud of his—and so were the people of Illinois. They *wanted* this Stevenson to remember his link to the first Adlai, and they sent him their precious mementoes of his campaigns as tokens of their faith and interest—buttons, luster plates, shaving mugs, ashtrays and bandanna handkerchiefs with pictures of Grandfather and Grover Cleveland in 1892 or with William Jennings Bryan in 1900. All sorts of things turned up—walking sticks, gavels, paperweights, torchlights and plug hats. A farmer and his wife brought in an old brown earthenware pitcher, and explained that when Grandfather was riding around Illinois, stopping for leisurely visits with constituents, he always sat under a tree in their side yard and drank buttermilk or cider served in that very pitcher. Adlai was rather envious at the thought of that relaxed, personal, olden-time kind of campaigning. Once he said, "Imagine—Grandfather could get along with a few good speeches and use them over and over, but now with the wire services and rapid reporting, a candidate is supposed to say something new every time he opens his mouth." There were several of Grandfather's famous stories my brother used himself (giving credit, of course). One was about the Kentucky lawyer who concluded his thunderous address to the jury with, "Now these, gentlemen, are the conclusions upon which I base my facts."

Adlai, a lawyer of quite a different breed, had made quite sure of his facts about the evils in the state government before he gave conclusions, and by midsummer, all of Illinois was learning how right he was. A gambler was murdered in Peoria, and when the *St. Louis Post-Dispatch* sent a reporter to investigate, officials tried to shunt him off. Immediately, most of the newspaper editors in the state got their backs up, and things got hotter and hotter. The *Post-Dispatch* reported in July, "The state as a whole is a mass of syndicated gambling operations. Dwight Green wants a third term as Governor. Yet he sits at the top of a State Government which presides over a vast, undermining corrupting underworld."

In theory, most people are against corruption and for reform, but sometimes I had the discouraged feeling, when Adlai outlined his program for good government, that the audience didn't much care. I went with him one day when he was to speak at a county fair. I think it was the first time his two older sons, Adlai III and Borden, appeared with him, and we were all perched on a raised wooden platform in a 100 degree broiling sun, at the edge of the race track where several thousand people sat. Borden and young Adlai looked rather dazed with the heat and the unaccustomedness of being on display, and I remember I felt like a poached egg. My brother was speaking very earnestly to his large audience in the grandstand sprawled along the race course about a program to remedy the neglect of rural roads and schools. Meanwhile, the horses were being led out for the trotting races to follow, the drivers were already sitting in their sulkies and the crowd was impatient. I thought indignantly, They think a political speaker is a fill-in before the main event. He's talking about the money they pay in taxes, and how it could be used to benefit them and their children, and they don't even care. Adlai suddenly halted his earnest speech, laughed and said, "Well, even if I'm running for Governor, I can't run in competition with horses." Then he sat down. The audience cheered; not even a horse got a bigger hand than the candidate for Governor, that day! I realized then that good politicians must know when to let go, without ever losing sight of their larger objectives.

My brother took a week off from campaigning that steamy summer to go to the Democratic National Convention in Philadelphia, where he seconded the nomination of our kinsman, Alben Barkley, for Vice-President.

In Illinois, there were still people who thought a candidate who put public welfare above party was too "impractical" to win, especially against so well-heeled an opposition. Money to finance the rest of Adlai's campaign was still hard to come by. There was too much of the wait-and-see attitude.

One August afternoon, a Bloomington house painter was putting a new coat of gray enamel on our front porch, and he and I got to talking about the old-fashioned political jamborees of the Gay Nineties. He said, "Your brother ought to have a big barbecue with free beer and entertainment."

There was no money for such an ambitious project in the Bloomington campaign fund, and anyway, I was sure my brother if I told him about it would veto the idea of wooing votes with beer. But the more the painter and I talked, the more I thought something like the old-fashioned political rallies should be done. Finally I decided that when Adlai came to Bloomington to speak we might have a big parade patterned on the torchlight procession that had welcomed Grandfather home after he was elected Vice-President.

I mentioned this idea to several people, and almost overnight, a wonderful thing happened. It ceased to be a political "stunt," and changed into a warmly spontaneous home-town tribute to Adlai. Republicans, Independents, old and new Democrats—everybody wanted to lend a hand. The League of Women Voters hauled their great-grandmothers' carefully saved clothes out of trunks in attics, to loan for costumes. Farmers came in to offer their prize livestock and old buggies, for the parade. Children brought in their pets, squealing, cawing, barking or braying, so we started a Pet Section and a Best Decorated Bicycle entry. Somebody found an old kerosene torch, and we had it copied, right down to the hinged lids with wicks.

When we suddenly realized that all the floats would have to be wired for electricity to show up at night, I went to one of the richest Republicans in town, an elderly lady cast in the same iron mold as another friend who'd explained to Adlai, "If God Himself were running on the Democratic ticket, I couldn't bring myself to vote for Him." I said to her, "We've just got to have fifty dollars more for wiring," and she reached for her checkbook and said, "Why, of course. I've known Adlai since he was a baby, and I think he deserves the biggest parade ever."

Alice Rawson Mulliken was the chairman, and her imaginative ideas and energy galvanized all of us. Tim, Ernest and I worked on a float in our back yard—Three Generations of Stevensons—with huge blown-up pictures of Grandfather, Father and my brother, and the slogan, "Stevensons Have Served the State and Nation." While we were frantically hammering nails into the boards for backing, the man who had enlarged the photographs came to our house to deliver them, and he stayed all afternoon, to help us finish our carpenter work.

My brother knew in a vague way we were planning a parade, but he was so busy campaigning around the state that he never came to Bloomington until the evening we'd set—September 16. We all went over to Mrs. Bohrer's on Franklin Square to assemble, and I'll never forget the expression on Adlai's face as a girl in a fringed buckskin Indian costume went past him, followed by a child leading a duck on a leash. Then a woman dashed by wearing a mammoth-brimmed Lily Langtry hat, and her plumes tickled Adlai's face and made his smile stretch even wider. When the handsome floats rolled into line and the marchers took their places for the mile-long pageant, my brother said in an awed tone, "I had no idea it was going to be like this. This is the most fun I've had in my long political career of eight months!"

Adlai rode at the head of the parade with Walter Bittner, in Walt's 1914-vintage car. In the procession behind him, there was everything from a man riding a bull, and cancan dancers cavorting, to a small, solemn boy leading a goat. One float was entirely covered with green branches, and the beautiful girl riding on it as Miss Evergreen City wore our mother's white satin wedding dress. I was wearing Great-grandmother Fell's Quaker bonnet, and was jouncing along on the Pioneer float with Florence Funk enjoying my one chance to be hauled by oxen. I saw Cousin Carl Vrooman stepping smartly along with the marchers, under a huge banner reading, "Bloomington's Best 'Ad.'"

There were more than 25,000 people watching that night; it was the biggest turn-out in Bloomington's political history. The parade ended at the courthouse square, and Adlai spoke there, where Great-grandfather Fell had addressed a meeting of grieving townsmen the day after Lincoln's assassination, and where Grandfather Stevenson had often spoken, too. My brother was introduced by our old friend, Republican Everett Ogilvie. There was no party line, no politics that night, just an affectionate tribute by a home town. Adlai was deeply moved, and he was very serious as he stood there on the platform above the vast crowd overflowing into the side streets and said:

I have Bloomington to thank for the most important lesson I have learned; that in quiet places, reason abounds, that in quiet people there is vision and purpose, that many things are revealed to the humble that are hidden from the great. . . . The spirit of Bloomington is the midland concept of Americanism, progress coupled with order, liberty without license, tolerance without laxness, thrift without meanness. . . . My home town has taught me that good government and good citizenship are one and the same, that good individuals make good towns and that nothing else does. Here I have learned that good communities make a good state and nothing else can.

Here from my parents and the immortal Joe Fifer, the friend of my boyhood, I learned that good government is good politics and that public office should double the responsibility that a man feels for his own home, his own neighborhood, his home town. I hope and pray I can remember the great truths that seem so obvious in Bloomington but so obscure in other places. . . .

All the top Democratic committeemen in the state had come down to Bloomington that evening, expecting to be mildly amused by our little homespun parade. They had scheduled a meeting right afterward, at the Illinois Hotel. When Adlai got home from that meeting, very late, he came into our bedroom, drew up a chair between Ernest's and my beds, and talked to us there in the dark. His voice was choked up when he told us, "Tonight was the turning point." The skeptical politicians, and there were many of them, had been impressed by the fullness and warmth of a home town's tribute. There was something in the air and they evidently sensed it. From then on, even contributions came in!

Adlai told us later about one funny incident that happened just after he got back to Chicago. He ran into a man he hardly knew, who said casually, "I just laid an election bet on you." When the man mentioned the amount of the bet, in five figures, Adlai nearly fell over backward. He told us, "I wasn't sure whether I was in, or that man was out— out of his wits!"

On Election night, Adlai was in his headquarters in Chicago, and a group of us who had worked in the campaign gathered in our Bloomington headquarters. Mary White, a telephone supervisor who had been one of the most effective volunteer workers and was state president of the Women's Trade Union League had had an extra phone installed, to receive returns. As the figures began to come in, we were all wildly excited, but I'll never forget the merriest, most radiant face in the room—Cousin Julia Vrooman's.

Adlai phoned us from Chicago to ask for the tally of votes by precincts and in the county. Joe Bohrer was the only one of us calm enough to give the information my brother wanted. Then I took the phone again and Adlai said matter-of-factly, "Well, that does it. We've won. I'll be making a statement now."

Only people who have put their whole hearts into a campaign know what a remark like that means.

Adlai was elected with the largest plurality of any candidate for Governor in Illinois history, 572,000 votes.

A few days later, my brother asked if he might come down to our farm with the Edison Dicks for a brief vacation, so Ernest and Ola and I went right back to North Carolina, to get ready for them. I remember Adlai's phoning me there to say rather apologetically, "Three reporters want to come too. Is it all right if I bring them along?" Once the idea of taking a vacation with the press would have stunned me, but by then, I was an old enough campaigner to say, "Of course." Adlai took our cook's room, and Ola moved out to our Civil War cotton gin, which we use as a garage and children's playroom.

Our log cabin sits on top of a small hill, with a view of pine forests for forty miles around. The furnishings are simple, very old pieces we've collected in Moore County. I think it was on that visit my brother looked around the living room and said, "I think this is just about the nicest room I've ever seen."

When he comes into our house, he walks about and savors things as if he were greeting old friends, and he notices if even one picture is changed. Then he goes off to change his clothes and get out on a horse. That fall was the only time he was ready to rest for a day or two, after the ten hectic months of incessant campaigning. Stretched out in the sun on the porch, he listened to the distant wail of a whistle on our little local line, The Aberdeen & Rockfish Railroad, and said dreamily, "How I love that sound. I always did." We set up a table under a tree, where he worked on his mail and memoranda, but sometimes I'd find him sprawled on the ground asleep.

He and Ernest and one or two of the newsmen played some golf that week. One afternoon I was following them around at the Pinehurst course, and Charles Wheeler of the *Chicago Daily News* was walking with me. He said suddenly, "With the plurality your brother got, he's going to be the next Democratic Presidential nominee."

I was so startled I must have gaped like a fish. Mr. Wheeler laughed. "You'll see," he said.

When I finally got up nerve to mention it to Adlai, he said, "Buffie! You mustn't pay any attention to remarks like that. My ambition and my only ambition is to be the best Governor Illinois ever had. And if you ever again hear such talk, promise me you won't encourage it."

I promised!

Chapter 12

AFTER ADLAI MOVED into the beautiful old Governor's Mansion in Springfield, in January of 1949, I saw more of him than at any time since we were children, because I stayed there frequently and served as my brother's hostess.

I won't try to pretend that the first year was easy—for any of us. In September, after the relentless ordeal of organizing a new administration and a six months session of the legislature, Adlai gave this statement to the press: "I am deeply distressed that due to the incompatibility of our lives, Mrs. Stevenson feels that a separation is necessary. Although I don't believe in divorce, I will not contest it. We have separated with the highest mutual regard."

My brother locks his deepest feelings inside himself, and I respect his reticence. I sensed that he was going through the most difficult period of his life, but he never discussed it, and no one had seen anyone work so hard as the new Governor. Months later, in a speech, he said, "I like my job; it has been worth the painful sacrifices."

Sometimes late at night I'd go down to his office in the basement of the Mansion, and find Adlai working in shirt sleeves at his desk, with his Dalmatian dog, Artie, sleeping at his feet. My brother would be reading through a mound of reports, or making notes on his ever-present long yellow pad. He'd look up with his warm, quick smile, take off the horn-rimmed glasses he wears for close work, and offer me an apple from the bowl of fruit on his desk. We'd talk for five or ten minutes—often about the news in family letters—and then I'd know he wanted to get back to state business. Once I said something about "You're at it twenty-four hours a day," and he laughed. "Buffie, you're exaggerating again. This job only take a seventy-five-hour week, but no less!"

The only times he arranged his schedule to take a whole day off were when his sons spent part of their school vacations at the Mansion with him. Alverta Duff, who came up from Bloomington several Christmases, watched my brother starting off one afternoon trap shooting, with young Adlai, Borden and John Fell, and she said, "I remember when the boys were little, Adlai would be down on all fours, while the boys climbed all over him, and all laughing their heads off. He's still the same kind of father."

This reminds me of the first speech Borden ever made, in the 1952 campaign, when he was a student at Harvard and went into Boston when Mr. Truman was speaking there at a Democratic rally. Somebody spotted my nephew in the audience, and they brought him up on the platform and insisted he "say a few words." Nineteen-year-old Borden put his hands in his pockets and said earnestly, "If my dad is elected and can be as good a president as he's been a father, I know the country's safe."

In 1949, Adlai was already being that good a governor, and Illinois could hardly hope for more, although there were patronage seekers who'd hoped for more. When he took office, there were 500 state police on the payroll, for example. The custom was that each new administration would turn these good jobs over to their own party followers. Adlai dumbfounded everybody by saying that from then on, the state police would be out of politics—they would *be* police. He asked that the men be selected and advanced on the merit system, and, if you please, that the jobs be divided equally between Republicans and Democrats! The howls were awful but the reform was fine. After the bill passed and the new police force was organized my brother used it, and mighty effectively, to smash commercial gambling and break the strangle hold that racketeers had had for many years. With his reconstituted police force he could also get at last effective and honest enforcement of the laws against overweight trucks.

When Adlai discovered that several state inspectors had taken bribes to permit the sale of horse meat as beef for hamburgers, he himself headed the investigation, fired the suspects at once and passed the evidence on to the prosecutors for action. One of these men, who'd had a high reputation for honesty, was an appointee of Adlai's, and my brother was shocked and upset, but he refused all suggestions to hush it up or shift the blame: "This is my responsibility and I want the whole mess made public and cleaned up openly."

As soon as he got wind of the counterfeiting of cigarette revenue stamps, he brought in a former F.B.I. man to conduct a secret investigation that got to the roots of the organized racket. Then the police, in a swift series of raids, caught the culprits red-handed. Adlai has said, "Corruption in public office is treason," and he dealt with it as ruthlessly as sabotage.

During his first months as Governor, he abolished 1300 unnecessary jobs, and raised the much-too-low salaries of other state employees. I remember how indignant he was when he found that workmen's compensation cases had piled up for literally years, waiting settlement. One of his first acts as Governor was to see that the backlog was cleared up, and from then on, most compensation cases were settled in three months instead of three years.

My brother believes strongly that each state should take care of its own affairs as much as possible, instead of being dependent on Federal agencies, but as he said, "Too many of the problems of states' rights have been created by states' wrongs." To help straighten out the mess of "wrongs" in Illinois, he set up a "Little Hoover" commission headed by Walter Schaefer, an old Chicago friend and one of the brilliant, experienced men he had persuaded to come to Springfield. Another was Carl McGowan, his top administrative aide, who had been a professor of law at Northwestern, and had worked with Adlai in Washington. Carl is a quiet, contained man with an integrity and inner force you feel even on meeting him, and a remarkably clear, concise mind and conscience. Whenever they were considering a new program, Carl, like Adlai, wanted to know not only "can Illinois afford it" but "can Illinois afford not to have it?" He helped Adlai with policy and program, and also advised on legislative strategy when the General Assembly was in session. Paul Powell, Democratic speaker of the House, did a fine job of lining up support for the administration's program.

The night our first legislative session adjourned, in June of 1949, I stayed down at the capitol till 5:30 A.M., to watch the finish. The sun was up and the birds were twittering when Adlai brought several of the legislators back with us to the Mansion. We all sat around the marble-topped table in the kitchen, having scrambled eggs and milk and coffee. As I listened to the men talking and joking, I had a good, warm feeling that even many of the politicians who had groaned at first over Adlai's highly unorthodox and non-partisan methods had come around to see that doing what's best for the people actually pays off politically.

In a radio report to the whole state, Adlai said:

In spite of difficulties, in spite of many disappointments, the Assembly enacted about two-thirds of the legislation I particularly recommended. I think I'm fortunate to have got that much of what I told the people I would try to do—especially when I proposed probably the most extensive and ambitious program any Governor has ever tried to enact in a single session. Maybe we tried to do too much all at once. Probably we did, but I think campaign talk should be more than sweet, deceitful words. It's easy to talk big and act small when the responsibility suddenly falls on you like a ton of coal.

When he took office, Illinois stood almost at the bottom of the list in the entire country, in state per capita aid to local schools, so he was especially happy to tell his listeners, in that same radio report:

. . . I think our major achievement has been in legislation pointing the way to better schools, approved by both houses almost unanimously. Not only have we provided more money than ever before [more than double] but with the advice of an advisory committee of experienced specialists we worked out reasonable and attainable permanent objectives for the Illinois common school system and the legislature adopted many of them. Our problem is not simply more and more money for schools, but how to make the most of it; how to provide our grade and high school children all over the State with basic education of a breadth and depth which will fit them for the world in which they must live.

He explained to voters why he thought the state needed to revise its eighty-year-old constitution, "to correct obsolete, wasteful and unjust practices of our governments—State and local." Adlai's bill asking that the people of Illinois be allowed to vote on constitutional revision was defeated in the Republican legislature. As a next-best substitute, he had endorsed the Gateway Amendment, permitting three amendments to the constitution to be placed before voters at one time. He told his radio listeners simply and clearly why he hoped they'd vote for it.

One of the many nice traits of my brother is his open-mindedness toward other people's ideas. Mrs. Laura Lunde of the League of Women Voters suggested we dramatize the Gateway Amendment, which would come before voters on a blue ballot, by having a Blue Ballot luncheon at the Mansion for the heads of twenty-three women's organizations. We even wanted all-blue food! My brother, instead of hooting at the notion, said, "Fine, go ahead." When I worked out the menu with the Mansion housekeeper, Mrs. Van Diver, and the cook, Gertie Dent, they were very cooperative, although I think they were a little dubious at first, wondering if we'd all be poisoned and turn blue. Gertie, who was a magnificent cook, produced everything from blue *Vichyssoise* to blueberry tarts. Adlai took time out from his crammed schedule to come in briefly and greet the ladies, and I was touched and pleased when I saw that in honor of our azure occasion, he was wearing a blue suit, blue pin-striped shirt and blue tie. Soon thousands of women were spreading the facts on the Blue Ballot throughout the state— and it passed.

222   *MY BROTHER ADLAI*

When it came to my ideas for supplying some much needed color to the Executive Mansion, Adlai kept an absolutely firm hand on the budget. "Economy's got to begin right here," he said. On one of our first evenings there, Ernest and I persuaded Adlai to take a before-bedtime walk, and as we came back to the Mansion, my brother exclaimed, "Why, the whole place is blazing! Lights on in every room— and nobody using them. I never want to see that again." He always turned out lights when he left a room, and the rest of us had to learn to do the same. Twice, bats got in and circled and swooped through the shadowy halls. Probably they liked his dusky lighting effects.

The twenty-eight-room Mansion is a beautiful old house, spacious, graceful, with a dignity reminiscent of the great Southern houses. The first floor was given over to "official" rooms; it was the custom for women's clubs and auxiliary groups upon request to use the music room and two front "parlors" for teas. The Governor's receptions were held there, and we used the big state dining room for official dinner parties. It had elaborate gold and crystal chandeliers and the walnut paneling had been enameled white, but what bothered me was the stained, dirty Scalamandré silk on the chairs. I got an estimate from an upholsterer on having them recovered, but Adlai took one look at the figure ($2000) and said, "No!" so I had them cleaned and dyed gold. In the family dining room, we had slip covers so we wouldn't spot the gold silk.

Our quarters were on the second floor, and Adlai had one of the large bedrooms opening off the center stair well. From my room, I could see the capitol dome, and the historic old house of John Todd Stuart, Lincoln's law partner. I had enthusiastic plans for repapering several of the bedrooms

which the former Governor's daughters had evidently decorated by tacking up school banners. Adlai nipped this ex-
penditure too. "Just put up a few pictures to cover those
marks on the walls."

It seemed sad to us that so many of the portraits and fine
old furniture that belonged to the Mansion's long past had
been removed. We finally fitted out one bedroom with gifts
to the state of early Governors' furniture. Adlai was eager
to have some pictures around, so I brought down some family
portraits from Bloomington. Jay Monaghan of the State
Historical Library loaned the Mansion the Waldo portrait
of General Shadrach Bond, the first Governor, and Healy's
beautiful one of Mrs. Richard Yates, the Civil War Governor's wife.

One of the first things Adlai did, when he became Governor, was to discourage the hanging of his picture in public
places in state buildings all over the state, an ancient practice
of which he highly disapproved. Once when he was making
up his Christmas gift list (and that's one time he forgets about
thrift), I suggested that several of his friends might like a
good photograph of him. He was appalled at the idea: "That's
a terrible kind of present to give." I said stoutly that *I'd* like
a picture, and he snorted. I considered it quite a victory
when he sent me up a memo one day months later: "Mrs.
Ives: [he addressed me very formally in office memos] Could
you put me in a cheap imitation leather bureau frame and
send one to each of the boys. A.E.S. P.S. Also one for you,
the attached."

The memos he sent on food amused me, because he had
an uncannily accurate memory for the number of duck, pheasants, baskets of home grown fruit or whatever friends and
friendly strangers had sent. One memo inquired wistfully,

"Mrs. Ives, what became of the goose I shot?" Another said, "Please check with Gertie. I think she must have six pheasants left. Would like two tomorrow when the B's are here for dinner." After he'd been out hunting, he must have wanted his bag of game to stretch, because I got a thrifty message, "One big duck should serve four people—four little people."

Adlai is of the school that likes wild duck and other game served very rare, as if it had barely walked past the stove. (I shudder involuntarily, as I write this.) He's very fond of fish, including fresh catfish, especially served with slaw. His esteem for turnips and squash is rather unusual. I think Gertie, the cook, was a little surprised at the Governor's enthusiasm for vegetables. His favorites are tomatoes, corn and eggplant. All through the summer, we had big platters of cold green beans, asparagus, beets—whatever was in season. The only request I relayed from my brother that caused the cook real anguish was, "May we have simple desserts sometimes?" She specialized in rich parfaits and pastries, and it broke her heart to give the Governor such piddling plain fare as baked pears or applesauce. But I noticed he never said no to her meringues filled with strawberries.

Dinner was usually at seven, unless a conference ran late. Adlai would come up from his office to join us for a drink beforehand—one bourbon and water. If there were no guests —and that was a rare day—sometimes he stretched out for five minutes on the sofa in the sunroom, relaxing. At dinner, the flow of good stories and good talk was a delight. His visitors —old friends and new—came from the four corners of the world and from all over the country. We had an incessant stream of newspapermen, domestic and foreign. Adlai's acquaintance from his travels and his years in Washington during the war and in diplomacy afterward was extensive and world-wide. Everyone seemed to come to Springfield—writers, statesmen, scholars, politicians, governors, congressmen, ministers, actors, labor leaders—and Adlai welcomed them all joyously. (But he kept a sharp and restless eye on the clock.) Of all his distinguished visitors, I think the one that caused the greatest excitement among my women friends in Springfield was John Mason Brown. How they envied me, having a brother who rated that witty, amusing John Mason Brown as an overnight guest. And I think André Siegfried's astonishing knowledge of Illinois political history interested Adlai most of all.

None of the staff slept in the house. The housekeeper and her husband, Captain Van Diver of the State Police, Adlai's driver and head of the police detail guarding the Mansion, lived in an apartment over the garage. The cook, butlers, houseman and two maids and laundress all went home at night. They discovered that when the new Governor said, "Breakfast at 8," he meant exactly that. He got up at 7:30, and if not very communicative in the morning, he is always bursting with impatience to get started at the day's work. I've seen him at 7 A.M. dashing from closet to bureau and putting things into a suitcase in his neat, compact way, before he took off on a trip so that he wouldn't have to think of it again. Once I protested that he wasn't taking enough underclothes and was briskly informed "these new textiles are easy to wash and simple to pack."

Punctuality, like neatness, is a passion of his. With several chores already ticked off, he'd sit down at the breakfast table at 8:00 on the dot, and eat with one hand while he went through the newspapers. He likes variety at breakfast, and he'd dive zestfully into codfish cakes or broiled tomatoes. He and I both gained weight on Gertie's cooking, so I started us on a reducing potion of yoghurt mixed into a glass of tomato juice, but I suspect my brother left out the yoghurt whenever he got a chance. He doesn't like "fad" foods, perhaps partly because we got such a dose of faddist health foods—if only vicariously—as children.

At the start, service even at breakfast was much too formal and slow for our taste; the table settings featured fancy lace mats and a centerpiece of roses so long-stemmed they drooped over to our plates. My brother O.K.'d my buying some plain blue linen mats, and gradually things looked and felt more homelike. I put a small table and chairs on the porch outside the dining room, and Adlai enjoyed having breakfast there in warm weather.

Promptly at nine, he'd go to his office in the basement. Two secretaries, Carol Evans and Margaret Munn, shared the next office; Carl McGowan and Bill Blair and sometimes another administrative aide were across the hall. Several members of the staff worked in the capitol building—Lawrence Irvin, Richard Nelson, Don Hyndman and William Flanagan. When the legislature was in session, Adlai, followed by Artie, often walked the three blocks to his office in the capitol—at a dogtrot. After William McCormick Blair Jr. joined the staff, in the summer of 1950, his tact and good humor and thoughtfulness smoothed out many a problem. He handled appointments, and the hundreds of invitations and requests that came to the Governor. I think Bill has a real genius for human relations.

The Governor and his staff and various "cabinet" members met every Thursday morning around the T-shaped conference table in his office. Adlai and one or more aides or visitors would lunch there on trays, or the Governor would have a men-only lunch in the dining room upstairs, with state officials, legislators or groups of visitors.

Fred Hoehler, one of the outstanding experts in the country, had agreed to come to Springfield to reorganize the Department of Welfare. (He had been in Europe as head of UNRA's Displaced Persons division.) To give just an idea of the "snake-pit" condition in state institutions when Fred took over, a bipartisan investigating committee had reported grimly that Illinois had one of the highest death tolls of patients who died in mental hospitals in suspicious circumstances. Many of the attendants were untrained political appointees. Adlai promised Fred Hoehler freedom from all political pressure in handling the work my brother called "our most important and poignant problem." Some 1100 new doctors, nurses and attendants were added to the seriously understaffed institutions without regard to their political views. New programs of research and organization of local clinics resulted in earlier diagnosis and more modern methods of intake, treatment and discharge. Patients, instead of all too often being left to sit hopelessly, shut up for the rest of their lives, could, in many cases, improve enough to go home. The administration opened a new research hospital to study the increasing problems of old age in a former army hospital in Galesburg, and experts from other states came to study what Illinois was doing. Another project close to my brother's heart was a new center for mentally ill children at the Peoria State Hospital. When Dr. Karl Menninger made an inspection tour in 1951, he reported that Illinois state institutions had improved so greatly during Adlai's administration that they were among the best in the nation. And, concerned with the way so many solvent patients were supported by the taxpayer in state hospitals, the Governor got through the legislature a bill which has permitted payment where possible and produced many millions for better care and facilities.

Somehow he managed to induce quite a few exceptionally able people to join the state service during his term. It was often said that man for man, my brother's administration was probably the ablest ever essembled in Illinois, and I am sure that such remarks pleased Adlai more than any praise for himself.

Hard as they worked, the Governor and his associates were never too busy to appreciate a joke. Once when they were discussing which way a taciturn legislator would vote on a bill, Adlai said it reminded him of the little boy who asked his mother if we all come from dust and return to dust as he had heard someone say in Sunday school. "Yes, that's right," she said. "Well," the boy remarked, "I've just looked under the bed and there's somebody there, but I can't tell you whether he's coming or going." When a bill was proposed requiring every room in every public building except schools and churches to have at least one cuspidor, J. Edward Day, one of his personal staff and an old and witty friend, commemorated the occasion by sending Adlai this doggerel:

> A bill has passed the Senate
> About which some are skeptical:
> It would give a legal mandate
> To a rather crude receptacle.
> For those among the public
> Who may not approve of this,
> We point out that good government
> Should not be hit or miss.
> We recommend approval
> For Libonati's legislation;
> We feel sure it will live up
> To our best expectorations!

Another impromptu "poem" that delighted Adlai was a verse saga all the newspaper women collaborated on, hailing his achievements as Governor. I'm sorry I can't remember it to quote. But I did copy part of a letter one of the staff members wrote Adlai on his fiftieth birthday, because I think it sums up the way people who worked with my brother felt about him:

> . . . My association with you has taught me that intelligence can be crossed with humility and fired by sincerity (only by mixing metaphors, however) to provide leadership—the only kind of leadership that even counts or ever helps. . . .
>
> Faith in others is most important in this world, perhaps in part because what we have seems to rapidly be disappearing. To create faith in a political leader is the hardest job I know of. You are doing it and in that knowledge I hold you in highest respect and admiration.

At birthday celebrations and other parties, Adlai's old friends often assembled in Springfield and did "stunts." Ed Day and Ellen Smith wrote amusing new lyrics to old tunes, and Ed McDougal and Carl McGowan played the piano. Somebody else had a guitar, and my specialty was doing imitations. Everyone wrote verses. We also spent some happy evenings in the music room while Louise Lanphier played Chopin and Debussy.

Adlai's first girl in Springfield, Mary Douglas Hay— "Dougie"—and her husband Don Funk, were old friends we enjoyed seeing. Adlai tried to get in some tennis occasionally with Carl or Bill or friends in town. Once he played in the city tournament, and the photographers were a bit embarrassed because they didn't even hear about it till a day later. He remarked that that was a blessing in view of his miserable performance. Sometimes he drove himself up to

Bill and Elizabeth Drake's beautiful farm at Elkhart, and played on their wonderful court. But of golf and riding there was precious little because the week was too full and on week ends he was usually away around the state working, inspecting or speaking.

During the State Fair each summer, so many visitors came to the Mansion we practically ran a hotel. In fact, when I planned the menus for a week ahead with Mrs. Van Diver, I'd make up a list of arrival and departure hours, and the maids would barely get the bed linen changed before a new batch of guests arrived. Having become imbued with a bit of my mother's Quaker thrift, I found myself thinking once, How wasteful to have to launder all these sheets when they've just been used one night!

The first time I started off with the Governor to the Fair, in the ten-year-old state Cadillac which Adlai thriftily refused to have replaced, a motorcycle escort screamed our coming. My brother thought that was entirely too ostentatious, and he asked Captain Van Diver please to "call off the bugles and drums." From then on, he rode without sirens.

Adlai was in his element at the fair when he could wander around seeing all the animals, the exhibits and all the "sights." Strangers would call cheerily, "Hi, Gov," or "Hello, Adlai," and he'd beam. He bought popcorn and we munched as we strolled. On the midway, he took a turn at the shooting gallery, and threw baseballs at baby-doll targets. Everywhere he stopped, the photographers usually surrounded him, but even that constant exposure he learned to take in his stride. He was especially interested in the sheep entered at the fair, because he raises sheep on his little home farm. In the art exhibit one time he was so taken with a modern oil painting—a boy with a rooster—that he tried to buy it, and learned it had already been sold to Ex-Ambassador Kennedy's daughter Eunice. That started a funny chain reaction: Eunice, who must have heard from somebody how much Adlai liked the painting, promptly sent it to him, and he had it hanging in his bedroom. Then when Eunice got married, Adlai sent the rooster back to her as a wedding present!

I think the part of the fair he enjoyed most was the horse show, and the thrilling performance one year of two famous five-gaited horses, Replica and Wing Commander. Bane Pierce, the announcer, was an old schoolmate from Bloomington, and once he asked me to present the blue ribbons to the winning riders. As I approached loaded with flowers and the cameras flashed, the horses shied and frightened me. My brother thought that was a great joke on me, as did the grandstands!

Each year, on Governor's Day at the fair, our delightful and beloved Kentucky kinsman, Alben Barkley, appeared with Adlai, and of course the crowd adored the "Veep," his stories and his speeches—as who doesn't? Once I recall Adlai told the crowd about the time he had to substitute for Barkley at a Democratic rally in Indiana, and he said, "I felt like the motorist who ran over a hog on the highway. The farmer was very irate, but the motorist finally calmed him down and said, 'Don't worry, I'll replace your pig.' 'Replace him!' the farmer shouted. 'You can't. You ain't big enough.'"

Another charming storyteller was our Aunt Julia Hardin, widow of a Presbyterian minister. One morning a Chicago political leader came to the Mansion for a breakfast conference with the Governor; Aunt Julia was already at the table, and my brother wondered what she and the politician would make of each other. He told me later that Aunt Julia began telling stories and the guest was so enthralled that when our aunt rose to leave, with a gentle, "Now I'll retire and leave you gentlemen to your business," the politician bowed over her hand like an old-world courtier. After she'd gone, he exclaimed, "Say, I never had such a break at breakfast!"

We always had relatives for Christmas, and our traditional noonday dinner of oyster soup, turkey with all the fixings, boiled turnips, and for dessert, plum pudding made by our cousin Nan Green in Danville, Kentucky. Days before, the two tall Christmas trees would be placed in the bay windows of the music room and living room, and we'd wind ropes of evergreen around the entrance-hall columns and the banisters, hang wreaths in the windows and decorate the mantels. Adlai and John Fell stuck Christmas cards in the bookcases, although the overflow had to lie in bushel baskets. The Governor wrote his own gift cards, and inscriptions in the books he sent as presents. (One year he gave at least a dozen copies of Jay Monaghan's *Illinois—A Pictorial History*.) He depended on me to choose gifts for the children of the staff and of other friends, and Mary Louise Day helped me gather cowboy gear, dolls and games. Once at the last minute Adlai said to me reproachfully, "But what about Carol Ann?" I looked blank. It turned out that Carol Ann was the small daughter of his caretaker at the farm, and I must confess I'd forgotten her, but my brother certainly hadn't.

He did his own choosing on gifts for his sons, and I remember he got John Fell a good gun one year and skis another. The boys would consult me ahead, about what "Dad" wanted. One of their presents to him was a waterproof corduroy hunting cap, and his staff gave him lined hunting boots.

On a snowy Christmas Eve, the children in a charity home in Springfield came to sing carols outside the Mansion. Adlai invited them in, and the cake and candy flowed freely. He had his arm around a small boy who asked trustingly, "Does Santa Claus live here with you?"

We always went to the midnight service at the Presbyterian church. Adlai greatly admired the minister, Richard Graebel, and liked his sermons all the year round, but the candle-lit Christmas service had a special beauty and the minister sang "Silent Night" in German alone in his fine warm voice. One of the memories I'll keep forever is that row of our four boys sitting there with shining Christmas faces, in the Lincoln pew with Ernest, Adlai and me. John Fell went to sleep on his father's shoulder.

When the household staff had all gone home, as they did on holidays, Adlai sometimes answered the phone himself; one Christmas night I beat the Governor to the phone and it was a man on long distance who told me he wanted to make a big contribution to the Democratic Party. It turned out that this was only the opening gambit. What he really wanted was the Governor to send a snowplow at once to clear his road. We had many gay and amusing incidents of that kind, and also some harrowing incidents on the eve of executions in the penitentiaries.

During holiday visits, Tim, young Adlai and Borden slept in an annex room back of the kitchen which they called the Casino, but John Fell, who was twelve when Adlai became Governor, always wanted to be in a room near his father. Often the three boys gathered in "Dad's" room with him, "to talk things over." Adlai has always discussed problems with his sons, and encouraged them to make their own decisions. As young Adlai once told a reporter, "It's been a kind of honor system." He inherits his father's taste for reading, and I have a mental picture of him sprawled on Adlai's bed with a book, while Borden looked over his father's new ties, and commented, "Aren't these too gaudy for a Governor?" (Adlai has very conservative taste in everything but ties—and, besides, the things people send him!) John Fell, who has the lively curiosity of Kipling's Elephant Child (although that's not the best simile for the son of a Democrat) was always busy examining new mementos and gifts sent to his father. I think he "borrowed" a sport shirt appliquéd with a two-foot-high donkey.

"Borrowing" was a euphemism for the annual Christmas-time ravaging of "Dad's" drawers and closets. And during the holidays Adlai always had a big house party and dance for the young people, when the boys invited their friends down from Lake Forest, Chicago and all over the state. Adlai moved into a butler's room, I went into a maid's room, and Ernest would go to a hotel to chaperon the young guests we couldn't wedge into the Mansion overnight. One of my end-of-December diary entries was:

> As usual, Adlai and I will move into the servants' quarters. For decorations tonight, in library, I have some fern sprayed white and am going to pin it on the green draperies. For the buffet supper, I'll give guests creamed chicken and oysters, a smoked ham that was sent to the Governor, small hot rolls, crab meat with mayonnaise, coffee, cake. Have had some embarrassment when total strangers phone, begging for invitations, but I just can't ask them.

Even the sofa in the sunroom became a bed during house-party time. In fact, so many girls wanted to stay overnight our last Christmas in the Mansion that they even offered to bring sleeping bags. I borrowed eight cots and ten mattresses from the 4-H clubs, and managed to put up twenty-three girls—without benefit of sleeping bags.

It must have been our first dance there, when we still felt a little new and stiff, that Adlai said to me worriedly, "Nobody's dancing. Let's you and I start them off." As he took me around for a few turns, he murmured, "Maybe we should show them how we do the Vernon Castle Walk!" Fortunately, the young guests took over the dance floor with sambas or mambas or whatever they do. Later in the evening, my brother pointed out a young man and his girl rapturously entwined on the shadowy stairs. "See that," he said to me. "Do you think it looks safe or had *you* better break it up?"

When John Fell was fourteen, he wanted to stay up for the dance and he wore a hand-me-down dinner jacket of his father's. It was so big on him that whenever a partner put her hand on his sleeve, the too-wide shoulders sagged down. John Fell explained to us cheerfully that he was wearing "the new off-the-shoulder fashion," to Adlai's great amusement.

At the Governor's big reception New Year's afternoon, the boys stood with their father in the receiving line—at least for a while. Like him, they are instinctively warm and friendly. Although shaking hands for hours can be a numbing chore, I've never once heard Adlai complain about it. He likes meeting and greeting people. (The only thing he dislikes is being mauled in a crowd. There are always a few frenzied admirers who seem to want to tear off a candidate's arm or leg, as a token.) The worst drawback of a receiving line is that you can't murmur more than a few polite words, even to close friends, without holding up hundreds of people waiting to shake hands. General Boyle, adjutant of the Illinois National Guard, stood beside Adlai, to introduce newcomers to him. Once he announced a name that sounded exactly like "Mrs. Plush-bottom," and Adlai rolled his eyes at me impishly, as he passed the lady on to me, while I struggled to keep a straight face. Another time, a small boy came down the receiving line with his parents, and asked the Governor longingly, "Would you give me your dog, Artie?" It was so obviously a case of real love that Adlai leaned over and said, "Wouldn't you just keep him for me, sometime?" Two years later, that small boy kept Artie while Artie's owner went on his trip around the world.

Even with the press of official entertaining piled onto his holiday schedule, Adlai would get in several sessions of trap shooting or bird hunting with the boys. He had rented his Libertyville farm to Marshall Field, Jr., and I think they missed the winter sports they've always done together there —ice skating on the Des Plaines River that runs by their house, or taking turns driving the truck and hanging onto a rope behind, skijoring over the snowy acres.

The four had one wonderful summer vacation trip together, while we were in Springfield. Adlai took all the boys to Jackson Hole, Wyoming, and they went on a ten-day pack trip through the country he loves. Our experienced camper friend from Bloomington, Ralph Heffernan, made the arrangements and they came back as brown as old cowhands, and entertained us uproariously with accounts of their adventures, and the fish that didn't get away. Adlai described their camp cook, Shorty Beal, a fabulous eighty-five-year-old ex-wrangler and cavalryman who could flip pancakes as high as his tall tales, over a campfire. His first remark to young Adlai was, "Don't laugh. I was born ugly. They turned me over three times to see which end to kiss, and then waited to see if I'd bark or bray."

The campers had spent their nights in sleeping bags, and their days on horseback, and before it was over, poor John Fell had to ease his saddle sores by riding with a rubber pillow tucked into his pants. Adlai and the boys were still kidding each other about their "rugged endurance," while they sorted the duffle bags that first evening back.

The trip I enjoyed most while Adlai was Governor was to Danville, Kentucky, to see him receive an honorary degree at Centre College, where our Great-grandfather, Reverend Lewis Warner Green, had been president before the Civil War. During that visit, my brother and I went to see Waveland, the beautiful brick house built in 1797 on the Wilderness Road by our Great-great-grandfather, Willis Green, after he married Sarah Reed—some say the first marriage of white settlers performed in Kentucky. It's now a large dairy farm, and the owners were extremely nice about letting us go through the fine old house and look our fill. Having been brought up on our Stevenson grandparents' tales of Kentucky, we were thrilled to see the places they'd loved.

In his address at the convocation ceremony, Adlai mentioned Grandfather Stevenson's being a student at Centre College:

> I have often thought that it was here at Centre that his flair for politics and his good judgment of people was clearly foreshadowed. For here he courted and won none other than the daughter of the President of the College—always sound strategy for a struggling student.

My brother became very serious, as he talked to his student-listeners about a liberal education:

> . . . You have a better chance than many to give a lot and therefore take a lot out of life. If we can't look to people like

you for leadership, for good judgment, for wise directions for yourselves and the convictions of our society, where can we look? For here at Centre which for 130 years has transmitted from one generation to the next the riches of Western civilization you have gotten some grasp of the basic principles on which our culture is founded—the concept of supremacy of the individual, the worth of the individual human being and the necessity for a climate of freedom in which these values may find means of expression. You have the basic core of a liberal education which can convert the possession of the influence and power you attain into a beneficent force instead of an evil one.

. . . There is the curious paradox that the man who is big enough to exercise wisely the power that comes with success is often also the man with the inner resources to lead a happy, useful life in obscurity. In either role he will be contributing to the well-being of his time and place—a fact which I am encouraged to believe that we have once again come to appreciate after a long period of worship of false and deceiving gods.

He spoke movingly about the dangers of "doubting our beliefs and believing our doubts," and told his listeners:

You cannot, you must not, stand aside from the great, the continuous decisions in your time, in your country, and in the world. . . . For these tasks and these exciting opportunities, use the equipment that God and this college have given you, and that your own industry each day improves. Use your heart and your head, and not your prejudices. You are more than the social animal Seneca spoke of. Man is a moral agent with the power of making choices affecting not only himself but countless others. And man can hope. Not animals, only mankind, can hope.

As I listened, it seemed to me that my brother's own convictions had become deeper and steadier than ever before. At the finish of the speech, Dr. Groves, the head of the col-

lege, presented Adlai with his degree, and emphasized he was
not doing it because of what our forebears had achieved, but
for all that my brother was doing in our own time.

Our old Danville cousins, Nan and Letty Green, who were
at the ceremony with us, had a forthrightness that delighted
my brother. When somebody asked them if they had a family
coat of arms, they said, "Certainly not. We were yeomen."

Our return flight to Illinois was rather harrowing, because
we flew through a bad storm. I was so frightened I just sat
and prayed, but Adlai read calmly, and made notes. The
pilot of the Governor's plane, Major Dan Smith, made a
skillful landing by radar control at Chicago, after the storm
blocked off the Springfield airport. Adlai had some appointments in the capitol he was anxious to get back for, but we
found we'd just missed a train and had several hours to kill,
so we went to the movie *Red Shoes*, and Adlai enjoyed it
enormously. I don't believe he went to the movies, in spite
of our urgings, half a dozen times in the four years he was in
Springfield.

Several months after that Danville trip which meant so
much to me, in July of 1950, we had a party that was perhaps his favorite social event at the Mansion—and I know it
was mine. My friend Louise Hickox Pickering and I decided
it would be interesting to have a Daughters of Ex-Governors
house party, and invite all those women who had lived in the
Mansion as children whom we could find. Most of the Governors had, of course, been Republicans, but this didn't
bother my brother at all. He knew that I was very eager to
have a book written about the first one hundred years of this
historic house, and I had the ulterior motive that our guests'
memories would contribute wonderful material on earlier
days.

At dinner one night I read Adlai excerpts from Bess Furman's fascinating book, *White House Profile,* because I wanted to use it as a kind of model for the history I had in mind. I read aloud the part about Thomas Jefferson furnishing twenty-three rooms of the White House and choosing each item himself; his large collection of French and Italian recipes was copied in his own neat hand—including one for ice cream that advised, "Jostle well on the knee." Adlai enjoyed hearing those human bits of history, and when the eleven Governors' daughters and one granddaughter arrived in the Mansion, he was as charmed with their "I remember" stories as I was. He made a brief, moving toast to them at dinner, and afterward we had a reception for Springfield people who were old friends of our guests. Hiram Sherman, who was visiting his mother, acted as master of ceremonies, and a singer did one song from the era of each "daughter."

Some of the women had tears in their eyes, as they walked from room to room. Mrs. Miller, eldest daughter of Governor Frank Lowden, said, "I remember when ex-President Taft slept in that bedroom, and we were having a young people's party downstairs and the chandeliers shook over our heads whenever he walked around." Our friend Benjamin Thomas made a recording as the women sat talking, and the whole thing was nostalgic and charming. Even though our book was never published, that house-party-into-the-past was one of the nicest things I've ever experienced. For weeks afterward, when a newcomer arrived at the Mansion, Adlai would say, "Get Buffie to tell you about the Governors' Daughters. I've never seen anything like it."

When members of the New Salem Lincoln League came to him and asked if they might put on an outdoor historical drama in Kelso Hollow in New Salem State Park, Adlai invited me to sit in at the conference, because he knew how much I love anything to do with theater. The state budget couldn't afford a cent of backing for the project, but Adlai and I both thought it was an exciting idea. My husband got so interested he helped the league raise the funds by private contributions, and the talented Kermit Hunter was commissioned to write a drama of the early settlers in Lincoln's village of New Salem.

I'd like to mention that Ernest, in his own quiet way, was constantly helpful. He had been a career diplomat for thirty years, doing important work abroad for the government— and he was such a popular man all over Europe that I had been simply "the wife of the consul-general." In Springfield, Ernest had no official capacity, and I think only a man with real grace of spirit could have adapted himself so good-humoredly to a background role. (Later in the Presidential campaign no one was more amused than Ernest when a newspaperwoman called him "the husband of the sister of the candidate.") He is devoted to Adlai, and he not only encouraged me to spend a lot of time at the Mansion, but he was able to ease the Governor's load by taking care of many family business matters, and he took care of visitors while Adlai was tied up in meetings.

At the opening of the outdoor drama, *Forever This Land,* Adlai said to my husband who had invested so much time and patience in it, "This is far beyond anything I'd even hoped for." His favorite part was the scene in which the settlers appeared before Governor Ninian Edwards and the legislators back in the dawn of his beloved Illinois. He often went back, with out-of-town visitors, during the two summers it ran. Brooks Atkinson, the drama critic of *The New*

York Times, flew out for a performance and loved it. Afterward, at the Mansion, he and Adlai sat in the kitchen at midnight in their shirtsleeves, eating watermelon and talking. Oriana Atkinson, his wife, has snapping dark eyes and a snapping wit, and is altogether delightful.

Once Adlai invited the entire Foreign Consular Corps in Chicago, with their wives, to come to Springfield, and even the ones who didn't know much English responded to *Forever This Land.* It was the first time a governor had entertained the foreign consuls in the capital; one thing that baffled some of them was the visit to New Salem Village. Looking around at the few crude reconstructed log cabins, a consul's wife said to me in bewilderment, "But where is the village?" At Lincoln's home, in Springfield, where Lincoln is still very much alive, another asked me earnestly, "This Abe they talk of—who was he?"

At the opening of Illinois' Sixty-Seventh General Assembly, in January of 1951, Adlai addressed a state legislature controlled by Republicans, and talked to them about the responsibilities of putting good government above politics and outlined another extensive legislative program. I've never seen a more intent audience. A Republican paper, the *Rockford Register-Republic,* commented later, "Accomplishments of the most recent general assembly were far-reaching, and they could not have been made without a mutual and healthy respect between the Governor's Mansion and the assembly halls in the capitol. . . . His courteous manner, dignity, and warm friendliness won considerable respect. Under Stevenson, state affairs have been conducted above-board."

As a result of the findings of his "Little Hoover" commission, the legislature passed seventy-eight bills to achieve greater efficiency without a raise in general taxes. Adlai had reorganized the Division of Highways, and Illinois was well along the way on its first big road-building program in thirty years. (When he took office, three thousand miles of highways were in need of repair or replacing.) To help finance this, the legislature finally followed the Governor's recommended increases in truck registration and gas taxes. After two years of discussion he at last got an agreement on the division of the revenue between the state, the cities, counties and townships by keeping everyone bottled up in his office—without drinks!—until 2:30 in the morning. He called it "agreement by exhaustion," a technique he learned from the Russian diplomats in London in 1945.

He vetoed any bill he thought was against the public interest, no matter what private pressures backed it. For instance, he vetoed five of nine bills presented by the Illinois American Legion, because he thought they were harmful for the state as a whole, and of course he was told that would lose him votes. He did the same to many other bills. In a report to the people, he said, "I know sound government ends when the leaders of special groups call the tune, whether they represent labor, capital, vets, pensioners, or anyone else." He vetoed an irresponsible increase in old-age pensions because it would have cost the state fourteen million dollars and the Republicans who pushed the bill through hadn't voted a cent to finance it. Even *The Chicago Tribune* hailed his "political courage" in saying no.

One I was especially proud of was his veto of a series of strongly supported bills requiring loyalty oaths. He said:

> Does anyone seriously think that a real traitor will hesitate to sign a loyalty oath? Of course not. Really dangerous subversives and saboteurs will be caught by careful, constant, professional investigation, not by pieces of paper.

The whole notion of loyalty inquisitions is a natural characteristic of the police state, not of democracy. Knowing his rule rests upon compulsion rather than consent, the dictator must always assume the disloyalty, not of a few but of many, and guard against it by continual inquisition and "liquidation" of the unreliable. . . .

The democratic state, on the other hand, is based on the consent of its members. The vast majority of our people are intensely loyal, as they have amply demonstrated. To question, even by implication, the loyalty and devotion of a large group of citizens is to create an atmosphere of suspicion and distrust which is neither justified, healthy nor consistent with our traditions. . . .

We must fight traitors with laws. We already have the laws. We must fight falsehood and evil ideas with truth and better ideas. We have them in plenty. But we must not confuse the two.

.. We must not burn down the house to kill the rats.

Another widely quoted veto in 1949 was on the Cat Bill entitled "An Act to Provide Protection to Insectivorous Birds By Restraining Cats." In his veto message, the Governor said:

It is in the nature of cats to do a certain amount of unescorted roaming. . . . The problem of cat versus bird is as old as time. If we attempt to resolve it by legislation, who knows but what we may be called upon to take sides as well in the age-old problems of dog versus cat, bird versus bird, even bird versus worm. In my opinion, the State of Illinois and its local governing bodies already have enough to do without trying to control feline delinquency.

The leavening of wit never concealed the real seriousness of his aims and accomplishments. More and more people talked to me about his "future." In one of our rare chances at a real talk, late one night, I said to my brother, "What are you aiming at? What would you like to do?"

He said, "Well, first I'd like to finish the job we've started here, which means another term, I suppose. And then I'd like to be president of some good university, but they're taking younger men these days and I'd be too old." (He was fifty-one!) He went on rather wistfully, "And of course I've always wanted to travel more, and know more about the unfamiliar areas of the world that will affect our future. But that takes a lot of time and money."

From my diary in August, 1951:

> Adlai has gained new stature in the political world. His entire independence that comprises his own sense of integrity—the rightness and fitness of things—has left him standing on a very firm rock. I rejoice to see this. He has a confidence now that he has never before had in his life. Senator Parrish stayed all night and after breakfast, I had a long talk with him. He said Adlai is the greatest Governor Illinois has ever had, that Democratic politicians at first resented his not playing the patronage and profit game but they have now come around to recognize the fact that good government is good politics. Parrish wants Adlai to run for President in '56. He wants him to be Governor again and then be way out front for the nomination in '56. Manly Munford, a day or two later, told me the general feeling among the press in Chicago is that Adlai is perfect Presidential timber.

When I returned to the Mansion in early December, after several months in North Carolina, I felt an even stronger Stevenson-for-President current in the air. At the first meal alone with my brother, I said "What's this talk about the Presidential candidacy? Is it possible you'd be nominated?"

He said quietly and briefly, "It's possible—but not proba-

ble." Then he pushed his chair back from the table in a firm
way that closed the subject.

A month later, in January of 1952, Adlai announced he
was a candidate for re-election as Governor. In his statement
to the press, he said:

> . . . I take great satisfaction in the progress we have made
> since 1949. But I have learned that the road is long and we
> have far to go before any of us, myself included, can in good
> conscience stop and rest.
>
> I invite the Republican party to nominate the best man it
> can find. It is of little importance whether the next Governor
> of Illinois is named Adlai Stevenson; but it is of the highest
> importance that he finish what we have started. No matter
> then who loses, the people will win.
>
> That is the kind of an election Illinois needs and deserves.
> I am gladly and proudly ready to take part in it.

But soon after that, a phone call came from the President.

Chapter 13

O NE EVENING in mid-January, we held up dinner until rather late, and when Adlai joined Ernest and me at the table, he seemed preoccupied, but I didn't wonder at that, he often was.

Several weeks before, there had been a tragic explosion at a coal mine in West Frankfort, Illinois, in which over a hundred men were killed. It was all the more tragic because Adlai had urged a law to ensure stricter mine inspection, but both union and owners had raised objections and held up passage of the elaborate bill he had worked out. Partly because of this, Congress was considering a bill to enlarge federal authority on safety inspection. My brother was against the idea. He felt that the state could and should do the job, and he had arranged to go to Washington to see Oscar Chapman, Secretary of the Interior, the head of the Bureau of Mines, and John L. Lewis, to discuss better safety measures. That evening at dinner, he said suddenly, "I just had a call from the President. He wants me to see him when I'm in Washington next week."

I suspected that the President might have something to talk about beside mine safety.

My brother went on, "I suppose it's impossible to meet in secret, and the press will be camping on the doorstep. They'll think it has something to do with the Presidential thing."

Ernest laughed and said, "Well, hasn't it?"

In the face of something so large and important, somehow we couldn't go on making chitchat at dinner. Ernest and I were leaving the next day for North Carolina, for what we'd planned as a peaceful rest in the sun. But by then, things were moving so fast that even in our remote cabin, we felt the repercussions.

After Adlai spent two hours alone with the President, the evening of January 22, reporters were busy throwing his hat into the ring. The less they knew, the more they guessed, and their guesses made headlines all over the country. That same week, *Time* magazine came out with a cover picture and story on Adlai. The article had been written weeks before, and had been planned as a regional piece on Illinois and its much talked-of Governor, but its appearance right after this meeting added to the spontaneous combustion of conjecture. My husband and I were deluged with hundreds of *Time* clippings on Adlai—some sent by the most unexpected people! My brother seemed launched toward the nomination, whether he liked it or not.

Finally I couldn't stand wondering any longer, so I phoned Adlai at the Mansion, to ask what had really happened at the meeting in Washington, and what he'd decided to do. He said, "Mr. Truman would like me to run, but I told him I was already running for Governor of Illinois." When I prodded him for more information, he said, "I can't tell you any more than that, Buffie; that's all there is to tell you."

But the newspapers went on speculating, and of course

Ernest and I did too. On our twenty-fifth wedding anniversary, we had champagne to celebrate and felt so buoyed up that we put in another call to Adlai. He was very brotherly: "Why have you called me this time?"

I said, "Because I can't stand the uncertainty."

"Why are you so concerned?"

Fortified by two glasses of champagne, I said, "Well, I'd like to know if I'm going to have a chance to get into the White House."

My brother laughed. "Oh, they'll probably let you in the side door." He knew I'd been working with the Moore County Historical Society to plan the reconstruction of one of the oldest houses around Southern Pines—the Shaw house. He said, "You take care of the Shaw house, Buffie, and I'll take care of the White House!"

From my diary, February 8, 1952:

> Adlai said the President had set a date in April when he would announce about his candidacy, but now it looks as though the date would be speeded up. Adlai wants to go and call on Pres. Truman again sometime soon and say he definitely cannot seek the nomination, but he can't get to him without being seen by the press and starting more speculation. Cruel that a President can't have a private talk.

Mr. Truman made his dramatic "I will not run" announcement at a Jefferson-Jackson Day dinner in Washington on March 29, and he'd barely finished his speech when all the reporters made a determined rush at Adlai who was sitting at the head table on the opposite side of the great armory. My brother told them exactly what he'd been saying all along—that he was only running for Governor. Instead of taking his no for an answer, Democratic leaders seemed more determined than ever to make him change his mind. In the midst of the frenzied pressures that week, Adlai, with his usual thoughtfulness, found time to write this note to my son, who had enlisted in the Air Force the summer before and was on the way to becoming a jet pilot:

> Dear Tim: Your mother writes me that you have been transferred to Texas, having successfully completed the course at Bainbridge. My utmost congratulations and genuflections. I think you have done a superb job and I am very, very proud of my beloved nephew. . . .

About that same time, Adlai had been asked to attend and speak at a big Democratic fund-raising dinner at the Waldorf. Averill Harriman was to be guest of honor, with the four or five other leading contenders for the Presidential nomination as star attractions. Adlai explained reasonably that since he wasn't a contender, he didn't belong in that group, and declined to come to the dinner. Immediately loud wails went up, and rent the long-distance wires. Politicians phoned him to report that the national television and radio networks were only interested in covering the dinner "if Stevenson is there. He's the big news." The Democrats pointed out to Adlai that they needed the fullest publicity coverage in order to raise funds, and that they couldn't get it unless he appeared.

My brother agreed to come, but to make his position absolutely clear, he gave this statement to the press as he took off for New York:

> I have been urged to announce my candidacy for the Democratic nomination for President, but I am a candidate for Governor of Illinois and I cannot run for two offices at the same time. Moreover, my duties as Governor do not presently afford the time to campaign for the nomination even if I wanted it.

Others have asked me merely to say that I would accept a nomination which I did not seek. To state my position now on a prospect so remote in time and probability seems to me a little presumptuous. But I would rather presume than embarrass or mislead.

In these somber years the hopes of mankind dwell with the President of the United States. From such dread responsibility one does not shrink in fear, self-interest or humility. But great political parties, like great nations, have no indispensable man, and last January, before I was even considered for the Presidency, I announced that I would seek re-election as Governor of Illinois. Last week I was nominated in the Democratic primary. It is the highest office within the gift of the citizens of Illinois, and its power for good or ill over their lives is correspondingly great. No one should lightly aspire to it or lightly abandon the quest once begun.

Hence, I have repeatedly said that I was a candidate for Governor of Illinois and had no other ambition. To this I must now add that in view of my prior commitment to run for Governor and my desire and the desire of many who have given me their help and confidence in our unfinished work in Illinois, I could not accept the nomination for any other office this summer.

Better state government is the only sound foundation for our federal system, and I am proud and content to stand on my commitment to ask the people of Illinois to allow me to continue for another four years in my present post.

I cannot hope that my situation will be universally understood or my conclusions unanimously approved.

I *can* hope that friends with larger ambitions for me will not think ill of me. They have paid me the greatest compliment within their gift, and they have my utmost gratitude.

That same week, Ernest had an emergency appendectomy, but he was so concerned about Adlai that the minute he could, he reached for a phone, and called me for news. I read Adlai's statement to him, and my husband was disappointed. I myself hardly knew whether I was glad or sorry. I really thought that ended the matter, and that one of the contenders at the Waldorf dinner would emerge in first place.

The evening of the dinner, I was sitting alone in our car at the Southern Pines railroad station, waiting for a guest to arrive. Ernest was still in the hospital, and I felt restless and a little lonely. I turned on the radio in the car, and heard my brother speaking. He was making an honorable proposal of marriage to his dinner partner and old friend, Mrs. Roosevelt! His brief speech sounded so gay and easy that I felt enormously relieved, and I thought, Well, at least we don't have to worry any more. He sounds happy to have it all finished.

Afterward, I read this account in *The Christian Science Monitor:*

> Practically everybody [at the dinner] said the same thing— What a shame "he" wouldn't run. There was no question who the "he" was. And when Governor Stevenson lightly stole the show in the speaking that followed, it was dropping worm-wood into the wound.

We got back to Springfield early in May. Adlai was over at the capitol at a conference the afternoon we arrived; I was unpacking when there was a knock on my door. It was my brother. "I just came over to say, 'Welcome home,'" he said.

I was so happy to see him, and I asked him to sit down so we could have a few minutes' talk. Somehow I had to say what I felt, because I knew he'd been holding to his decision, and I wanted him to know how much I admired him. "I think you're a great man," I said. "I think you'll never have greater popularity than you have right now." He looked at me, smiling, and said quietly, "You do, do you? Well, back to work." And he left.

The next day, he went off to fill several speaking engagements. From my diary, May 6: "The papers are buzzing with the hit Adlai is making on the West Coast where he has gone to visit the Illinois 44th Division in camp and make speeches in Oregon and San Francisco. Adlai has within himself something so big, and now that it has flown out, people all over the land are catching at it."

The night he returned, he kept us laughing all through dinner with his account of the tour and the split-second schedule of appearances that required an official to have "the wind of an Olympic runner and the timing of a cuckoo clock." I remember he gave us a wonderful description of a remarkable old lady, aged ninety-five, the widow of our kinsman, Theron Fell, with whom he'd had a good visit in Portland. Adlai was amused because a reporter had said, "I guess Oregon's the one state in the union where you don't have any relatives." And then the delightful ninety-five-year-old cousin popped up!

I went down to my brother's office a few evenings after his return. There was a small mountain of letters heaped on his desk, and he was trying to read his way through them. He showed me one from a stranger in San Francisco, enclosing a check for $25. The man wrote that he had heard Adlai speak there and felt that every citizen should be given a copy of that speech, and to please accept his small contribution to a reprint fund. My heart warmed to that stranger, because I think the speech Adlai gave at the Commonwealth Club is one of the finest he ever made. It contains the very essence of his political beliefs. For instance, he said:

. . . It is not the lower order of the genus "pol," but it is you, the people, who have fouled the nest. Your public servants serve you right; indeed often better than you deserve. . . . Look to yourself and your fellow citizen, particularly the loudest complainer about sin, sickness and corruption in our public life. He probably tried to fix a parking ticket, to say the least, that morning and probably succeeded. Public officials, from top to bottom, from the high and the hazy to the low and the lazy, do not corrupt each other. We, the people, corrupt them. Behind every fix is the fixer, behind every bribe is the briber, behind every lobby and influence peddler is someone who wants the influence. . . . It seems to me that Government is like a pump, and what it pumps up is just what we are, a fair sample of the intellect, the ethics and the morals of the people, no better, no worse.

. . . As a Democrat, an office holder, an aspirant for re-election, I do not, I have not, I will not condone, excuse or explain away wrongdoing or moral obliquity in public office, whoever the guilty or whatever their station. One dishonest official is one too many. A dishonest official is as faithless to his party as he is to his office, and our political parties must never founder on the rocks of moral equivocation. But I do not blush for the Democratic party's record of probity and fidelity to public trust during twenty years in Washington. . . . And I am reminded of what Justice Charles Evans Hughes said during the Harding era scandals: "Neither political party has a monopoly on virtue or rascality. Let wrong be exposed and punished, but let no partisan Pecksniffs affect a 'holier than thou' attitude. Guilt is personal and knows no party."

. . . It is just as important to recognize and support the good as it is to root out and punish the bad. We do not lose faith in the banking system because a few bankers turn out to be embezzlers.

. . . And speaking of corruption, how about the corruption, the dishonest and reckless abuse of our freedom of expression? The "hucksters of hysteria," the contemporary exponents of irresponsible accusation and guilt by association do more grievous injury than all the miserable thieves and opportunists that foul the public nest, because they corrupt the minds and hearts of men with passion, poison and prejudice.

The letters from people responding to such speeches—and to the unshakable honesty of the man who had made them—were almost frighteningly appreciative. Many of the ones I read begged my brother to run for President. They said his country needed him, and the appeal was all the more moving because it came from housewives, preachers, office workers, businessmen—all kinds of private citizens.

Adlai's mail jumped from about 100 letters a week to 300 a day; inevitably, a few were just plain silly. These included the letters from foolish women. The staff had to set up a file marked "Proposals." One woman gave her qualifications in this businesslike way: "I am a nice eligible lady offering my services as a wife. I could serve you in kitchen or drawing room. You need somebody to look after your clothes." Several of the women wrote him how much they loved children and dogs!

The rumors about mythical romances flew thick and fast. I answered the phone one night, and a reporter said he was calling to check on the Governor's forthcoming engagement. I asked who the woman was, and the reporter mentioned the name of somebody my brother had met exactly once. Every week the rumors tossed up new fiancées for Adlai to marry. Once he said, "They must think the plural of spouse is spice."

The matrimonial rumors were mild, compared to the swarms about the Presidential nomination. Top newsmen and commentators were descending on the Mansion every hour. Two writers were there to gather material for books on my brother. The *Life* men arrived and photographed the Governor upstairs and down, with and without dog, and even sitting under a tree. There were long-distance calls every few minutes—and calls in person from dozens of influential politicians. The gist of their arguments was that Adlai simply couldn't reject the highest gift his party had to offer—that he mustn't let the Democrats down. I knew my brother felt a strong sense of responsibility to his party, but he also felt deeply responsible to the people of Illinois.

He had a hard time convincing people that he really meant it when he said that being Governor of Illinois was his only ambition, and that anyway he couldn't in honor seek the nomination for President while asking the people of Illinois to re-elect him Governor.

He went quietly ahead doing his enormous job as Governor, but it was like trying to work in the midst of a hurricane. My own jitters got so intense that I started smoking. The first time my brother saw me with a cigarette, he said in an astonished tone, "What are you *doing?*" I said piteously, "I'm calming my nerves."

Usually, I get a deep sense of peace and fulfillment from the Illinois prairies in the beautiful late spring and summer, but that year, whenever I drove from Bloomington to Springfield, my mind was so torn that my eyes hardly took in the beauties around me. I remember thinking sadly, Why I didn't even notice the peonies in bloom, or the color of the soy bean fields.

The war in Korea was an even more somber worry. My son was learning to fly jets, at Bryan Air Base. In June, young Adlai graduated from Harvard, joined the Marine Corps and left for his training at Quantico. I knew my brother must have discussed the Presidential boom with his sons, and that he was thinking a great deal of the effect on them. Once when I complained about the Mansion being like a goldfish bowl, Adlai said, "If you think this is bad, imagine what it's like for a President. And think of the constant, pitiless glare of publicity on his children."

One afternoon I was entertaining several hundred Democratic women of Sangamon County at a garden party on the Mansion lawn, and I went to my brother's office to ask if he'd come out and meet the guests. But when I found him that late afternoon he was in his bedroom lying down. I had known, of course, that he'd been under terrible pressure for months, but this was the first time I'd seen him with his defenses down. He was obviously worried and nervous.

I said, "I think you have to relax and go with the stream of history. You can't go against it."

The babble of three hundred women all talking at once came through the window, and reminded me why I'd come. Adlai smiled faintly. "Do you think I should go down and see them?" I said he'd better get some rest. That was one time he accepted my advice. In a day or two, he was as energetic—and as self-contained—as ever.

During the Republican convention, we had a dinner party in the garden one night, and Ernest brought out a little portable radio so we could listen to the speeches. Adlai was calm and relaxed, and he told us very much the same thing he told the press at the Governor's Conference in Houston on June 30, when there was much speculation in the press that he would run against Taft but not against Eisenhower:

I hope to stay in Illinois as Governor. My work there is not finished and it is very important to me. I am not being coy or trying to select my opponent. I have not participated nor will I participate, overtly or covertly, in any movement to draft me. Without such participation on my part, I do not believe that any such draft can or will develop. In the unlikely event that it does, I will decide what to do at that time in the light of the conditions then existing.

Something that happened the day before the Democratic convention opened is a revealing example of the public concern over Adlai's making a decision if he was forced to. The Reverend Harrison Ray Anderson of the Fourth Presbyterian Church in Chicago sent an urgent special invitation asking my brother to attend the service that Sunday, July 20. Ernest, John Farwell and I went with Adlai, and it was a strange experience, because the entire sermon seemed to be directed at my brother. It was titled: "How Men Know God's Will." The text, from The Epistle of James 1:5, was: "If any of you lack wisdom, let him ask of God, that giveth to all men liberally, and upbraideth not; and it shall be given him."

At one point, the Reverend Anderson looked straight at my brother as he said, "When making decisions, don't look back. . . . Think how those decisions will be viewed one hundred years from now." He also made a pointed remark about consulting trustworthy friends for advice. It seemed to Ernest and me that the entire congregation was staring at Adlai, whenever the minister made one of these references, but my brother was listening so attentively he didn't notice. All he said afterward was, "Good sermon; he has helped me." But he seemed very thoughtful.

That week of the convention, he was staying with several aides at the home of Bill Blair's parents on Astor Street, a big, quiet house that had been closed for the summer. Within twenty-four hours of Adlai's arrival, that "quiet retreat" was the hub of attention. To accommodate the hordes of reporters and photographers waiting there for any news, the telephone company put up five phone booths along the side-walk. Inside the house, the one line was so endlessly busy that one day Mr. Blair, Senior, calling from his office repeatedly, couldn't even get through to his own home.

Ernest and I had been loaned the Ed McDougals' apartment just around the corner on Lake Shore Drive, and we were swamped with the overflow of messages intended for Adlai. Our phone would begin shrilling before 7 A.M., and it never let up. Every time I went around the corner to "Blair House" the crowds were bigger, until finally the police had to close off the block. The first time Ernest and I had to push through and be identified by the security officer guarding the door, I had a sorrowful feeling that my brother was an encircled man, and would never be the same person again. But when I got inside, there was Adlai acting exactly the same as always, unruffled, smiling and hard at work in his bedroom, while everyone else was chattering or watching television.

The night before the convention opened, I went to a Democratic women's dinner at the Palmer House, and at first the only person I knew in the vast crowd was the bright and beautiful Jane Barkley, the Vice-President's wife. I was impressed and a little envious because a woman from Alabama who sat at the same table with me seemed to know everybody there. Finally Adlai appeared, and the photographers asked him to pose beside a life-size donkey made of ice. Adlai said something about it being the coldest Democrat he had ever met, and then suddenly the press "found" me, and came at me firing volleys of questions: "Will your brother be nominated? Will he accept a draft? Do you have a dog? Do you like politics? What do you do in Springfield? Would you be his hostess in Washington? Is your hair natural? What are your hobbies?" They were smiling and friendly and I liked them, but by the time they'd finished asking, "What do you and your brother eat?" I felt like saying "Raw fish." When dinner was finally served that night, I had lost my appetite!

The next morning, I was co-hostess, with the Illinois state chairwoman, Blanche Fritz, at a breakfast for Democratic women. Our guests of honor were the lovely, gentle Eugenia Anderson, Jane Barkley and Mrs. Elizabeth Conkey, our National Committee woman.

Afterward, we all rushed to the amphitheater in the stockyards, to hear Adlai, as Governor of Illinois, welcome the delegates.

. . . Here on the prairies of Illinois and the Middle West we can see a long way in all directions. We look to east, to west, to north and south. Our commerce, our ideas, come and go in all directions.

. . . You are very welcome here. Indeed, we think you were very wise to come here for your deliberations in this fateful year of grace. For it was in Chicago that the modern Democratic story began. It was here just twenty years ago in the depths of shattering national misery at the end of a dizzy decade of Republican rule that you commenced the greatest era of economic and social progress in our history with the nomination of Franklin Roosevelt. . . .

But, our Republican friends say it was all a miserable failure. For almost a week pompous phrases marched over this landscape in search of an idea, and the only idea they found was that the two great decades of progress in peace, victory in war, and bold leadership in this anxious hour, were the misbegotten spawn of bungling, corruption, socialism, mismanagement, waste and worse. They captured, tied and dragged that idea in here and furiously beat it to death.

After listening to our misdeeds awhile I was surprised the next morning when the mail was delivered on time! Our friends were out of patience, out of sorts and, need I add, out of office.

But we Democrats were not the only victims here. First they slaughtered each other, and then they went after us. And the same vocabulary was good for both exercises, which was a great convenience. Perhaps the proximity of the stockyards accounts for the carnage.

The constructive spirit of the great Democratic decades must not die here on its twentieth anniversary in destructive indignity and disorder. And I hope and pray, as you all do, that we can conduct our deliberations with a businesslike precision and a dignity befitting our responsibility, and the solemnity of the hour of history in which we meet.

. . . And—above all—let us make our decisions openly, fairly, not by the processes of synthetic excitement or mass hysteria, but, as these solemn times demand, by earnest thought and prayerful deliberation.

It is an unusual moment in our history when three men whose names are up for President of the United States should be blood kin. These men were Senator Richard Brevard Russell of Georgia, Vice-President Alben Barkley of Kentucky and Governor Adlai E. Stevenson of Illinois. Somehow it brought to my mind Adlai's ancestry—Southern and Scotch-Presbyterian on his father's side, and Northern, Quaker and Unitarian on his mother's. But, I thought, isn't that the story of America? And I wanted to see Senator Russell whom I had never met. Later he came to Springfield but they only gave me about five minutes to talk to him!

Ernest and I spent every waking hour at the convention that week, and we lived mostly on sandwiches. We were in Adlai's box, with the Edison Dicks, the Hermon Smiths, Mrs. Harriet Welling, Aunt Letitia and other friends of his who came and went. Adlai was a delegate, but the first time he took his seat with the Illinois delegation on the opening evening, there was such a commotion that from then on he stayed at the Blairs' house and watched the proceedings on television. His ever-capable secretary, Carol Evans, typed on a bridge table upstairs. Bill Blair proved himself a masterful executive and kept things going smoothly. He dealt skillfully with the press and the deluge of calls and callers with a tact, patience, and good sense that never deserted him and astonished me.

Bill's grandmother, Mrs. Joseph T. Bowen, the matriarch of Chicago and a very old lady, lived in the house next door, and she never even whimpered when the beautiful velvety lawn between the two houses was trampled to mud by the waiting reporters, television and radio men. She was a great philanthropist and champion of good government, and she kept saying, "You keep in the fight, Adlai. Go to it, Governor!" My brother couldn't save her lawn, but having been a reporter himself, he worried about the press having to keep such long vigils out there, without news.

Early one morning Bill phoned me to say that Adlai wanted to have a top secret breakfast conference with two men in a half hour in our apartment, and they'd use the service elevator. I don't know what went on at the conference because I stayed out of the way. When I got down to the street the ever-vigilant press had picked up the scent, and there were thirty or more at the front door. One woman stuck her head into our car and asked me, "Is Harriman up there?" I said truthfully, "If he is, I didn't see him."

Later that week, I saw Marie Harriman, and she was very funny describing her experiences as the wife of a candidate. As Adlai's sister, I had thought I was having a hectic time at the convention, but it was child's play compared to all that she, Jane Barkley and Mrs. Kefauver went through.

Adlai's name was placed in nomination on Thursday. I

had overheard just one snatch of conversation at Blair House, which I suppose is pertinent to that. My brother was talking on the phone to a Democratic governor. I heard him say, "Don't. Don't do it. I mean that. . . . Thanks, but I mean it." From everything I saw and heard, I'm convinced my brother tried to the last to avoid the nomination, and to satisfy his prior obligation and his own desire to run for re-election as Governor.

By Wednesday night, he still didn't know whether he'd be drafted, but it began to look that way and he settled down to work in earnest at a table in his bedroom. I went to Blair House Friday evening to have dinner with him and Borden and John Fell. (Young Adlai was at Quantico.) The boys knew their father might be nominated that night, but they still didn't know quite what to make of it. Adlai seemed so relaxed he made us all feel more natural, and soon the boys were joking with him just as always. My brother kidded me about the way I'd "posed" for television that day at the convention, when I'd leaned over the side of the box to speak into a microphone, and the camera had shot me from behind. Adlai said, "I saw you on television, Buffie—but only the posterior view. You'll have to learn to protect your rear flank."

A friend had advised me to get dressed up for the evening session at the convention, "because you'd better be prepared for anything that happens." So I zipped out of my light cotton, put on a black silk, and went back to the Coliseum. By that time, I had an odd sense of detachment, rather as if I were an outsider watching an historic event unroll.

Adlai was nominated at 2 A.M. on the third ballot—I think about the only such draft in such circumstances in our political history. I was taken up to Mrs. Truman's box, where

Perle Mesta, Secretary Snyder and several other people were seated. I felt in a haze as hot white lights flashed on us, and above my head floated one small balloon lettered "KEFAU-VER." Mrs. Truman has such grace and naturalness, and I remember how warm her smile was, but I have no recollection of what anybody said. It was three o'clock in the morning when a great roar went up from that weary, sweltering crowd, and below me I saw my brother walk in, with the President. My throat was tight, and I thought of Mother and Father, and wished they could have been there. I heard my brother's voice saying: "Better we lose the election than mislead the people. . . . I ask of you all you have. I will give you all I have . . . in the staggering task that you have assigned to me. I shall always try 'to do justly and to love mercy, and to walk humbly with my God.' " It was a struggle not to cry.

Later I was escorted to one of those cell-like rooms behind the seat tiers, and Ernest appeared, beaming. Borden and John Fell came over, wearing the widest smiles I've ever seen. I met Mrs. John Sparkman and her beautiful young married daughter, and thought they were charming. All the senators there were being very cordial to me. Somebody came up and offered to be my secretary, and I said innocently, "But why should *I* have a secretary?"

When we drove back to Blair House with Adlai, through the silent city, there were still crowds waiting in front to cheer him. Inside, we celebrated with a few close friends; my brother, with a smile, asked for a glass of milk. Even Herman, the Blairs' butler, seemed to have lost a bit of his impassive calm, as he served the guests.

I think Adlai was up the rest of the night, what with the "imperative" calls and conferences. I had a few hours sleep, and then three important calls came in, from people who couldn't reach Adlai on the phone because of the never-ending busy signal, and asked me to take messages to him. I jumped into a dress and shoes—there wasn't time for stockings, girdle, or make-up—and dashed around the corner to Blair House. As soon as I'd panted out the messages, Bill Blair said, "Come on. We're just leaving for the convention. Jump in the car."

I was sandwiched in the back seat between Adlai and Averill Harriman, who were discussing who the new chairman of the Democratic committee should be. In the midst of this fascinating conversation, the thought flashed through my head, I don't even have on lipstick!

When Senator Sparkman was nominated for Vice-President a bit later that Saturday morning, I was right out at the front of the rostrum with him and my brother, waving gaily, still without stockings or lipstick!

Adlai's train stopped in Bloomington on the way back to Springfield on Sunday, and Alverta Duff was at the station, with crowds of friends. She presented Adlai with a floral horseshoe and told him, "If you can't get a good cup of coffee in the White House, you just send for me."

At Springfield, twenty-five thousand people were waiting to greet their Governor who had just been nominated for the Presidency. I think that meant more to Adlai than any other ovation. He had tears in his eyes, as he spoke to them in the shadow of the courthouse.

On Monday night, when the full realization of his situation must have engulfed him, he slipped out of the Mansion by a side door, through the bushes and down the side street to Lincoln's house and there, with the astonished caretaker's permission, he sat for an hour in the darkened living room.

MY BROTHER ADLAI

No one knew about his midnight visit until it slipped out months later, I think from the sharp-eyed state policeman who trailed him.

There was no time for meditation after that and it was his last quiet hour. The new Democratic candidate had no headquarters, no staff, no campaign plans, not even a treasurer for the National Committee. An aide said much later, "You hear of people starting from scratch, but there wasn't even a scratch, when we started."

On the first motor caravan of the campaign, the staff was still so new at that kind of thing that the candidate's car was unmarked, and Adlai sat wedged in with several other men. Onlookers kept asking each other, "Which one is Stevenson?"

Chapter 14

FROM MY DIARY August 9, 1952: "Sat in on Governor's tour-planning conference. They discussed Adlai's major speeches, topic, time, and place. How Adlai kept his humor—once winked at me in glee."

I remember that a visitor used the phrase, "the call of Destiny," and Adlai laughed and said, "Oh, come now, let's not be too grandiloquent."

By that time, all of us around him had a feeling that whether he won or lost the election, his words would be part of history. I began saving every scrap of memo he sent me, and then I'd go into his office and find his wastebasket stuffed full of crumpled yellow sheets covered with his hasty handwriting—speech drafts he'd casually thrown away. Almost any morning, that wastebasket could have been a collector's item.

He was just as casual about his personal safety. Ever since the nomination, Jim Daley, a security officer from the Chicago police force, had been near him twenty-four hours a day. When the Governor worked late at his desk by the basement window, the venetian blinds were usually up, and he'd have made an ideal target, but I'm sure he never gave

it a thought. Once they caught a man crouching in the
bushes outside, and after that, two more police were added
to the guard. I learned later that Adlai's only reaction was,
"Don't tell Buffie. She'd worry."

Fortunately, our nervous systems adapt so fast that the
improbable soon seems normal, and I found that there
wasn't time for personal worries in a day jammed from
8 A.M. to midnight. From my diary August 10: "Have had
newsreel, TV, interviews, photographers in Mansion and
Bloomington—even invitations for *me* to speak! Had huge
American Legion lunch on lawn today. Worked at mail and
A's gifts with secretary. Now thank Heaven I have one.
Phones never let go. [The Mansion hadn't even a switch-
board, when the Presidential nominee came back from Chicago. We soon got one!] House full of men, conferences in
every room."

Ernest sat in on one very special conference, along with
several aides and, I believe, Wilson Wyatt, Adlai's personal
campaign manager and an old friend. My brother was to see
Mr. Truman on August 12 and wanted to go over some
main points before that meeting. Ernest told me afterward
Adlai had decided that if he were elected, he would immediately go to Korea, and also to Japan and India, countries
he felt were of crucial importance in the Far East struggle
against communism. Adlai wondered whether he should
discuss this plan with Mr. Truman at this time in view of
the increased danger that it might somehow become public.
He felt firmly that disclosure of his plan to go to Korea
made during the campaign would look as though he were
trying to make political capital out of that tragic war. Two
months later, when Eisenhower made his "I will go to
Korea" pronouncement, I was traveling on the campaign

train, and I was the one who told Adlai. He was in his compartment working as usual on the next speech, and when I rushed in and blurted out the news, he said mildly, "Well, I've known for quite some time where *I'd* go and *why.*"

In his first major speech of the campaign, which he gave before the American Legion convention in New York that August, he said:

... We talk a great deal about patriotism. What do we mean by patriotism in the context of our times? I venture to suggest that what we mean is a sense of national responsibility which will enable America to remain master of her power—to walk with it in serenity and wisdom, with self-respect and the respect of all mankind; a patriotism that puts country ahead of self; a patriotism which is not short, frenzied outbursts of emotion, but the tranquil and steady dedication of a lifetime. These are words that are easy to utter, but this is a mighty assignment. For it is often easier to fight for principles than to live up to them.

Patriotism, I have said, means putting country before self. This is no abstract phrase. Unhappily, we find some things in American life today of which we cannot be proud.

Consider the groups who seek to identify their special interests with the general welfare. I find it sobering to think that their pressures might one day be focused on me. I have resisted them before and I hope the Almighty will give me the strength to do so again and again. And I should tell you now, as I would tell all other organized groups, that I stand to resist pressures from veterans, too, if I think their demands are excessive or in conflict with the public interest, which must always be the paramount interest. ...

True patriotism, it seems to me, is based on tolerance and a large measure of humility.

There are men among us who use "patriotism" as a club for attacking other Americans. What can we say for the self-styled patriot who thinks that a Negro, a Jew, a Catholic, or a Japanese-American is less an American than he? That betrays the deepest article of our faith, the belief in individual liberty and equality which has always been the heart and soul of the American idea. . . .

It is always accounted a virtue in a man to love his country. With us it is now something more than a virtue. It is a necessity, a condition of survival. When an American says that he loves his country, he means not only that he loves the New England hills, the prairies glistening in the sun, the wide and rising plains, the great mountains, and the sea. He means that he loves an inner air, an inner light in which freedom lives and in which a man can draw the breath of self-respect. . . .

I had gone to New York the day before my brother spoke, because the Women's Auxiliary of the American Legion had asked me to "say a few words" at their luncheon. When I consulted Wilson Wyatt, whose wise advice I valued all through the campaign, about this invitation, he approved heartily, so I swallowed my nervousness and said yes. I was amused to see in *The New York Times* that Mrs. Eisenhower had declined to speak, but that when Mrs. Campbell, the president of the Auxiliary, said that Mrs. Ives had accepted, Mamie quickly did, too. That was my first solo appearance before a large group, and it took all the nerve I had to get up on the platform before several thousand women and choke out a few remarks. Afterward, the ladies generously presented Mrs. Eisenhower and me with gift certificates entitling us to a hat made by Mr. John, the milliner. I was delighted at the prospect, but I never could snatch time, in that campaign fall, to try on hats. Sometimes I've wondered if Mrs. Eisenhower ever got hers.

After the luncheon, I went back to the Biltmore to see if my brother had arrived. On the seventeenth floor, I found a great mob of people pushing down toward the end of the corridor. When I spotted the Mayor of New York and the reporters whose faces were already becoming almost as familiar to me as relatives', I knew Adlai must be there. I identified myself to the plain-clothes men, and got into the suite where typewriters were already clacking away. Bill Blair came out of a room with his hands full of papers. As usual, he seemed to know who everybody was, and was quietly checking names against the appointment sheets. Between callers, I slipped in to have a minute's visit with Adlai. He had a little blue envelope in his hand, and he said to me gaily, "You wouldn't know who this is from, would you?" His eyes were twinkling. "Marlene Dietrich." (By this time his fan mail must be almost rivaling hers!)

I sat with him in an open car when we were rushed across town to Madison Square Garden for his speech. Adlai was becoming reconciled, through necessity, to screaming sirens and motorcycle escorts, and in fact, he commented admiringly on the way the New York police handled this job, and their superb timing. As for me, that dash through stop lights, with sirens screaming and people turning to stare, was a childhood dream come true. I was ashamed to tell anyone what fun it was, especially when it always made Adlai bite his lip. On one such ride, he gave me an amused look and said, "Buffie, you're the one who should have been a politician."

From my diary: "Day after we got back from New York, Mr. Karsh came to do photographs of the Governor and me, and I think his results were really quite good. He didn't keep Adlai posing. [I don't believe anything bores my brother so much as being photographed or painted.] Karsh just let him walk in and turn and sit down and then he quickly snapped it. With me, it was more trying. I posed for over 2 hours under very hot lights. Sunday before we left for church, I had to pose again for the A.P., and a *Saturday Evening Post* man was interviewing me, then I had to go out and pose with Adlai for I.N.S. Guests for lunch—some distinguished writers, all talking about the campaign. In afternoon, I worked with my secretary, saw *Post* man again, drove to Bloomington. Thus the days go by—full—too full."

The Democratic National Committee officials had already met at the Mansion, for a two-day conference around the long table in the state dining room. My hurried diary notes recorded: "18 for lunch—40 for buffet dinner. Sat in on an evening meeting. Interesting to watch A's quiet face, quick smile and occasional humor. Senator Sparkman dropped off to sleep for a minute, right at the meeting, and others showed fatigue too. I like Sparkman very much—such a *good*, thoughtful man."

Another entry mentions: "Had to quickly organize buffet for 80—the campaign staff. Interesting to meet the group who handles the appalling load of mail. Several experts have come to help."

When Adlai was organizing his campaign staff, soon after the convention, they rented a big old house a block from the Mansion, as headquarters. My brother said to an aide, "Maybe some of the staff can sleep there and even get a cook, and that will be cheaper than a hotel."

Within three weeks, the staff had mushroomed so fast that they had to take over two floors of the Leland Hotel, too.

Newton Minow, who had come to work July 1, said, "Things were happening so fast that anybody who'd been around twenty-four hours was a veteran."

A good many of the staff were volunteers, and a more selfless, devoted lot I never saw. Once when my brother was speaking to a group of Volunteers-for-Stevenson, he said, "One of the greatest satisfactions I have had has been the support of people like yourselves—people who may wear a party label over their hearts but never over their eyes—but most of all, and most important of all, who want nothing for themselves." Adlai's old friends from 1948, Jane Dick and "Dutch" Smith, headed the Volunteers-for-Stevenson—this time not just in Illinois, but in forty-eight states. Joe Bohrer, heading the McLean County group, was another old friend who did a fine job. In Chicago, our lifelong friend Margaret Willing Farwell and her daughter Joan were two of the hard-working volunteers. Stephen Mitchell, a fine Chicago lawyer and one of Adlai's original nonprofessional boosters in 1948, assumed the chairmanship of the Democratic National Committee at Adlai's request, and a happy choice it was, too.

By September, the campaign was off on the right foot—but the wrong shoe! At a Labor Day rally in Flint, a photographer caught a picture of a hole in Adlai's shoe that became famous. (I'd persuaded him to get a new gray suit, by bringing a tailor right to the Mansion, but he kept on wearing those old shoes because they were so comfortable.) He was sitting on a platform with one leg crossed over the other when the photographer shot him from below—and the resulting footage, hole and all, was rather conspicuous. The next year when he was in Southern India and got word that the photographer had won a Pulitzer Prize, Adlai cabled him: "Congratulations. I'll bet this is the first time anyone ever won a Pulitzer prize for a hole in one."

But I think what he told the great crowd of auto workers in Detroit that day was much more newsworthy:

> . . . Contrary to the impressions fostered by some of the press, you are not *my* captives, and I am not *your* captive. On the contrary, I might as well make it clear right now that I intend to do exactly what I think right and best for all, for all of us—business, labor, agriculture—alike. And I have no doubt that you will do exactly what you think best at the election.
>
> You are freeborn Americans—a proud and honorable station, carrying with it the right and the responsibility to make up your own minds—and so am I. So if either of us thinks in terms of captivity, let's agree right here and now on a mutual pact of liberation. . . .

In Flint, later the same day, he said:

> . . . We must stop treating labor and management like fighting cocks, taking sides and egging them on. This kind of fomented disagreement isn't good. It is magnifying honest differences of opinion into artificial barriers between large groups of people. We are talking ourselves into a kind of class hatred. And there can't be class hatreds or group antogonisms in a healthy democracy. . . .
>
> You know, here in Flint, from your own experience, how unemployment can strike suddenly and unexpectedly. And you know also how intelligent, imaginative work—such as Governor Williams and Senator Moody have done recently— can improve an unemployment situation. The spectre of unemployment and depression haunts everyone who has to work for a living, and that's most of us these days. The Democratic party is proud of the steps it has proposed and the country has taken these past twenty years to conquer this recurrent

misfortune. But, like peace on earth, the goal has not been won. And, like the quest for peace, we must keep everlastingly at the cause and cure of economic disaster.

Both General Eisenhower and Adlai spoke at the National Plowing Contest at Kasson, Minnesota, that week, and my brother said later in Phoenix, "After my distinguished opponent had given his speech, I began to wonder if he didn't think it was a plowing-under contest. At least, he spent most of his time plowing under the farm platform of the Republican party. For my part, I didn't have to plow under the Democratic farm platform; I could stand on it. In fact, I am perfectly willing to have the General try and stand on it too—though I wish he would be a bit more careful and request permission of the copyright owners."

I think my brother's regard for his adversary got some rude jolts that month. First, General Eisenhower publicly endorsed Senator Jenner of Indiana who had called General George Marshall "a front man for traitors" and "a living lie." From long observation Adlai had developed a profound respect for George Marshall and he naturally expected Eisenhower to tolerate no such slander of his former superior officer and benefactor. Instead it was reported that after a visit from Senator McCarthy, General Eisenhower had even cut out all mention of Marshall from a speech in Wisconsin. And then there was the famous "peace conference" with Senator Taft where again party harmony emerged as apparently the first objective of the "great crusade." Adlai remarked: "I shall not argue that it is necessarily fatal to change horses in mid-stream. But I doubt if it is wise to jump on a struggling two-headed elephant trying to swim in both directions at the same time."

In September, when my brother returned from his first campaign trip to the West Coast, I accompanied him on a motor caravan through New England. The second day was dismally rainy, and we were riding in open cars. The raw wind whipped at my feathered hat until most of the feathers blew all over the countryside, and I ended up looking like a wet plucked hen. The people who'd turned out to greet "our candidate" were huddled in damp clumps. To add to my discouragement, a lady in the car kept trying to show me how to wave. She'd say, "You should have seen Mrs. Roosevelt. *She* knew how to wave. Don't try to wave *at* anyone, just wave. The people don't really know who you are—but it's friendly to wave."

So I braced myself for the next town, and found I was making large circular sweeps of my arm, great rolling gestures. "Oh, dear," my kind mentor said. "That's not natural." She took my arm and began to pump it up and down, with my hand flapping. The rain came faster, the wind blew harder. At the next stop, in front of a high school, I asked my teacher if I could please go into the Ladies Room. She looked doubtful, but gave me two minutes. I used up this allotment trying to find my way in the school basement, and I was wishing gloomily that I could get lost and stay lost.

The high spots made up for those low points. At Hartford, Connecticut, Adlai made a magnificent speech on atoms for peace. At Springfield, Massachusetts, he spoke from a platform built up over the crowds, and said cheerfully, "I've been accused of talking over people's heads, but this is the first time I've actually been able to do it!" In even those brief, impromptu talks, he had an unquenchable humor and patience and conviction, and everytime I watched his listeners respond to it, I felt refreshed.

Somewhere in Connecticut on that trip, he received what he thought was about the most amusing of all the hundreds of presents: a portrait of himself made up like George Washington, in white wig and ruffled cravat. After muttering something about making "a silk purse out of a sow's ear," he said to me that there was evidently little the Democrats couldn't do and nothing they wouldn't do for their candidate.

I loved the reception in New Haven, on the Yale campus. I hadn't seen that place since my brother was at school nearby, and what a difference in our visit this time! From my diary: "I learned that day how to squirm through crowds and get right up to the ropes and even under—when I wanted to. Crowds all try to keep up with Adlai, who always has walked too fast, so it takes some doing to get up to the front before he speaks."

My next diary entry was September 20: "Flew to Quantico for Ad's ceremony."

Young Adlai was receiving his commission as second lieutenant in the Marines. (He later commanded a platoon of tanks in Korea.) My brother had been invited by the commandant to speak to the "graduating class." He refused to make political capital of the wretched war in Korea and the dangers the boys faced, his own son included. A volunteer member of his staff, Willard Wirtz, told me that when it was suggested to Adlai that he point out in his speech what a strong personal reason he had for ending the war, "you never heard anyone say no faster."

Earlier that month, he had spoken out with real passion against those who called Korea "a useless war." Adlai thought —and still thinks—that Mr. Truman's decision to defend Korea was one of the major and most courageous moves to halt communism. And at Quantico he said:

. . . In one way or another each generation has to fight for its freedom in the conditions of its time. Our times are hard— as hard as any in our history. We, your fathers, have asked you to make ready to fight so that you and your children may walk upright and unafraid. . . .

Why must you defend your country when your country seems to lie in peace around you? Is it because of some mistake made in the past by those older than yourselves—some failure of foresight in decision? Is it for that you must offer the sacrifice of the young years of your lives?

Certainly there have been failures and mistakes. . . . But it is not to make good the errors of the past that you are here but to make good the promise of the future. . . . It is to affirm and to establish the faith that a peaceful world can in truth be built, that you and the thousands upon thousands of young men like you have been asked to serve your country with the hope and promise of your lives.

My own son was standing beside me at Quantico wearing his newly earned Air Force wings, and I knew that meant he'd soon be flying jet fighter-bomber missions in Korea. Tim had a month's leave, and he spent a large part of it with the campaign tour, making himself useful but inconspicuous. The only time he wore his uniform on leave was that day at the Marine base.

My diary continued:

September 21st: In New York again. Mrs. Marshall Field gave a tea for the Volunteers-for-Stevenson, "to meet Mrs. Franklin D. Roosevelt and Mrs. Ernest L. Ives." It's hard for me to believe my name would be linked with the wonderful Eleanor Roosevelt's. Before we left the party, she and I were having a press conference together. She took it naturally and seemed so easy with the presswomen asking rather leading questions. It was a wonderful experience for me.

I told Mrs. Roosevelt how she'd even been held up to me as a model on how to wave.

That was a momentous week for me. The next day, in Washington, Mrs. Truman invited me for tea, with a few of her close friends. Although I'd met her on nomination night, this was the first time I'd really talked to her, and I thought I'd never seen a sounder woman in all my life— with a lovely dignity and humor and naturalness. She wore a light blue silk dress, and I decided no photographs do her justice, partly because they don't show how graceful she is.

I have met several wives of very important statesmen who frankly fell below my expectations. I remember thinking once or twice, Well, I'd hate to see *her* represent our country as a President's wife. But with Mrs. Roosevelt and Mrs. Truman, I felt a sense of pride that our country should have them as First Ladies.

From Washington I went to North Carolina, where I'd been invited to speak. My diary reports:

> Sept. 23rd: Flew to Raleigh. Met by Mrs. Scott. Had a press conference in Hotel; got along pretty well; Spoke after Sadie McCain introduced me and she said such nice things it made me want to cry. Very big audience. Valerie Nicholson and Arnette met me at the hotel and drove me to Southern Pines. Seemed so good to be with these dear old friends again.
>
> 24th: Reception at Shaw House by our Historical Assn. was the most complimentary thing that ever happened to me! Vera Clay for News Week interviewed this A.M. out at the farm. Averys drove me to Ashboro for a rally and I was showered with gifts, a hat, baskets of dried flowers, paper rack and stockings. I made a "speech."
>
> 25th: Drove to Goldsboro with K. McCall. All restful and agreeable. Talked to Woman's Club. Took plane at Raleigh for Washington and then train to Indianapolis to rejoin the campaign. Met Adlai at Gov. Schrickers'.

26th: Wonderful picnic at the Barkleys in Paducah and Adlai spoke—then to Louisville. Fine reception! I went to the Bingham's cocktail party for the press.

28th: Springfield. Went to church with Adlai and Ernest. Lovely to be in our own beds but, oh!, such a lot of mail.

29th: We drove to Urbana for reception. Interesting talk with some professors about "X." ("X" was a topflight newspaper man who had been covering Ike and had decided he couldn't vote for him.)

October 1st: Big national Volunteers-for-Stevenson doings. Thirty-eight states represented at conferences in Springfield. Dinner at Leland, then reception at Mansion.

Oct. 3rd: Tim and I left home at 7 A.M. to join the party at airport. In Ohio all day and home after midnight! Glorious weather. Drove in motorcade with three mayors from Kentucky into Cincinnati. Wonderful lunch meeting. Thence to Columbus to Governor Lausche's. What nice people! Relaxed. Pleasant dinner. Amusing to be in Taft territory, and he talked in Columbus too but it didn't hurt our crowds.

4th: At work all day at the Mansion with all others off on a trip. I am very weary and glad to just stay and do my mail, etc. A month from today and it's all over, in or out! It has been and is a fascinating experience.

On October 9, we took off for a three-day plane tour; Adlai was to speak in Oklahoma, Texas, New Orleans and Florida. The campaign party traveled in three DC 6's, with Fred Jaberjahn piloting the candidate's plane. Members of Adlai's staff, including several aides and two secretaries, a press-relations man and photographer, sat up front; six seats had been removed to make room for typewriters and mimeograph machines. In the back were Adlai, Carl McGowan, Ernest, myself and visitors who came aboard from time to time. Aunt Letitia, who was seventy-three and had never flown in her life, joined us in St. Louis, and she was the greatest campaigner I ever want to see. No matter how bumpy it got, she never once complained, although when the hostess came by with our trays, she'd murmur, "Oh, just a little tea, please." Adlai, who was sitting across the aisle from her, always writing or conferring, would look over with a smile and ask, "Are you all right, Aunt Letitia?"

"Oh, yes, dear boy," she always said. "Why don't you rest your eyes a bit?" He'd laugh and go back to the relentless work.

The crowds were so dense that when we got off a plane we couldn't even carry a small suitcase; it took two hands, and then some, to get through. I had a tiny leather case that held make-up and aspirin—two basic necessities on campaign tours!—and sometimes I managed to cling to it. We'd file down the ramp ahead of Adlai into the mobs below, and police or local Democrats would take us in tow. Then a great shout would go up as Adlai appeared and the crowds surged forward.

Our first stop on that trip was Oklahoma City. At a luncheon at the hotel there, Aunt Letitia sat by an agreeable man and enjoyed herself immensely. Finally she asked him, "Which one is the Governor of Oklahoma?" He said, "Why, you're sitting beside him." She thought this was a great joke on herself.

When Adlai spoke in a park there, she and I sat in the front row. Afterward, people came up to shake hands, and one old man said to Aunt Letitia, "I voted for your father. I remember you."

"How nice of you," she said. And in a quick aside to me, "Buffie, your slip's showing."

In San Antonio, we went to a big Democratic women's reception, and the hostess asked us to "make a little talk."

Aunt Letitia mounted a chair, and she told her listeners
about the contrast between olden-time campaign trips and
today's. "I find air travel very satisfactory," she said serenely.
"We Stevensons have been in retirement since 1892, but
now we are emerging." At that, who should come through
the door but Adlai. It couldn't have been better timed if
they'd rehearsed it.

When our plane approached New Orleans, the mimeograph machines were still ticking away to turn out copies
of the speech Adlai was to deliver that night, which the
press had to have the moment we landed. The pilot circled
the city slowly three times, until the last page was finished,
and the mystified crowds waiting below must have wondered
if we were in trouble. Newspaper versions of Adlai's speeches
were often quite different from the spoken ones, because he
was so pressed for time he went right on writing or rewriting
up to the last minute. Often, while he was being introduced,
Adlai would be sitting beside the podium still scribbling on
his speech.

When we drove into New Orleans from the airport that
night, it was already dark; in the city, marchers walked beside our open cars down Canal Street, carrying kerosene
flares. It was a beautiful sight, but the fumes from the flares
were so strong that we choked and coughed. I saw Adlai
wipe his streaming eyes while he went on waving from his
perch on the top of the back seat. In spite of the fumes, I
was deeply moved by that procession; our cars traveled exactly the same route my brother and I had taken with Grandfather Davis on the streetcar, as children.

We were due at a dinner party at Antoine's, and I hated
to face all those people in the same tired navy jersey dress
I'd worn since early morning, but there wasn't time to

change. I wouldn't have missed that dinner—or meeting the other guests—for anything. Mrs. Isadore Newman, of the Volunteers group, had asked me to tell her some of Adlai's favorite dishes, so we ate baked pompano and Antoine's flaming cherry dessert, but my poor brother was having conferences at the hotel, and had to miss the dinner.

He always had a good appetite, even just before a speech. He'd say, "Oh, all I want is a sandwich," but I noticed that if a hot dinner was put before him, he'd dive right in. I can still picture him with a tray and a copy of a speech side by side on the small table by his chair, in a hundred hotel bedrooms. There were so many decisions to be made at each stop; long-distance calls waiting "stacked," local politicians bringing problems to be hashed out, delegations to meet and the endless procession of speeches to work on. One of my diary entries is: "He and I are so different. When I'm hurried, I'm sharp, and he never is—he's as kindly as ever."

He spoke that night in New Orleans in Beauregard Square. The soft air, the beautiful trees, the intensely receptive audience, all these made it a thrilling hour. I was very proud when he didn't hesitate to express his honest convictions on the Tidelands oil question, right in Louisiana. He ended his speech with a few sentences in French, and I'd been flattered because he'd asked me to "check" that part when he was writing it. He delivered it with a flawless French accent, *I* thought! The charming Mrs. Russell Long sat beside me on the platform, and I was happy to see a favorite congressman friend of ours, Hale Boggs.

Back in our hotel, the electricity had gone off, and Aunt Letitia's luggage had been misplaced. She went to bed in my dressing gown. Friends, as always, crowded into our rooms, and we chatted by candlelight. Aunt Letitia must have lain there praying patiently, in true Presbyterian style, for a chance to sleep, but she never complained.

At dawn the next day, we left for Florida. In Tampa, Ernest, Aunt Letitia and I were riding in a big car behind the candidate's, and our driver was so busy telling me he'd been born in Bloomington that he got out of line in the procession. This must have rattled him rather badly, because he shouted to the traffic man, "Hey, you've got to let me back into line. I've got Mamie in the back seat!"

Aunt Letitia said, "Well, Buffie, that settles it. You'll have to wear bangs now."

When we rejoined Adlai, somebody had just thrust a huge, live fish into his arms and asked him to pose with the flopping thing for photographers. We Americans seem to expect a candidate to be saint, superman and buffoon.

After that strenuous three days, I went to Bloomington to give a reception for state candidates, and then Ernest and I flew out to meet Adlai in San Francisco. When I arrived in a room high in the Fairmont Hotel, I wanted to rush right to a window and look at the magnificent view, surely one of the loveliest in the whole world. But the presswomen were already waiting for me right there, so I dodged into the bathroom long enough to fix up my haggard face and comb my hair. After the interview, a chef came in with a beautiful cherry pie with Adlai's name written on top. He said he'd read that it was my brother's favorite dessert. The security men wouldn't let strangers into the candidate's room, so I took that culinary work of art in to him. There were a lot of men there talking in huddles, and they looked rather surprised to see me come sailing in with a pie.

Adlai said recently that the rally in San Francisco's great Cow Palace that night stands out in his mind as one of the peak moments of the campaign. The people had been pouring in since early afternoon, when the doors opened, and the overflow crowds out front were so thick that our party got separated in the rush. The Democratic chairman had to climb over a back fence to get in! Adlai made one of his best speeches, I thought, and there was an electric excitement in the air. All our spirits soared; I think we really felt victory might be around the corner. To climax the evening, we went to Chinatown afterward to see a marvelous parade and fireworks in honor of the candidate.

At eight the next morning we assembled sleepily to leave, and I was sad to see that beautiful pie still uncut. My brother often mourned the waste of food, on our tours—especially cherry pie. In each hotel, such tempting buffets were spread out, or elaborate *hors d'oeuvres,* and too often there wasn't time for even a taste. I remember Adlai, as he left a hotel room, looking back at an untouched salmon, and saying, "Put that in your handbag, Buff."

When I went down to get into the car I was assigned to, it seemed to have disappeared, and my brother called to me to jump in with him. During this few seconds' delay, a woman rushed up and said, "Oh, Governor, I used to live in Illinois. Do let me shake your hand." Of course, Adlai reached out and shook hands. Just then, the sirens started up, and our car began to move off slowly. The poor woman shrieked, "Oh, my diamond ring—it's gone!" The police stopped the car and we looked at each other aghast, as the photographers shouted happily, "Just one more shot of the lady who lost her ring shaking hands with the Governor." We drove off still wondering about the mysterious disappearance, but Adlai couldn't help seeing the funny side, and told the story later on himself.

This reminds me of another "jewelry" story. A New York jeweler had sent my brother a rhinestone-donkey pin which Adlai gave to me, and I wore it constantly as a good-luck emblem. In Texas, I was startled to see accounts in the papers of "Mrs. Ives' donkey made of diamonds." In Texas, even rhinestones are bigger and better!

After all the Dixiecrat shouting I was happy to find there were still so many Texans who were Stevenson supporters. Their hospitable welcome buoyed us up—in Dallas, Fort Worth and Houston. In the La Mar Hotel in Houston, the crowds were so large and vociferous the whole place was in an uproar. Adlai said to an elevator operator, "I guess you'll be glad when this is over." The girl answered feelingly, "I'll be glad when that man gets to wherever he's going." Then she recognized him and was nearly paralyzed with embarrassment.

In Fort Worth, the Democratic women had made attractive little white parasols with "Gladly for Adlai" written in red and blue, to raise money for their campaign fund. They presented me with one I carried on our final whistle-stop tour. There were many other ingenious souvenirs—bracelets, kerchiefs, and so on—that local women's groups made and sold, all over the country.

I was interested to learn that local groups could earmark the funds they'd raised for special projects, such as a telecast or advertisements, and the Democratic National Committee financed major campaign expenditures, including plane and train trips. Neale Roache of the committee was responsible for all travel arrangements for our twelve-day whistle-stop tour, and I'll never know how he managed things so smoothly. Wilson Wyatt's assistant, Victor Sholis, traveled with us, along with liaison men and aides. There were about sixty of us in the party, plus eighty or ninety newspaper, radio and television men and women, filling six cars in all. A fan sent Adlai a Whistle-stop tie, red with semaphore signals and railroad tracks, and of course there were donkey neckties of many colors.

In the candidate's car, there were five compartments: Adlai had one for an office and one for sleeping; the security officer, Jim Daley, and Carl McGowan and Bill Blair, occupied the others. The car also had a small diner, seating twelve. At each stop, three phones were hooked up around the dining-room table, and telephone conferences went on endlessly. Adlai was impressed with the meals that the chef, William Banks, turned out in his tiny adjoining kitchen in the midst of this hubbub. He used to peer into that little galley and say, "How do you suppose he manages?" The chef's squash pie made such a hit I asked for the recipe.

Ernest, Aunt Letitia and I, along with two secretaries and members of the immediate official staff, were in the next car. Then came two club cars where visitors sat when they rode with us for a few hours. (In each state, we received a five- or six-page mimeographed sheet listing the names of people who would board the train at various stops.) Behind were the press cars. Most of the reporters piled out at each whistle-stop, to listen to Adlai talk informally to the crowds from the observation platform at the end of his car. Somehow he managed to say something different almost every time, even when the stops were twenty minutes apart. If he didn't, the reporters would make faces! Once they went further than that. Adlai received a birth announcement saying "My name is Jimmie. I am two days old, but I am already for Stevenson." My brother was so amused at this he told a whistle-stop audience the story, remarking, "Evidently it's not time for a change—for little Jimmie." The crowd loved it, so Adlai repeated it all that day, with variations. The next morning, he received a note from the reporters, with a dollar bill attached by a safety pin: "We have just cut little Jimmie's throat—here's a dollar to bury him." Adlai laughed and took the hint, and the Jimmie story was interred forthwith.

But at each stop he introduced several live members of his family, until I was afraid the press would get up a collection to bury us, too. At the end of his remarks, we'd line up and pop out on cue. For instance, he'd say, "This is my sister, Mrs. Ernest Ives, who keeps me out of trouble." The first time somebody called, "Hi, Buffie," I peered at the faces below searching for someone I knew! After that, I welcomed those friendly hails from strangers. Aunt Letitia drew cheers, and well she might.

At nearly every stop, somebody would present me with orchids, and the little compartment I shared with Ernest soon looked like a tropical jungle. I even had orchids pinned to the curtains. I couldn't bear to throw them away, and I couldn't wear the same flowers at the next stop for fear the welcoming committee there would have another bouquet ready.

Even without the floral offerings, that "room" was rather crowded quarters for two, for twelve days. Ernest and I each had one coat hanger, but when I wanted to change my clothes, I'd crouch down, drag my suitcase out from under the seat, and pull out a dress. I had a navy blue jersey and a knit ribbon silk that I wore most of the time, and I blessed their wrinkle-proof endurance. I read in the papers that

Mrs. Eisenhower said she was getting fat on the Republican campaign train, and that she'd heard Mrs. Ives was getting thin and she couldn't understand how I did it. A press-woman told me she had a maid along to take care of her clothes, and I used to think of her occasionally when I was down on the floor groping for my suitcase.

Nobody would claim that whistle-stop campaigning is straight bliss. For the candidate, it is almost inhuman, and yet heartening too, because the crowds have a spontaneity and variety that's endearingly American. These were citizens who came down to a train of their own free will to look over a candidate—to cheer him or even heckle. The hecklers were few—and mostly very young—and Adlai took them on so good-humoredly it was fun to watch. Once three bobby-soxers stood right below him waving big "I Like Ike" placards. Adlai said to them, "I like Ike, too. And now that we've agreed on that, won't you put those things down so we can talk?" The bobby-soxers giggled sheepishly, lowered their banners, and listened. My favorite was the little boy in Spokane who got rattled and screeched: "Hooray for Stevenhower." Adlai laughed out loud and said, "I think that young man is going to be a great diplomat." In many towns, he received large placards covered with Ike buttons and signatures, with a heading: "I Liked Ike—but I've switched to Stevenson."

Like Senator Wayne Morse, a lot of people evidently couldn't stomach the way the Republican Old Guard seemed to be taking over, or the Nixon-McCarthy type of campaigning. On the third day of this whistle-stop journey, in Cleveland, Adlai answered them in a speech that brought us many happy personal reactions. Even European friends sent heartening messages approving my brother's stinging indictment of such campaign tactics.

In that speech he also went into detail about the deposition he had given, by court request, in the trial of Alger Hiss. He had become acquainted with Hiss in 1933 in Washington, when they both worked in the Agricultural Adjustment Administration. He never saw him again until they met twelve years later in the State Department. He had never known Hiss socially, or been in his home. When he was asked to say what Hiss' reputation had been in the government circles when he knew him, Adlai answered truthfully, "Good." As a lawyer, he feels strongly that every citizen has a duty to give testimony in a court, and give it honestly. He feels too that to withhold honest testimony for fear it may be embarrassing is cowardice, and that an official who would do such a thing doesn't deserve public respect. And he thought that Mr. Nixon, as a lawyer, was hardly honoring the profession—or the profession of politics —when he made constant references to that Hiss deposition and charged my brother with "bad judgment," carefully omitting to mention that both Eisenhower and John Foster Dulles were on the board of trustees which re-elected Hiss president of the Carnegie Endowment Fund. In fact, Adlai pointed out in his speech:

. . . In December, 1946, Hiss was chosen to be president of the Carnegie Endowment by the Board of Trustees of which John Foster Dulles was chairman. After Hiss was elected, but before he took office, a Detroit lawyer offered to provide Mr. Dulles with evidence that Hiss had a provable Communist record. No such report or warning ever came to me. Under date of December 26, Mr. Dulles responded. Listen to what Mr. Dulles said:

"I have heard the report which you refer to, but I have

confidence that there is no reason to doubt Mr. Hiss' complete loyalty to our American institutions. I have been thrown into intimate contact with him at San Francisco, London and Washington . . . Under these circumstances I feel a little skeptical about information which seems inconsistent with all that I personally know and what is the judgment of reliable friends and associates in Washington."

. . . Alger Hiss, General Eisenhower and Dulles continued as fellow-members of the Board of Trustees until after the conviction of Alger Hiss.

I bring these facts to the American people not to suggest that either General Eisenhower or John Foster Dulles is soft toward Communists or even guilty of the bad judgment that the General's running mate charges against me. . . .

But I know and you know that we do not strengthen freedom by diminishing it. We do not weaken communism abroad or at home by false or misleading charges carefully timed for election purposes. For I believe with all my heart that those who would beguile the voters by lies or half-truths, or corrupt them by fear and falsehood, are committing spiritual treason. . . .

While I'm on that subject, I want to mention another, later time when Adlai spoke out passionately against McCarthyism, in March of 1954. He spoke as a statesman, not as a politician, and he spelled out the dreadful dangers in flouting democratic procedures and trespassing on the President's prerogatives. I think that speech was a catalyst. The "anything for harmony" policy was sorely strained already. A little later, Senator Flanders criticized McCarthy on the floor of the senate; then the Army released its list of the McCarthy-Roy Cohn uses of pressure, resulting in the Army-McCarthy hearings. That marked the beginning of the end of a sorry episode, and I'm deeply proud of my brother because he never lost his nerve or tempered his convictions.

After a major speech in a city, and the crowds and lights and blaring sirens, we'd get back on the train for the night, and as it went through the quiet, sleeping towns, they gave back a feeling of peace and serenity. Then the tempo of the next day would catch us up again. I'm giving one morning's schedule here, as a sample:

Saturday, October 25, 1952

6:55 A.M. EST	Lv.	Albany, New York.
8:00 A.M. "	Ar.	Hyde Park Station, and motorcade to Franklin D. Roosevelt Memorial.
8:05 A.M. "	Ar.	Franklin D. Roosevelt Memorial. Governor Stevenson will place wreath on Roosevelt's grave, and then drive to "Val Kill" for breakfast with Mrs. Roosevelt. Wire service representatives and photographers will go with Governor. Balance of Party to proceed to Nelson House, Poughkeepsie—and wait.
8:25 A.M. "	Ar.	Val Kill.
8:55 A.M. "	Lv.	Val Kill.
9:00 A.M. "	Ar.	Nelson House, Poughkeepsie. Governor Stevenson will address Rally from Balcony.
9:10 A.M. "	Lv.	Nelson House and board train.
9:15 A.M. "	Lv.	Poughkeepsie.
10:35 A.M. "	Ar.	Rensselaer (Yard Stop).
10:55 A.M. "	Lv.	Rensselaer (Boston & Albany RR).
12:20 P.M. "	Ar.	Pittsfield, Massachusetts. Leave train and speak from Platform near Station.
12:35 P.M. "	Lv.	Pittsfield.

And on and on.

When our train reached Hyde Park, I looked out and there was Mrs. Roosevelt, hatless, with her Scottie on a leash, waiting just like any other hostess to collect her guests at

the station. Her son Franklin and his wife were there too—
an attractive, tall young couple. In Mrs. Roosevelt's simple,
charming house, three small round tables were set up in
the dining end of the living room, and we relaxed over
scrambled eggs, bacon, coffee and muffins. I noticed that our
hostess, who knows so well the tight timetable of campaigners, kept an unobtrusive eye on the service and made sure
that more hot muffins and coffee arrived promptly. It was
such a gay, easy half-hour. We knew that John Roosevelt
had come out for Ike, and Mrs. Roosevelt told Adlai that
one evening when John and his wife were out, neighbors
went in and filled their whole house with Stevenson banners
and buttons!

Seeing my brother and Mrs. Roosevelt together, I had a
strong sense of their mutual respect and appreciation. I
knew Adlai admired her, not just for her qualities as a
person and a citizen, but because of his experience with her
sound judgment, tactfulness and enormous vitality when
they worked together in the U.N. As for my husband that
day, Ernest was almost speechless with pleasure, meeting the
person he thinks "is the greatest woman of our times, and
one of the great women in history."

Over breakfast, our hostess and Adlai were exchanging
funny stories on the rigors and rush of campaigning. A few
days later, when she introduced him at a luncheon in New
York given by women Volunteers-for-Stevenson, she referred
to that, and my brother asked her if she could please tell
him how a candidate ever found time to get his hair cut.

For time and money saved, I think that luncheon for
2,500 women was outstanding: each guest was given a box
lunch, and when we opened our "shoe box," on top of the
waxed-paper packets of food was a smart silk handkerchief

with the candidate's picture on it—I think a gift of the Ladies Garment Workers' Union.

Adlai talked to his audience about many serious issues, from education to atomic warfare, and he said, "There are some areas of political life about which women, I believe, feel more keenly than men. Anything that strikes at the security or traditional teachings of home and family is a matter of deep concern to women, even more than to men." He also told them, "I will not promise miracles—I leave that to someone else."

When we left the Commodore Hotel after the luncheon, his car went off first with the usual wailing of sirens, and a group of us remained chatting on the sidewalk. Suddenly the sirens sounded again, motorcycle cops escorted a long black car to the curb, and I thought, Why, Adlai's come back for something. Instead, out of the car stepped General Eisenhower and Governor Dewey! At that, the Volunteers burst out laughing and set up a chant, "We want Stevenson." One of the reporters following them leaned over and muttered, "We do too!"

In the evening, Adlai was one of the speakers at a rally in Madison Square Garden, and among the star performers were, as I recall, Humphrey Bogart, Lauren Bacall and Mercedes McCambridge. In fact, there were so many speakers that the program was running overtime, and it had to be hurriedly revised to fit the radio time limit. I was sitting near Mrs. Roosevelt on the platform and she whispered that her ten-minute allotment had been cut down to five, then to one minute. She was as easy and gracious as ever, about this. In painful contrast, there were others who droned on and on—until someone switched off the lights!

The Garden was filled to the rafters, with standees jamming the aisles, and just before my brother spoke, I was appalled but also amused to see Adlai's son Borden thread his way onto the crowded platform, with a Roosevelt grandson, Susie Hinchcliffe, and lovely Adrienne Osborne who is now my daughter-in-law. Borden looked so trusting that some kind-hearted person managed to wedge in four more folding chairs.

All three boys joined us in Boston, during a week-end stop there. Young Adlai, who was on leave, arrived beaming, and told us, "The taxi driver who brought me here is so strong for Dad he didn't even want to let me pay the fare!"

We never had any problem with wasted food, when the boys were around. Borden had said expansively to some of his Harvard classmates, "Come on up and see Dad." While they were waiting in his suite, I noticed their eyes rolled toward the buffet supper laid out. They were much too polite to mention hunger, but when they were urged, how they dived in. John Fell didn't let the fancy basket of fruit sent up by the management go to waste, either. I have such grateful memories of that hotel staff—and many others— whose thoughtful courtesies went far beyond fruit.

Our second day in Boston, a Sunday, after church in Cambridge and a large luncheon party with Governor Dever, we started off on a motorcade that went on for about six hours and seemed to cover all of eastern Massachusetts. Aunt Letitia and I were in a car with the Governor's sister, Marie Dever. Somehow the driver got separated from the rest of the party, so we three eventually had tea at a roadside hamburger stand, and never did get to a tea being given in our honor. Some truck drivers sitting next to us at the counter were so gallant, and such Stevenson fans, that we had a nice time anyway.

On October 30, the ninth day of whistle-stopping, we arrived at Pittsburgh. I was worried about Adlai that day. There had been a riot in a state prison at Chester, Illinois, and the mutinous convicts held seven guards as hostages. My anxious brother was keeping in touch with Lt. Governor Dixon and the department head by phone, and he had complete confidence in their ability to handle the situation, but as Governor, Adlai felt that the responsibility was his, especially if lives were in jeopardy. Advisers had been begging him not to go to Illinois, and interrupt the campaign tour. On top of his serious concern over the riot, Adlai had a tooth that had been troubling him, and he looked exhausted.

After his speech in Pittsburgh's Hunt Armory, we returned to a hotel suite with Mayor Lawrence and many other people. I took a long-distance call for my brother; it was Wilson Wyatt, phoning from New York. When I went looking for Adlai, I couldn't find him anywhere. An aide took me aside and told me the Governor had slipped away, to fly that night to the prison in a special plane.

We were a desolate lot of campaigners, straggling back to the railroad yard around midnight. I joined Jane Dick, India Edwards, the vice-chairman of the National Committee, and her assistant, Katie Louchheim, who were traveling on the train. We were sitting on Mrs. Edwards' berth looking very dejected, when Senator Fulbright came by. He had offered to pinch-hit for Adlai, and he said in his quiet, charming Southern way, "Now, girls, tomorrow we'll be going to work early, and I'll need your help. Everyone will have to do his best."

Our first stop was at 7 A.M., in Cumberland, Maryland,

and the miners who'd gathered at the train that cold, raw morning were disappointed not to see Adlai, but Senator Fulbright was wonderful. At about ten-thirty, we stopped at Silver Springs, and then came the most hideous moment I've ever experienced. A great crowd had assembled, and children and grownups had already rushed onto the tracks when suddenly the train started to back up—right into those people. It was sheer horror, to be so helpless. Just in time, somebody inside got to an emergency stop-cord, and thank God, nobody was hurt. We were trembling so much we could hardly make our little speeches.

As the train was pulling out, a man reached up and thrust a tiny puppy, a Chihuahua, into my arms. "For Stevenson," he yelled. Being a dog owner myself, I called anxiously, "What shall I feed it?" but we were already speeding down the tracks. The puppy was sick, and a campaign tour is nothing to wish on a dog! When we stopped in Wilmington, we sent it to a veterinary, and finally arranged to have it taken back to the too-impetuous owner. The last I heard of that dog he had been presented to Mamie in the White House.

From Wilmington we went to New York, hoping that Adlai would get there in time to do a television speech he was scheduled to make. He had arrived at the Illinois prison at four that morning, and conferred with the Lt. Governor and other officials through the dawn. The rioting convicts had a radio, and so they knew from news broadcasts that the Governor had come. Within a few hours, armed police advanced on the east cellblock where 339 convicts held their seven hostages. An official read the ultimatum, calling for immediate release of the hostages "or the police will enter and use any force necessary to restore order." After a little disorder and a couple of shots, at 11:47 A.M., the hungry hostages staggered out unharmed. Adlai, with prison officials, went into the cellblock to see the convicts, and then visited the liberated guards in the hospital, before taking a plane back to New York.

He was raced from the airport and across town in what must surely be the record for the run, and reached the television studio just as the chairman, Adolph Berle, was rising to introduce him. While the rest of us were sitting down to dinner afterwards, in a private dining room at the studio, Adlai was in the next room with a dentist working on his broken tooth. We'd barely had time to bite into those luscious steaks before we had to leave for a big night rally in Brooklyn. My brother grabbed a cheese sandwich, ate it in the car—and broke his tooth again!

At the Brooklyn Academy of Music, police zoomed off and came back with a dentist who patched him up in a dressing room just in time to make another half-hour speech, the last of a long day and the end, thank Heavens, of forty hours without sleep and with little food. Oh, I was thankful our whistle-stop tour was almost over! Chicago was the final stop; the boys were on hand to greet their Dad, and Adlai's tired face lit up when he saw them standing there.

The next morning, Sunday November 2, my brother, our good friend Art Moore, Ernest and I drove from Springfield up to Bloomington, to the Unitarian Church. Dr. Walker chose a moving passage for the responsive reading, and his sermon was excellent. It seemed so odd to see reporters sitting there busily taking notes, in the little church Adlai and I had gone to since childhood. My thoughts went back to the funeral service there for our darling Grandfather Davis, and I remembered the purple iris and lilacs heaped on his coffin. I was jolted back to reality by seeing a woman thrust a piece of paper at Adlai for an autograph—in church!

When we got outside, I asked my brother if we might invite the reporters and photographers to come home with us for a drink. Until then I'd felt shy about making overtures, even to the ones I would have most liked to be friends with. Now this was almost the end of our road, after thousands of miles traveled together, and it was nice to be able to sit down and visit.

After lunch, Adlai went upstairs to his old room and took a nap. Alverta tiptoed in, pulled down the shades and put a blanket over him. When we had to rouse him, an hour later, it was good to see him so relaxed again. He went off in a hail storm, for a motorcade procession ending with a reception at the Bloomington Armory. Then he left for Springfield after a nice little speech to his "home folk" and shaking a lot of hands. By eight o'clock I was in my own bed—what bliss!

I stayed in Bloomington one more night so that I could vote there. Before listening on the radio to my brother's speech that Election Eve, from Chicago, I wrote in my long-neglected diary:

> The sun has been streaming in all day, through the bare branches of the trees. There seems a peace in this house. It is hard to realize that in these very rooms Adlai grew into manhood. Qualities he expresses now were not only given but developed by Mother's and Father's influence. It is hard to put your finger on a spot in the past and say, "At this point, or that, we recognized certain greatness in this boy." But it is very honest and easy to say that he always was a special sort of person. He was always decent and he was fair, and for some reason or other, we all began early to turn to him. This is a peculiar word, this word "greatness." I suppose what I would

rather say would be his goodness, his compassion and his bril-
liance of mind, and now, tomorrow, the people in this land
will go to vote for him for President of the United States. Who
is more qualified, I don't know and I can't imagine. I used to
be afraid of his sensitiveness, and that the political storms and
treacheries and vulgarities and slanders would be impossible
for him to bear, but I have been mistaken. There is a fortitude
and resolution and a stern core that makes him able to look
with pity, if not with contempt, on some of the machinations
of his fellow-men in the heat of a campaign battle. But he will
never stoop to tricks, and playing on the passions and prejudices of the voters. So, if he should win tomorrow in spite of
all the handicaps of twenty years, etc., I think it will be that
the people have recognized his sincerity and his honesty of
purpose. And if he doesn't win, "living doesn't end."

Like millions of my fellow-countrymen, I tuned in to hear
my brother conclude the campaign.

In this city of Chicago, in the early hours of a July morning
last summer, I accepted the nomination of the Democratic
party for the Presidency of the United States. By the calendar
that was just fourteen weeks ago. That is not so long as time is
measured, but to one who has spent weeks, as I have, writing,
traveling, yes, and listening, to countless thousands of the
American people, it has been a long, long time.

The end has now come, the cheers and jeers, the tumult and
the shouting are almost over, and these are the last words I
shall speak to you before the balloting begins tomorrow
morning.

Anyone who runs for office wants to win. I want to win, of
course; but, win or lose, if I have kept faith with myself during the campaign, then I can await tomorrow—and the day
after—and all the days after that—in good temper and sober
contentment.

. . . I said when I accepted the nomination—let's talk sense
to the American people. . . . Talking sense is not easy. It means
saying things that sometimes people don't like to hear; it means

risking votes, and candidates are not supposed to do that. It means saying the same thing in all parts of the country and at all stages of the campaign.

. . . Win or lose, I have told you the truth as I see it. I have said what I meant and meant what I said. . . .

I have asked you for your support for my candidacy. I ask you now for support of our common faith in this country. The confidence we've inherited is our greatest wealth, the source of our strength.

Whatever the electorate decides, I ask that we close our ears, once and for all, to the cowardly voices of hate and fear and suspicion which would destroy us; that we dedicate ourselves, each one of us alone and all of us together, to that belief in ourselves, that trust in each other, on which the greatness of our country rests. For, believe me, the future of the world depends on it.

Adlai voted at Half-Day, near his Libertyville home, flew back to Springfield and was already at the Mansion when we got there at noon. He and his staff were cheerfully making forecasts of the outcome. Each one wrote down his prediction on how the electoral votes would be split, and the slips of paper were sealed in a large envelope and put in the safe. I know what my brother's guess was, but I think I'll leave the telling to some future biographer.

That evening, we heard the returns in the Mansion. The bad news started early, but I simply couldn't take it in. Sometime about midnight, I went downstairs to Adlai's office. He was writing something, and he looked up and said, "I'm going to make a statement."

"What for?" I asked numbly.

He laughed. "To concede. What else?"

Borden remarked, "By the time I pay up my bets at college, I'll be broke for a year!"

We drove over in the car with Adlai to the Leland Hotel, where he was to make his statement to a multitude of friends and press, and on the way, he laughed and said he was reminded of the Lincoln story about the little boy who stubbed his toe and said, "It hurts too much to laugh—and I'm too old to cry," and asked if we thought it would be all right for him to use it.

And he did use it, in his brief speech, after he'd said:

> . . . The people have rendered their verdict and I gladly accept it.
>
> General Eisenhower has been a great leader in war. He has been a vigorous and valiant opponent in the campaign. These qualities will now be dedicated to leading us all through the next four years. . . .
>
> I urge you all to give to General Eisenhower the support he will need to carry out the great tasks that lie before him.
>
> I pledge him mine.
>
> We vote as many, but we pray as one. With a united people, with faith in democracy, with common concern for others less fortunate around the globe, we shall move forward with God's guidance toward the time when His children shall grow in freedom and dignity in a world at peace.

Some friends came back with us to the Mansion, and we were so downcast that Adlai insisted we all have a glass of champagne to celebrate "our defeat." After everybody had gone, I went into my brother's room. He'd just gotten to bed. "How are you?" I asked, trying to sound matter-of-fact.

He said, "Oh, I'm all right. I've no regrets. I didn't ask for any of this, and I've done the best I could."

A curious thing happened, those next weeks. It was as if people wanted to tell him that in defeat he had won some larger victory. The letters and telegrams and cables poured in by the bushel. Even thousands of Republicans wrote Adlai to thank him for the kind of campaign he had conducted and to express regret that they couldn't vote for him, usually because they thought it was time for a change of party in Washington. Total strangers kept phoning long-distance to say, "Don't be discouraged. Don't give up. Your country still needs you."

It seemed that a great many people had plans for him, too; he was offered dozens of jobs of all kinds. Instead, he wanted "to drop out of sight for a while" and carry out his plan to go to the Far East and on around the world. Once the word was out he quickly received so many invitations from other countries to speak, that he had to adopt a rigid policy so as to avoid any possible embarrassment to the new administration: "I'm not going on a speaking tour—it's a listening tour!"

The fan mail came from the four corners of the earth. It was of all kinds, brilliant, thoughtful, emotional, amusing, pathetic, illiterate. I'll always remember the man who wrote that he was very worried about his wife, because she'd taken the election so hard: "She sits and cries for hours, and when I ask her what's wrong, she points to your picture on the mantel and sobs, 'It's him.' "

Adlai answered, "Tell your wife not to worry—'him's' all right!"

The only time I saw him come near breaking down—for even a moment—was the day he made his farewell address to the Illinois legislature, in January of 1953. He had wanted so much to finish the job he'd started as Governor.

As we drove off for the last time from the Mansion, full of the shadow of so many official families for ninety-six years, we saw the staff hurriedly remaking the beds where the new occupants would lie in our places that night. At the station, many of the people who came to see him off were weeping. A small girl who couldn't have been more than six tugged at his coat and asked tearfully, "Aren't I ever going to see you again?"

On the train, Adlai looked out over the black prairie earth; he stretched out on the seat and suddenly he said, "Thank you for everything, Buffie. I couldn't have done it without you."

No words have ever meant more to me.

Chapter 15

Postscript written in the summer of 1955.

W E DROVE up to Adlai's farm at Libertyville recently to spend a week end with my brother. As our car came through the gate, black-faced sheep munching grass peacefully wandered away from the road, and Artie, the Dalmatian, emerged dripping from the river to greet us.

His master, like most commuters with a day off, was working around the place. He had on dungarees, a plaid shirt and a ruddy new layer of sunburn, and he'd been chopping out some unwanted brush. His modern square-lined house looks over a grove of wonderful old sugar maples, with the river beyond, and shrubbery had sprung up so thick and fast it blocked off the view.

Adlai loves his great maples, and a fine, ancient burr oak. One of the perennial excuses he gives me for not redecorating the house is, "The tree surgeons keep me broke." When he's working in his library, at the big, oblong desk that was once a dining-room table, he takes a ten-minute break and goes out for a quick walk under the trees to the river and back. The first day he could get outdoors, when he was convalescing after a kidney stone operation, I found him busily cleaning up fallen branches.

Like Father, Adlai is too much on the go to be a real gardener, but he takes pride in the big vegetable garden his caretaker tends, and he always lets me know at mealtimes if "this came out of the garden." This summer we had squash, green beans, corn and tomatoes. Last winter my brother looked at some apples in a bowl and said, "But these aren't ours!" I said I'd bought them in town because the apples on his trees were wormy. Adlai said thriftily, "Well, the cook can cut out the worm holes and use what's left for applesauce." The sheep aren't for show, either; they mow the tall grass, and end up at the stockyards or in the deep freeze. Sometimes I say meaningly, "You don't want to have mutton for dinner again, do you?" The answer is, "Why not?"

Adlai has breakfast at 7:30, and then drives five miles to catch the eight o'clock electric train for Chicago and his law office. At dusk, when he gets home, sometimes he and Artie take a last stroll along the narrow, winding river. Often we sit on the porch under the yellow awning, and watch the sunset. In the living room, Artie stretches on the hearth, and if it's cool, Adlai lights the log fire. "Those maples are good to the last."

My favorite room is the big basement study that's full of his mementos. The crimson rug is a gift from old King Ibn Saud. Adlai first saw it lying on the desert sand—a "red carpet" rolled out for him—surrounded by camels and Cadillacs, when his plane landed in Saudi Arabia.

A Malay tribe gave him the blowpipe and quiver of poison darts. There is a handsome model of an old Adriatic sailing ship from Tito and primitive art from darkest Africa. A

Lincoln collector gave him a famous letter to General Meade. A Frenchman sent him a fascinating handwritten order of Napoleon. Somebody else sent the romantic, official campaign photograph of Lincoln which Adlai says "is so retouched it looks like Lord Byron." There's a large framed water color of the house in Los Angeles where my brother was born. Faded brown tintypes of our grandparents mingle with snapshots of all three sons—and a photograph that John Fell took of his father and lovely Queen Elizabeth.

The newest photograph is a wedding picture of young Adlai and pretty Nancy Anderson, taken in Louisville when they were married this summer. Adlai entered the date in the vellum-bound Bible that has recorded births and marriages and deaths in our family for over a hundred years.

At the far end of the room, a film projection screen rolls down for home movies, or to show the boys' color slides. Hundreds of books line two walls to the ceiling. Adlai has arranged them in classified sections, so that he can "find what he wants when he wants it—almost." A huge stack of scrapbooks about himself were compiled and sent by a kindly and competent woman in the East who has evidently made a career of it—one each month!

The unusual map on the wall was a present from the pilot and crew of Adlai's 1952 campaign plane. It shows all the territory he covered, and all the stops, and when I glance at it now, I think, Was it possible?

Adlai still flies a lot, partly on business, and his farm at Libertyville has become a stopover for all kinds of travelers. One week end when I was there this summer, it seemed as though practically everybody enroute to the United Nations tenth anniversary meeting, in San Francisco, wanted to see my brother. The chairman of the board of a great London paper called, and the Japanese Minister of Health phoned for an appointment. Then it was an official from Burma. Adlai talked on the phone to an old friend, the Foreign Minister of France, Monsieur Pinay, and they made a date to meet in New York. A delightful couple from Oregon came for the night.

When I hear visitors talking at the farm with my brother, one of the things that impresses me is that they seldom discuss the past. I'm an old reminiscer myself, and I love to look back, but Adlai and his callers are concerned with today—and tomorrow. They talk about race problems in South Africa, ways to halt the drop in farm incomes, a new housing plan in France, more flexible tariffs, the chances for democracy in a reborn Argentina—a blueprint for atom control.

As I write this, I have no idea what will happen in that future. In going over my old scrapbooks, to collect some material for this book, I came across a newspaper clipping from July of 1952: reporters had asked me what I thought my brother's prospects were, and the answer I gave is just as true now: "I don't know what God has in store, but when anyone is as faithful to ideals as Adlai is, he's bound to wind up in a serious job."

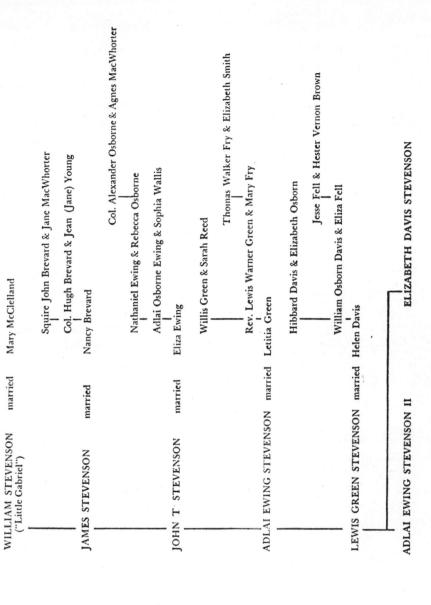

WILLIAM STEVENSON ("Little Gabriel") married Mary McClelland

Squire John Brevard & Jane MacWhorter

Col. Hugh Brevard & Jean (Jane) Young

JAMES STEVENSON married Nancy Brevard

Col. Alexander Osborne & Agnes MacWhorter

Nathaniel Ewing & Rebecca Osborne

Adlai Osborne Ewing & Sophia Wallis

JOHN T. STEVENSON married Eliza Ewing

Willis Green & Sarah Reed

Thomas Walker Fry & Elizabeth Smith

Rev. Lewis Warner Green & Mary Fry

ADLAI EWING STEVENSON married Letitia Green

Hibbard Davis & Elizabeth Osborn

Jesse Fell & Hester Vernon Brown

William Osborn Davis & Eliza Fell

LEWIS GREEN STEVENSON married Helen Davis

ADLAI EWING STEVENSON II   ELIZABETH DAVIS STEVENSON